INSPIRE / PLAN / DISCOVER / EXPERIENCE

IRELAND

IRELAND

CONTENTS

DISCOVER 6

EXPERIENCE DUBLIN 54

EXPERIENCE IRELAND 122

NEED TO KNOW 300

Left: Vintage Guinness signs decorate a pub wall
Previous page: The Cliffs of Moher, County Clare
Front cover: The island of Little Skellig seen from Skellig Michael

DISCOVER

The Ring of Kerry, from Valentia Island

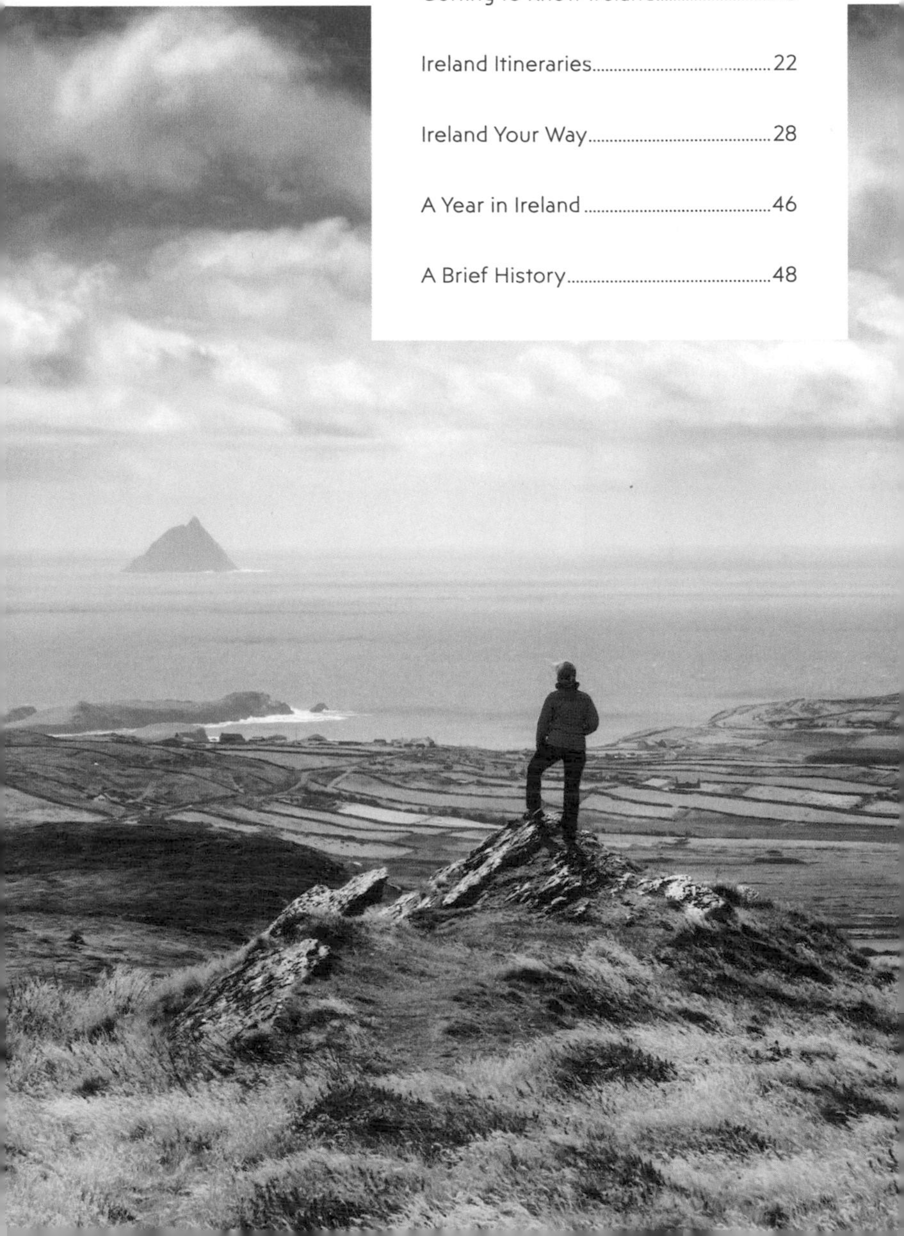

WELCOME TO
IRELAND

Rugged coastlines and lush green landscapes. World-class museums and cosy pubs packed with locals only too happy to prove that their reputation for Celtic charm is well deserved. Culture and craic; the Emerald Isle provides both in spades. Whatever your dream trip to Ireland includes, this DK Eyewitness travel guide is the perfect companion.

1 St Colman's Cathedral rising above the colourful fishing boats moored in Cobh harbour, County Cork.

2 Ornate, tight-packed graves in Glasnevin Cemetery, Dublin.

3 Mussenden Temple at sunset, perched on a cliff edge along Northern Ireland's north coast.

Ireland is a small island, but a spectacular one. Divided since 1921 into Northern Ireland and the Republic of Ireland, there are dazzling locations aplenty across both countries, from the famed Cliffs of Moher to Antrim's stunning Causeway coastal route, one of Europe's most dramatic drives. Hollywood agrees, and visitors may recognize Ireland's natural beauty from the sets of *Star Wars* and *Game of Thrones*.

The cities, too, will not disappoint. Once battle-scarred, Belfast today is a rejuvenated place, with a fast-developing foodie scene and Cathedral Quarter's impressive array of quirky bars and nightlife. In Dublin, trace the footsteps of the city's most famous literary sons, from James Joyce to Oscar Wilde, or spend an afternoon exploring the lush expanse of Phoenix Park. In the west, Galway's colourful streets always offer a lively welcome, while Cork city counts picturesque waterways and the nearby Blarney stone among its many attractions.

Small enough to travel easily around, Ireland can still overwhelm with the sheer number of unmissable sites on offer. We've broken the island down into easily navigable chapters, with detailed itineraries, expert local knowledge and colourful, comprehensive maps to help you plan the perfect visit. Whether you're staying for a weekend, a week or longer, this DK Eyewitness guide will ensure that you see the very best Ireland has to offer. *Céad míle fáilte* – a hundred thousand welcomes from one of the friendliest islands on earth. Enjoy the book, and enjoy Ireland.

REASONS TO LOVE
IRELAND

Its scenery is spectacular. Its people are great craic. Its history is emotive. Ask anyone from Ireland and you'll hear a different reason why they love their country. Here, we pick some of our favourites.

1 THE CRAIC

Roughly translated as good times with friends, this is at the very root of Irish friendliness. An indefinable and irreverent humour, it prompts many a return visit to Ireland.

2 SCREEN-WORTHY LANDSCAPES

From Spielberg to Kubrick, and *Star Wars* to *Game of Thrones*, Ireland's jaw-dropping landscapes have long been fertile ground for filmmakers.

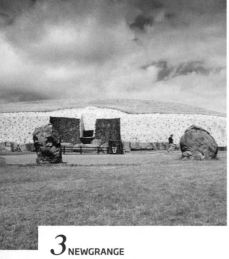

3 NEWGRANGE

Explore Newgrange *(p248)*, older than Egypt's pyramids and just as mysterious. It's one of the world's most important prehistoric sites, and the oldest known solar observatory.

THE GIANT'S CAUSEWAY 4
Visit Northern Ireland's only UNESCO World Heritage Site, the surreally beautiful Giant's Causeway, formed from thousands of interlocking basalt columns *(p276)*.

TWO CAPITAL CITIES 5
Barely a two-hour drive apart, visitors to Ireland are easily able to experience the pleasures of both Dublin *(p54)* and Belfast *(p266)* – each offering their own rich history.

BURGEONING LOCAL FOOD SCENES 6
Once with a reputation for mainly meat and potatoes, Ireland is now in full culinary bloom. Head to the capitals for creative chefs and great local ingredients.

ANCIENT CASTLES 7

The Irish countryside is littered with castles. Some are no more than rubble and ruin, while others remain as magnificent as when they were first built – with histories to match.

TITANIC BELFAST 8

This award-winning museum, housed in a striking modern building, is a triumph of innovation (p274). It is located in Belfast, where the doomed ship was originally built.

9 WORLD-CLASS DISTILLERIES

Ireland is a whiskey-lover's paradise. Home to top distilleries like Bushmills and Jameson, it's the perfect place to sample the good stuff.

10 TRAD SESSIONS

Traditional music is the life-blood of Ireland. Sessions can range from a full band belting out knee-slapping jigs to a single mournful singer bringing an entire pub to silence.

SURFING THE SLIGO COAST 11

Ireland's Atlantic coast is world-renowned as a top surfing spot, and there's no better place to experience this than the golden beaches and clean waves of Sligo *(p238)*.

CELTIC HERITAGE 12

Ireland's rich tradition of storytelling embraces a heritage steeped in enchantment. Most tales originated over 2,000 years ago, and Irish mythology remains a link to the ancient past.

EXPLORE
IRELAND

This guide divides Ireland into eight colour-coded sightseeing areas, as shown on this map. Find out more about each area on the following pages.

Belmullet
Ballycastle
Ballina
Achill Island
Foxford
Newport
Clare Island
Castlebar
Westport
Inishbofin
Leenane
Clifden
Cashel
Knockferry
Galway
Galway Bay
Ballyvaughan
Aran Islands
The Burren

Atlantic Ocean

Ennis
Kilkee
Killimer
Tarbert
Tralee

Dingle Peninsula
Dingle
Dingle Bay
Killarney

CORK AND KERRY
p154

Valentia Island
Ring of Kerry
Kenmare
Tahilla
Glengarriff
The Skelligs
Durrus
Leap
Mizen Head
Baltimore

WESTERN EUROPE

NORWAY
SWEDEN
North Sea
DENMARK
IRELAND
UNITED KINGDOM
GERMANY
CZECH REP.
AUSTRIA
Atlantic Ocean
FRANCE
SWITZ.
ITALY
PORTUGAL
SPAIN

SCOTLAND

Tory Island

Inishowen Peninsula

Rathmullan
Buncrana

Aranmore

Portrush
Ballycastle

Coleraine
Cushendall

Letterkenny

NORTHWEST IRELAND *p224*

Derry~Londonderry

Stranraer

Stranorlar

Strabane

NORTHERN IRELAND

Glencolmcille

Donegal

Ballymena

Larne

Carrickfergus

Kilcar

Lough Derg

NORTHERN IRELAND *p262*

Omagh

Lough Neagh

Antrim

Bangor

BELFAST

Ballyshannon

Donegal Bay

Lower Lough Erne

Dungannon

Lisburn

Enniskillen

Upper Lough Erne

Monaghan

Armagh

Portadown

Dundrum

Sligo

Ardglass

Newcastle

Tobercurry

Cavan

Dundalk

Kilkeel

Boyle

Carrick-on-Shannon

Ardee

Knock

THE WEST OF IRELAND *p206*

Longford

THE MIDLANDS *p244*

Kells

Slane

Irish Sea

Roscommon

Trim

REPUBLIC OF IRELAND

Athlone

Kilbeggan

Shannonbridge

Tullamore

DUBLIN *p54*

Portumna

Birr

Naas

DUBLIN

Lough Derg

Portlaoise

Kildare

Wicklow Mountains

Bray

Enniskerry

Roscrea

Abbeyleix

Wicklow

Nenagh

Carlow

Rathvilly

Arklow

Shannon

THE LOWER SHANNON *p184*

Kilkenny

SOUTHEAST IRELAND *p124*

Gorey

Limerick

Adare

Tipperary

Cashel

Enniscorthy

Kilmallock

Cahir

Carrick-on-Suir

New Ross

Wexford

Mitchelstown

Ballymacarbry

Waterford

Rosslare

Fermoy

Lismore

Mallow

Saltee Islands

Youghal

Cork

Ardmore

St George's Channel

Cobh

Kinsale

0 kilometres 50

0 miles 50

N

GETTING TO KNOW
IRELAND

Today's Ireland comprises many different parts: 2 countries, 4 provinces, 32 counties, and innumerable towns and villages. While the celebrated Irish craic is everywhere, each area has a history and essence distinctly its own. Becoming familiar with each region will help when planning your trip.

DUBLIN

PAGE 54

Ireland's capital has a wealth of attractions, most within walking distance of each other – from Trinity College to Christ Church Cathedral, there are historic sights at every turn. Southeast Dublin is home to Grafton Street's attractive shops and much of Ireland's cultural heritage, including the National Gallery and National Museum of Archaeology. Southwest Dublin juxtaposes the modern bustle of Temple Bar with stark reminders of the city's past in Viking Dublin. North of the River Liffey are some of the capital's finest Georgian streetscapes, jostling for attention alongside great museums and shops.

Best for
World-class museums and vibrant nightlife

Home to
The Book of Kells, within Trinity's Old Library

Experience
An evening of traditional music in lively Temple Bar

SOUTHEAST IRELAND

PAGE 124

Blessed with the warmest climate in Ireland, the Southeast is one of the most beautiful regions in the country. County Wicklow, the "Garden of Ireland", is home to breathtaking mountain scenery and several major historic sites, while the counties further south showcase gently rolling hills, lush farmland and imposing medieval castles. It's also a golfer's paradise, with multiple championship courses dotting the region.

Best for
Magnificent manors and estates

Home to
Kilkenny, one of the country's most historic and pleasant towns

Experience
A stroll through the mystical monastic settlement at Glendalough

CORK AND KERRY

PAGE 154

Comprising nearly half of the historic province of Munster, magnificent scenery has attracted visitors to this region since Victorian times. Rocky headlands jut dramatically into the Atlantic, and colourful fishing villages nestle in the shelter of the bays. County Kerry offers stunning landscapes and a wealth of prehistoric and early Christian sites, whereas Cork's gentle charm and culinary heritage has enticed many a casual visitor into becoming a permanent resident.

Best for
Picturesque seaside towns

Home to
The historic Skellig Islands, which have also doubled as a Star Wars filming location

Experience
The culinary delights of West Cork

→

PAGE 184

THE LOWER SHANNON

In the three counties that flank the lower reaches of the Shannon – Ireland's longest river – the scenery ranges from the rolling farmland of Tipperary to the eerie limestone plateau of the Burren. Visitors flock here for medieval strongholds and atmospheric towns, or the bustling riverside resorts that promise a more laid-back stay. Along the west edge of the region lie the spectacular Cliffs of Moher, Ireland's most-visited natural attraction. The area also boasts a thriving traditional music scene, particularly in the small villages of County Clare.

Best for
Impromptu Irish trad sessions

Home to
The Cliffs of Moher, one of the most dramatic stretches of Ireland's west coast

Experience
A luxurious stay in the Neo-Gothic Adare Manor

THE WEST OF IRELAND

This is the heart of Connaught, Ireland's historic western province. The region lives up to its image as a traditional, sparsely populated land with windswept mountains and a countryside speckled with low stone walls and peat bogs. Yet it also encompasses Galway, a vibrant university city whose youthful population brings life to the medieval streets and snug pubs. At the mouth of Galway Bay lie the three Aran Islands, whose starkly beautiful landscapes, ancient churches, forts and monuments draw hordes of day-trippers.

Best for
World-class horse racing

Home to
The austere Aran Islands

Experience
A pint of the black stuff in one of Galway's cosy pubs

→

NORTHWEST IRELAND

PAGE 224

Towering cliffs, deserted golden beaches and rocky headlands abound along the rugged coast of Donegal, which incorporates some of Ireland's wildest scenery. Despite the remote landscape, locals are known for their unpretentious friendliness and lilting accents. To the south, Sligo is steeped in prehistory and Celtic myth, with its legacy of ancient monuments and natural beauty enriched by associations with the poet W B Yeats. By contrast, Leitrim is a quiet county of unruffled lakes and waterways.

Best for
Long walks along unspoilt beaches

Home to
Slieve League, one of Europe's highest sea cliffs

Experience
Monstrous waves off the coast of Sligo, a surfing hot spot

THE MIDLANDS

PAGE 244

The cradle of Irish civilization and spiritual home of the Celts, the Midlands encompass some of Ireland's most sacred and symbolic sites. Much of the region is little visited, but the ragged landscapes of lush pastures, lakes and bogland reveal ancient Celtic crosses, gracious Norman abbeys and Gothic Revival castles. There's fun to be found indoors as well; the Midlands is home to a number of Ireland's most renowned whiskey distilleries, including Kilbeggan in Westmeath and Tullamore in Offaly.

Best for
Prehistoric sites

Home to
Newgrange, Ireland's most important passage grave

Experience
Whiskey-tastings in the historic Kilbeggan Distillery, which dates back to 1757

NORTHERN IRELAND

Northern Ireland has sights from every era of Ireland's history, as well as some magnificent natural scenery. The north coast offers the most striking examples of the latter, with the extraordinary volcanic landscape of the Giant's Causeway, or Mussenden Temple's serene cliff-top location. Back in Belfast (the country's lively capital), history – in the form of colourful political murals and the Titanic dockyard – sits neatly alongside a flourishing contemporary food scene and quirky nightlife options.

Best for
Stunning coastal scenery and great local restaurants

Home to
The Giant's Causeway

Experience
A pub crawl through the cobbled streets of Belfast's Cathedral Quarter

←

1 Coumeenole Beach, Dingle Peninsula.

2 St Kieran's Street, Kilkenny.

3 A food stall at Cork's English Market.

4 Whiskey on display at the Jameson Distillery Midleton.

Ireland is a treasure trove of things to see and do, and its relatively small size means that you can navigate the island easily. These itineraries will inspire you to make the most of your visit.

2 WEEKS

Across Ireland

Day 1

Explore Dublin – *pick a day from the city itinerary (p58)*.

Day 2

Head south out of the city towards Enniskerry, to explore the beautiful house and gardens of the Powerscourt Estate *(p132)*. Break for lunch in the Avoca café, before enjoying a scenic drive along part of the Military Road through the windswept Wicklow Mountains. There are plenty of stunning spots to pause en route, including at Powerscourt Waterfall, the tallest in Ireland. Finish the day in Kilkenny with dinner at Matt the Millers, a lively local pub.

Day 3

Head towards Waterford, Ireland's oldest city *(p140)*. Spend the morning at the Museum of Treasures, which tells the story of the city's rise and fall, before having lunch at the Granary Café. Follow the coast road to Youghal, with its medieval town walls and imposing clock tower. From here, it's a short drive to the Jameson Distillery Midleton *(p175)* – take a tour and sample some of their fine whiskey. Round off the day with a quick visit to Blarney Castle *(p175)* to secure the gift of the gab, before spending the night in Cork City *(p158)*.

Day 4

Start the morning with a trip to Cork's English Market, where you can pick up breakfast – and perhaps a picnic lunch –

at one of the stalls. Then head for Kinsale *(p179)* and spend a couple of hours wandering the streets of this charming historic town. When you've had your fill, travel along the coast past tiny villages and lovely seascapes towards Bantry *(p172)*. This is a perfect place to spend the night, with plenty of good restaurants and live music on offer most nights during the summer.

Day 5

Take the stunning trip over the Caha mountains via Glengarriff to Kenmare *(p170)*, a great base for exploring the Ring of Kerry *(p182)*. Stop for lunch at one of the town's many restaurants – try Maison Gourmet for sandwiches and delicious baked goods – before driving around the peninsula, breaking at one or two of the little villages en route to enjoy their pectacular scenery. Spend the night in Tralee *(p168)*, a small town best known for its international Rose of Tralee festival.

Day 6

Next morning, drive around the beautiful Dingle Peninsula and stop in Dingle town *(p169)* for a seafood lunch in Out of the Blue. Set aside a few hours to explore this colourful town, before taking the ferry out to the Blasket Islands; now uninhabited, they once supported a strong Gaelic community and culture. Back on the mainland, the Dingle Skellig Hotel is a good place to stay, located just a few minutes from the town, with unbeatable views.

→

Day 7

Follow the winding coastal roads through Kilkee, Milltown Malbay, the Cliffs of Moher (p190) and Doolin for their elemental, windswept views and pleasant villages. Doolin is home to some excellent traditional music – and makes a perfect lunch stop. The afternoon can be spent exploring the Burren's (p188) lunar-like landscape, which is riddled with excellent hikes, before settling in the lively town of Ennis (p197) for the night.

Day 8

Turning south, spend the morning in Limerick (p201), admiring the amazing collection of antiquities in the Hunt Museum, and the austere St Mary's Cathedral. In the afternoon, visit the beautifully restored Bunratty Castle and Folk Park (p192). A great family day out, the folk park has meticulously recreated 19th-century rural life in Ireland and is well worth a visit. Next, move on to Galway city (p210), and spend the evening in one of the restaurants or bars lining Quays Street.

Day 9

From Galway, follow the coast roads through Roundstone and Clifden, which have some spectacular ocean views. Visit the magnificent lakeside castle of Kylemore Abbey (p218) where you can have a light lunch alfresco, before a walk (accessible through the visitors' centre) in the beautiful, sprawling Connemara National Park. After a few hours among its mountains and forests, end your day in the smart little town of Westport (p214).

Day 10

Spend the morning visiting the beautifully renovated 18th-century Westport House. Next, head to Achill Island to enjoy gorgeous seascapes, before moving on to Sligo (p238) for lunch in the quirky Vintage Lane Café. Spend the rest of the afternoon wandering the town. Be sure to check out the Sligo County Museum, which houses a fine collection of W B Yeats memorabilia, while the town's Model Arts & Niland Gallery has wonderful paintings by his brother, Jack B Yeats.

1 Fanad Head
Lighthouse in Donegal. ↑
2 Bunratty Castle and Folk Park.
3 Westport town, County Mayo.
4 Northern Ireland's north coast.
5 A Belfast bar.

Day 11

The coast of Donegal is one of the least visited and most beautiful areas of Ireland. From Sligo, spend the day driving the narrow roads of Donegal, with frequent breaks to enjoy the spectacular scenery. For truly stunning views, make for Horn Head where, if the weather is fine, you can take a dip at nearby Killahoey Strand. End the day's driving in Derry (p280).

Day 12

Spend the day on North Antrim's spectacular coastline. Head north to the golden sands of Portstewart Strand (p284). Grab lunch in Harry's Shack (p279), located right on the beach, before heading 32 km (20 miles) east to the Giant's Causeway (p276) to explore Northern Ireland's only UNESCO World Heritage Site. Then continue along the coast to the lesser-known Gobbins Cliff Path, a remarkable guided tour that winds out towards the Irish Sea (book in advance; www.thegobbinscliff path.com). As evening approaches, continue south to Belfast (p270) for a gourmet dinner in the Muddlers Club.

Day 13

From Belfast, follow the coast road east towards Bangor, pausing in Holywood for a filling breakfast in one of its excellent cafés – we recommend the Bay Tree. Then spend the rest of the morning at the intriguing Ulster Folk and Transport Museum (p294). Further east is Mount Stewart (p295), a grand stately home where you can break for lunch and explore the lovely gardens. Head back to Belfast for another night of fine dining and cocktails (p271 and p272).

Day 14

On your last morning, travel south to Newgrange and the Boyne Valley (p248), the cradle of Irish civilization, to visit the mysterious and ancient passage tombs at both Newgrange and Knowth. Then stop by the nearby Hill of Tara (p256), a site of huge importance within Celtic mythology. This will take up a good chunk of the afternoon, so afterwards set your route back towards Dublin for a good dinner, before finishing in the Stag's Head with some well-deserved drinks.

7 DAYS

On the Wild Atlantic Way

The Wild Atlantic Way is one of the world's longest defined coastal touring routes, running from Ireland's most northerly point in County Donegal to the most southerly point in County Cork. There are myriad ways to take on this extraordinary journey, and this suggested itinerary focuses on the southern half of the route.

Day 1

Start your road trip in the picturesque seaside town of Kinsale (p179), famed for its gourmet restaurants and beautiful harbour. Upon leaving town, the road passes the 17th-century Charles Fort, a star fort dramatically located on the water's edge. Head for Schull, breaking in the tiny coastal village of Baltimore (p173) en route.

Day 2

From Schull, take the stunning trip over the Caha mountains via Glengarriff to Kenmare (p170). The town's Irish name, Neidín, is translated as "little nest" and

it lies snugly at the head of the River Kenmare. It's a great base for exploring the area; devote the rest of the day to touring the Ring of Beara.

Day 3

Still in Kenmare, spend the next day driving around the Ring of Kerry. It's a popular tourist route so don't expect isolation, but there are plenty of opportunities to veer off the beaten track and take in broad bays, coves and craggy cliffs. Surrounding villages also offer spectacular scenery; set aside an hour or two to explore Sneem, or the picturesque Waterville.

1 Dingle Peninsula, County Kerry.

2 Colourful pub signs in Kenmare.

3 Shops and restaurants in Kinsale, County Cork.

4 Achill Island's Keem Bay.

5 A street in the centre of Galway city.

Day 4

From Kenmare it's a 40-minute drive to Killarney *(p164)*, breaking at Ladies' View, from where it seems as though the whole of Kerry is laid out below you. Pick up some fresh fish and chips from Quinlan's Seafood Bar, and then continue on to the bustling seaside town of Dingle *(p168)* and the charming array of quaint eateries and artisan shops.

Day 5

Spend the morning driving around the ruggedly beautiful Dingle Peninsula, dotted with remnants of early Christian churches and monastic settlements. Then head north, taking a scenic driving break aboard the Killimer-Tarbert ferry before following coastal roads through Kilkee and Miltown Malbay to see the breathtaking Cliffs of Moher *(p190)*. It's a further 90 minutes to Galway, where you'll find a warm welcome in the lively university city *(p210)*.

Day 6

From Galway it's just over 70 km (43 miles) to Clifden *(p216)*, colloquially known as the capital of Connemara. This will be your base for the day, from which you can explore the protected parkland of Connemara National Park and the majestic Kylemore Abbey *(p218)*. Follow the Sky Road as it loops scenically around the north side of Clifden Bay, and pop into Dan O'Hara's Homestead, where exhibits explore Connemara's history *(p217)*.

Day 7

Press on northwards to reach Croagh Patrick, Ireland's holy mountain *(p215)*. After a steep and tricky ascent, you'll be rewarded with magnificent panoramas of the surrounding countryside. Drive further north to visit Westport, and pass a couple of hours at the beautifully renovated Westport House *(p214)*. Spend the rest of the day exploring the sandy beaches and dramatic cliffs of Achill Island, Ireland's largest island.

Dramatic Coastlines

Ireland's edges offer some of its most spectacular scenery. Perched at the tip of Northern Ireland's north coast, the Giant's Causeway is a UNESCO World Heritage Site *(p276)* and truly one of the most unique landscapes in the world. Its stone prisms slot together almost too perfectly, so myths abound regarding the site's formation. The breathtaking Cliffs of Moher *(p190)* line County Clare's west boundary; have your camera at the ready to capture the sheer cliff face rising majestically from the crashing Atlantic below. Further south, off the coast of Kerry, lie the jagged Skellig Islands *(p162)*. Home to a group of monks during the 6th century – and to Luke Skywalker more recently – the islands house a cluster of distinctive beehive huts.

→

Waves crash against the hexagonal stone prisms of the Giant's Causeway

IRELAND FOR
NATURAL BEAUTY

Ireland's scenery is one of the country's greatest attractions, with the sheer variety on offer almost as impressive as the vistas themselves. The fabled emerald can be glimpsed throughout Ireland's rolling hills, while the rugged coastlines and pristine beaches also offer plenty for the eye to delight in.

Wicklow's Mountainous Scenery

Known as the "Garden of Ireland", Wicklow can at times feel more like the Garden of Eden. Glassy lakes lie hidden amid mountains and waterfalls tumble through lush forests and valleys of eye-popping green. Head for the Wicklow Way, Ireland's oldest walking route, to take in some of this diverse terrain.

←

A couple take in panoramic views of Wicklow, looking south towards Wexford

TOP 5 UNMISSABLE HIKES

Bray to Greystones Cliff Walk, Co Wicklow
A coastal walk suitable for families (2.5 hrs).

The Barnavave Loop, Co Louth
An intermediate mountain trek (4 hrs).

Coomloughra Horseshoe, Co Kerry
Ridge walk for experienced hikers only (7 hrs).

Cliffs of Moher Coastal Path, Co Clare
An easy route around this attraction (1–3 hrs).

Glenariff Forest Park, Co Antrim
Various trails through woodland (1–2 hrs).

Donegal's Golden Sands

With over 1,000 km (620 miles) of coastline, Donegal harbours a wealth of unspoiled beaches, many with Blue Flag status. Gorgeous stretches of sand are paired with brisk waves – perfect for surfing – while the county's remoteness means you may often have the place to yourself.

→

Narin Strand near Adara, in County Donegal

Atlantic Playmates

Kerry's coastline might seem like an unlikely whale-watching spot, but over a third of the world's whale and dolphin species have been recorded in Irish waters, and many marine tours are available here. Those in luck may spy orcas, humpback whales and basking sharks.

→

Glimpse of a humpback whale's tail, as can be spotted off Kerry's coast

Watch the Sunrise at Newgrange

Built over 5,200 years ago, the fact that this incredible structure even exists is remarkable; the only building materials available then – including tools – were made of stone. A Neolithic passage tomb, it also acts as an ancient solar observatory; every year on 21 December the sun aligns perfectly with the structure, illuminating a deep inner chamber *(p248)*.

→

The ornately carved entrance stone at Newgrange

IRELAND FOR
HISTORY BUFFS

Ireland has an intense relationship with the past. Everywhere you look there are reminders of its rich and often turbulent history: Iron Age hillforts, Norman castles, winding medieval streets and colourful political murals. In Ireland today, history is at once revered, celebrated and hotly debated.

TOP 5 FAMOUS WOMEN IN IRISH HISTORY

St Brigid, 6th Century AD
Ireland's only female patron saint.

Grace O'Malley, 1530–1603
A pirate queen.

Lady Gregory, 1852–1932
Played a key role in the Irish Literary Revival.

Countess Markievicz, 1868–1927
Most significant female figure in the 1916 Rising.

Mary Robinson, b 1944
Ireland's first female president.

Take a Black Cab Tour of Belfast's Murals

One of the city's unmissable attractions, visitors are taken on an intimate and eye-opening tour of some of Belfast's most iconic landmarks *(p273)*. Local guides who lived through the Troubles explain the significance of the murals, as well as giving valuable insight into the wider conflict.

A Walk Around Dublin

Dublin offers many excellent walking tours. One of the most popular is run by a local historian and takes in the 1916 Easter Rising's most relevant sites. Thoroughly engaging, it's a great way to see the city. Tours run daily from March to October; less frequently during winter months. A Michael Collins walking tour is also on offer, as are more general tours of Dublin's history.

→

The ancient chapel at the Rock of Cashel

↓ Dublin's GPO, a key sight on the 1916 walking tour

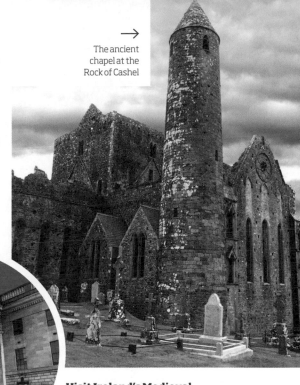

Visit Ireland's Medieval Past in Tipperary

One of the country's most important historical and archaeological sites, the Rock of Cashel *(p194)* is a spectacular collection of medieval buildings, including a 15th-century castle, a 13th-century Gothic cathedral and a 12th-century round tower.

Discover Treasures in Waterford

Waterford's historic "Viking Triangle" is the city's cultural and heritage quarter. It is home to three museums – Reginald's Tower, the Medieval Museum and Bishop's Palace – known collectively as the Waterford Treasures. These relate the city's history, from its AD 914 foundation through to the 20th century.

↑ Political murals along the Falls Road in Belfast

→

A Franciscan friary in Waterford's Viking Triangle

> **INSIDER TIP**
> **Cheers!**
>
> *"Sláinte"* is a common toast used in Ireland, particularly in the Republic. Pronounced "slawn-che", and accompanied by a raised glass, it translates literally as "health".

IRELAND
ON TAP

Celebrated for its atmosphere, friendly locals and genial bar staff, the humble pub is the beating heart of Irish social life. Wit is washed down with whiskey or Guinness in what often feels like an extension of the family home, and a visit is a must for any curious visitors seeking out the "real" Ireland.

Pubs of the Past

The first incarnations of Irish pubs included medieval taverns, coaching inns and shebeens, or illegal drinking dens. Brewing and distilling flourished under colonial rule, and the sumptuous Edwardian or Victorian interiors of some city pubs are a testament to these times. The oldest pub in Ireland today is Sean's Bar, a low-ceilinged watering hole in Athlone that dates from around AD 900.

→

Sean's Bar, the oldest pub in Ireland, is located next to Athlone Castle

Pubs Today

Modern Irish pubs are still a key part of local life, often acting as social hubs for small towns and villages. A smoking ban has been in place across Irish and Northern Irish pubs since the noughties, causing plenty of beer gardens to pop up as a result. Pubs are largely family-friendly during the day, and can be great for hearty lunches. The food may vary, from toasted sandwiches to Michelin-level fare. Most are somewhere in between, with a solid line in comfort food.

← The Crown Liquor Saloon, a Victorian gin palace

TOP 4 IRISH PUBS

Kyteler's Inn, Kilkenny
An atmospheric stone-walled pub that dates back to 1263.

Stag's Head, Dublin
This authentic Victorian drinking spot is a stone's throw from Temple Bar.

The Crown Liquor Saloon, Belfast
An iconic city bar with original gas lamps.

Tigh Neachtain's, Galway
This Galway pub offers great trad music.

↑ A round of Guinness, with the thick creamy heads denoting a good pint

Befriending the Locals

While Irish pub etiquette is informal, the practice of "rounds" – buying drinks for those in your group, which each person will then reciprocate – is widely observed. Leaving before your turn to order will be frowned upon, so if you'd prefer not to get involved in a round, speak up!

↑ A typical pub in Ireland, at the heart of local social life

Traditional Music Festivals

These usually take place widely throughout Ireland and are very popular. *Fleadh Cheoil*, held in a different city each year, is the world's biggest traditional Irish music festival, with over 500,000 fans flocking to the event in 2019. Other specialist festivals include the Willy Clancy Summer School in quaint Miltown Malbay, which focuses on musical teaching and includes talks on the language and culture of the area. Dublin's Tradfest is one of the most accessible weeks in the traditional music calendar, with free events held in unique venues around the city.

→

TradFest Gala Night at the Printworks, in the courtyard of Dublin Castle

IRELAND FOR
MUSIC LOVERS

Ireland is the only country in the world to have a musical instrument – the harp – as its national emblem, and the nation's love of music and its role in society is difficult to exaggerate. Live trad is a key aspect of the country's heritage and there are countless opportunities to see this performed.

TRADITIONAL INSTRUMENTS

There is no set line-up in traditional Irish bands. The violin, or fiddle, is probably the most common instrument used, along with the flute and the tin whistle. Percussion is often provided by the *bodhrán*, an ancient frame drum with a goatskin head, while *uilleann pipes* – Ireland's equivalent of Scottish bagpipes – account for woodwind. The harp has been played in Ireland since the 10th century, with a revival in the noughties, though these unwieldy instruments remain rare due to their astronomical price.

Irish Dancing

Dancing plays an important role in Irish trad music, with the lively beats compelling listeners to move their feet. Many melodies are derived from centuries-old reels, jigs and hornpipes, nowadays mainly performed at *céilís* (dances) or *fleadhs* (festivals). Such events often offer the opportunity to pick up a few steps for yourself.

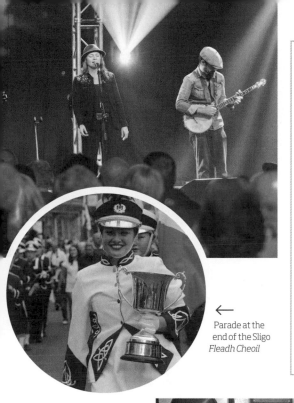

TOP 5 IRISH MUSICIANS

The Dubliners
Lively folk band with a 50-year career.

Van Morrison
Northern Irish singer-songwriter, best known for his 1967 hit "Brown-Eyed Girl".

Thin Lizzy
Hard rock band fronted by Phil Lynott.

U2
World-famous Dublin rock band who formed at school in the 1970s.

The Cranberries
Limerick-based band whose debut album propelled them to fame in the 1990s.

← Parade at the end of the Sligo *Fleadh Cheoil*

Pub Trad Sessions

Pubs are well known as a breeding ground for impromptu trad sessions. One of the things you may hear is *Sean-nós* (pronounced "shan-nos"), which literally means "old style", and refers to a traditional type of unaccompanied singing. Usually performed in Gaelic, this art has been passed down orally from generation to generation. Even for non Gaelic speakers, hearing a hush fall over the pub and the bare, melodic voice can be hugely moving.

↑ Traditional Irish music session in a pub in Doolin, County Clare

↑ An Irish dancing troup in traditional costume

Be Inspired by Science

In Belfast, W5 *(www.w5online. co.uk)* is an award-winning science centre with over 250 exhibits; robotics, engineering and live demonstrations will keep your kids entertained for hours. In Dublin, the Museum of Natural History – part of the National Museum *(p74)* – also offers family-friendly exhibits for budding scientists.

→
Children play in
W5's interactive Discover area

IRELAND FOR
FAMILIES

With its abundance of castles, nature parks and the country's inherent Celtic mysticism, Ireland is a veritable playground for kids. Most attractions are family-friendly, leaving the weather as your only worry. (Of course, in Ireland, this *is* a worry – but luckily there are plenty of indoor activities available also.)

EAT

Gaillot et Gray
Pizzeria offering wood-fired sourdough pies.
D4 59 Clanbrassil St Lwr, Dublin 454 7781

€€€

The Market Bar
Tapas spot with table games for children.
D4 14A Fade St, Dublin marketbar.ie

€€€

Captain Americas
A menu of burgers and pizzas, plus a kid's club.
D4 44 Grafton St, Dublin captain americas.com

€€€

The Windstar, a twirling ride in Tayto Park ↑

Visit the Animal Kingdom

Dublin Zoo *(p112)* is one of the oldest and most popular zoos in the world. Home to over 400 animals and with 70 acres to explore, it makes for a perfect family day out. Many animals are rare species, and activities and talks take place regularly to help children and adults learn more about the creatures.

→

A family visiting the Dublin Zoo

Travel Back in Time

Combining a restored 15th-century castle and 19th-century folk park, Bunratty Castle *(p192)* is as close to time-travel as you're likely to get. Kids will love the farmhouses, fishing huts and costumed characters bringing village traditions to life.

←

The magnificent Bunratty Castle in County Clare

Enjoy Theme Park Thrills

Ireland's only theme park, Tayto Park is just a 30-minute drive from Dublin and home to Europe's largest wooden roller coaster. There are plenty of other attractions, including a 5D cinema, a dinosaur exhibition and a bird-of-prey sanctuary.

Experience Fairies and Folklore

Set in the gorgeous Slieve Gullion Forest Park, the Giant's Lair in Armagh is a magical adventure playground packed full of activities, all based on local legends.

↑ Carved details along the Giant's Lair, an enchanting children's trail

Take to the Water

As expected of an island, Ireland offers a wealth of watersports. Head to the west coast for unmatched surfing opportunities - beginners can opt for one of Bundoran's many surf schools, while experts usually flock to Mullaghmore *(p239)*, which is home to one of the world's biggest breakers. For kite surfing, head to beautiful Achill Island to ride on the flat waters of the lake or the waves on the beach with the Pure Magic Kite School *(www. puremagic.ie)*. Further south, sea kayak by starlight in West Cork *(www.atlanticsea kayaking.com)*; for a more urban experience, try wakeboarding in the heart of Dublin *(www.wakedock.ie)*. Ireland's first cable wake park is suitable for all levels, so slither into a wetsuit and skim through one of the city's busiest districts.

$\longrightarrow$

Surfers at the
Bundoran Beach
in Donegal

IRELAND FOR
OUTDOOR
ADVENTURES

Ireland is an excellent destination for thrill-seekers; its varied landscapes offer a host of activities. It's no secret that world-class surfing is easily found along the coastline, but from hiking to biking and beyond, inland Ireland also provides many opportunities to get your endorphins flowing.

Hiking Heaven

Walking enthusiasts will enjoy exploring Ireland's gorgeous landscapes. Spend a day rambling the Cuilcagh Way in Fermanagh, a 20-mile (33-km) boardwalk trail nicknamed the "Stairway to Heaven" for its breath-taking views. More dramatic still is the Gobbins Cliff Path, set high above the Atlantic *(www.thegobbins cliffpath.com)*.

$\longleftarrow$

The Gobbins Cliff Path, a scenic coastal route near Islandmagee, Antrim

On Two Wheels

Ireland offers a great range of routes for cycling, from easy loops to scenic multi-day tours. The Ring of Kerry is a sizeable undertaking, stretching over 180 km (112 miles), but the glorious views will help you forget your burning calves. The rugged Aran Islands (p212) are perfect for a day trip; bikes can be rented on the islands or brought across on the ferry from Rossaveal. For something more high-octane, head to the Ballyhoura Mountains, which have Ireland's largest network of mountain-biking trails (www.visitballyhoura.com).

→

Cycling up the Gap of Dunloe, a narrow mountain pass near the Ring of Kerry

Scale the Heights

An emerging Irish trend that offers a more unusual adrenalin rush is sea stack climbing. Summiting these steep, off-shore columns can be more challenging than inland climbing as the stacks tend to be formed from softer, erodible rock. Donegal-based company Unique Ascents (www.uniqueascent.ie) offers a guided package to anyone with a head for heights. Other above-ground thrills include Ireland's longest zipline and a treetop adventure walk, located within Castlecomer Discovery Park in Kilkenny (www.discoverypark.ie).

←

Sea stack climbing near Gweedore in Donegal

Yeats Country, Sligo

Despite spending much of his life in England, W B Yeats always acknowledged Sligo as his native and spiritual home. The landscape inspired some of his most famous poetry, including "The Lake Isle of Innisfree" and "Under Ben Bulben", one of his final works. Although originally buried in France, Yeats' body was moved to a Sligo church-yard almost a decade later.

→

A striking statue of
W B Yeats, which stands in
the middle of Sligo town

IRELAND FOR
BOOKWORMS

Ireland's literary heritage is truly remarkable, with four Nobel prize winners –
in Bernard Shaw, Yeats, Beckett and Heaney – before even mentioning the
likes of Wilde, Joyce, Swift, Stoker and C S Lewis. Book-lovers will enjoy the
regular festivals, museums and re-enactments that honour these luminaries.

CONTEMPORARY WRITERS

Today Ireland still punches well above its weight in terms of talented writers – with William Trevor, master of the short story, and the hugely popular Maeve Binchy two of the best-loved and most recognized. Among the finest living authors are Anne Enright, Ireland's inaugural Laureate for Irish Fiction, and John Banville (both Man Booker Prize winners), while Colm Tóibín's quietly brilliant writing leapt to the world's attention after his novel *Brooklyn* was adapted into an Oscar-nominated film.

Charlie Byrne's Bookshop

Charlie Byrne's is one of Ireland's most popular independent book-shops. With over 100,000 books stocked on every topic imaginable, this bibliophile's paradise offers a good supply of author-signed titles, and also runs a number of book clubs.

→

The book-lined interior of
Charlie Byrne's in Galway

INSIDER TIP
Joyce Location

Sweny's Pharmacy in Dublin has been preserved in its original 1850s style and still sells *Ulysses*-style soap.

Dublin Literary Pub Crawl

This award-winning tour follows the footsteps of famous writers through the pubs they frequented. Professional actors perform the works of Joyce, Beckett and others over a hugely entertaining and enlightening couple of hours.

 Joyce statue by Ian Pollock in a Dublin pub

↑ Exterior of Seamus Heaney Homeplace Museum

Seamus Heaney Homeplace

Opened in 2016, this stunning museum *(p293)* celebrates the life and work of Ireland's most beloved poet. There are interactive exhibitions, personal stories and hundreds of insightful artifacts, creating a fitting tribute to a titan of world literature.

Dalkey Book Festival

Held in the beautiful seaside village of Dalkey in June, this is an intimate literary festival with events hosted in pubs, cafés and even a medieval graveyard. There is always a fantastic line-up, leading Salman Rushdie to describe it as "the best little festival in the world".

→ Event at the Dalkey Book Festival, which has run since 2010

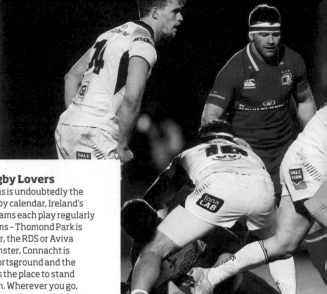

→ Ulster take on the Leinster rugby team at the RDS

A Nation of Rugby Lovers

While the Six Nations is undoubtedly the highlight of the rugby calendar, Ireland's four professional teams each play regularly in their local stadiums – Thomond Park is the home of Munster, the RDS or Aviva stadium houses Leinster, Connacht is based at Galway Sportsground and the Kingspan Stadium is the place to stand up for the Ulstermen. Wherever you go, expect a raucous atmosphere and plenty of post-match pints and analysis.

IRELAND FOR
SPORTS FANS

Ireland offers a wealth of variety for sports fans; all major international team sports are played, though most popular are the two uniquely Irish ones of Gaelic football and hurling. Horse racing attracts fanatical support, while Ireland is also a world-renowned golfing destination.

The Home of Hurling

There are few more thrilling sports to watch live than hurling. Billed as the world's fastest team sport, hurling combines aspects of hockey, lacrosse and baseball, and can trace its origins back to prehistoric times. Watching this high-speed, high-scoring game taking place at Croke Park is an unforgettable, heart-pounding experience.

← Galway takes on Waterford in an All-Ireland hurling final

TOP 5 MOMENTS IN IRISH SPORT

1978
Munster rugby team defeats the All Blacks.

1985
Barry McGuigan wins world featherweight boxing title.

1987
Stephen Roche wins the Tour de France, Giro d'Italia and World Championship in a single season.

1990
Ireland reaches the quarter-finals of the Soccer World Cup in Italy.

2011
Rory McIlroy wins the US open, with a record 16 strokes under par.

← A beachside course at Tralee Golf Club, Kerry

Sample World-Class Golfing

Home to some of the world's best courses, as well as a third of all coastal links, Ireland is a dream golfing destination. Expect spectacular scenery and sprawling golfing estates, such as Antrim's Royal Portrush Golf Club, host of the 2019 British Open Championship. With such resources it's no surprise that Ireland regularly produces champion players, including Rory McIlroy and Shane Lowry.

→ World Series Hurdle Day at Punchestown Festival

A Day at the Races

Horse racing has a rich history in Ireland. Kildare's Punchestown Festival is one of the highlights of the racing calendar. Events at the Curragh in County Kildare or the Leopardstown in Greater Dublin also offer the opportunity to don your gladrags, while Laytown, just north of Dublin, hosts a unique race along the beach.

Belfast's Blossoming Food Scene

Perhaps the island's most exciting foodie destination, Belfast *(p270)* perfectly encapsulates Ireland's wider culinary ambitions. Top chefs use local and seasonal ingredients to create stunning dishes, while any number of quality cheap eats can be found around town – check out St George's Market for a great selection.

←

Tempting dish from Coppi, a contemporary Italian restaurant in Belfast

IRELAND FOR
FOODIES

Ireland's humble gastronomic beginnings are a thing of the distant past. It's now a top foodie destination, thanks to a wealth of talented chefs working with great local ingredients. While the highest concentration of gourmet restaurants is in the main cities, fine cuisine can be found across the island.

TOP 5 MUST-TRY IRISH FOODS

Irish Stew
Meat-and-root-veg stew, slow cooked for hours.

Ulster Fry
Ups the carb count with tasty soda farls and golden potato bread.

Galway Bay Oysters
The wild Atlantic and freshwater combine to give flavourful oysters.

Brown Bread Ice Cream
A luxury in the 1800s, now a modern classic.

Boxty
Popular fried potato dish that's part pancake, part hash brown.

The English Market, Cork

A covered fruit and veg market established in 1610, this is one of the oldest municipal markets in the world. Now a bustling hub offering all manner of delectables, the sheer variety of traders makes it a pleasure to explore.

→

The covered English Market in Cork, packed with delicious produce

 INSIDER TIP
Budding Chefs
Check out Cork's renowned Ballymaloe Cookery School for a huge range of courses.

Sample a Gourmet Pub Lunch

Ireland's first Michelin-starred pub, the Wild Honey Inn, is located at the edge of the Burren (p188). The pub also has 14 comfortable rooms on site – a great option for those keen to fully indulge in chef and co-owner Aidan McGrath's sublime locally flavoured menu.

↓ Refined bistro cooking at the Wild Honey Inn

↑ Cheese Stall at Temple Bar Market, one stop on the Dublin Tasting Trail

Hit the Tasting Trail

This is not only a great introduction to local cuisine, but one of the best ways to explore Dublin (p54). A three-hour stroll around the city takes you to eight different venues, where you can meet producers, taste samples and learn about both the historical and current food scenes.

Galway's Famous Food Festival

The world's longest-running oyster festival is held in Galway (p210) every September, with three days of sea-food trails, shucking competitions, tastings, demonstrations, music and family events. Established in 1954, the event now draws big names from across Ireland and further afield.

→ A participant in Galway's Oyster Festival

A YEAR IN
IRELAND

As a country that values the craic above all else, it's little wonder that Ireland offers a packed calendar of festivities. Whether you're after music gigs, sporting events or festivals rooted in tradition, there are numerous celebrations to be found throughout the year.

Spring

March heralds Ireland's most famous festival, St Patrick's Day. Though spring can be wet, the Irish refuse to let their spirits be dampened and toast the national holiday in honour of the country's patron saint on 17 March with a wave of Guinness and green-themed celebrations throughout the Emerald Isle.

1. St Patrick's Day parade in Dublin

Summer

Hot weather can't be guaranteed to arrive with summer, but when it does the Irish make the most of it. Pubgoers spill onto the streets and it's the perfect time to sample the country's outdoor delights, such as surfing in Donegal or the scenic drives and walks of the Wild Atlantic Way. In Dublin, locals celebrate James Joyce's renowned novel *Ulysses* on Bloomsday

THE TWELFTH

The 1690 Battle of the Boyne, when Dutch Protestant King William of Orange defeated English Catholic King James II, is celebrated as a public holiday on 12 July in Northern Ireland. Although interesting, Orange Order marches are also contentious, heightening Catholic and Protestant friction.

in mid-June with readings and re-enactments, while in Northern Ireland bonfires are piled high and the Orange Order marches to commemorate the Battle of the Boyne.

2. Scenic Slea Head coastal road, Dingle Peninsula, on the Wild Atlantic Way

Autumn

Temperatures drop and the days begin to shorten in autumn, but there's no shortage of entertainment. This season sees a range of festivals across the island, with music lovers especially spoiled for choice. Electric Picnic is a popular Laois-based music-and-arts event – the largest of its kind in Ireland – while Cork and Wexford play host to a jazz and an opera festival respectively. Galway city's long-running Oyster Festival is a wonderful celebration of delicious local seafood.

3. Picnicking in the gardens of Johnstown Castle during the Wexford Opera Festival

Winter

Ireland's winter months can be stormy and bitter. Most years pass without snow, but it's still a time to huddle inside by a crackling fire with a glass of mulled wine. Christmas celebrations sweep the country come December, with most cities offering a festive market.

In February, sports fans follow Ireland's progress in the Six Nations rugby tournament.

4. Belfast's Christmas market and (inset) typical Christmas fare

TOP 4 QUIRKY FESTIVALS

Tedfest
Father Ted TV show fans gather on Inishmore for this convention in February/March.

National Leprechaun Hunt
Adults and kids search for "little green men" hidden in the country-side around Carlingford in mid-May.

Puck Fair
One of Ireland's oldest festivals is held over three days in August in Kerry. A wild mountain goat named "King Puck" presides over the fun and entertainment.

Durrow Scarecrow Festival
This popular scarecrow competition is held in July/August in Laois.

A BRIEF
HISTORY

Ireland's relative isolation has cut it off from many major events experienced by the rest of Europe. Its history is one of internal strife, invasion and reconciliation, with the island divided into the Republic of Ireland and Northern Ireland since 1921. Despite this, Ireland's influence worldwide belies its diminutive size, from mass emigration prompted by the Great Famine to a remarkable literary heritage.

Prehistoric Ireland

Until about 9,500 years ago Ireland was uninhabited. The first people were hunter-gatherers and left few traces of permanent settlement. The 4th millennium BC saw the arrival of Neolithic farmers and herdsmen who built field walls and monumental tombs such as Newgrange. Metalworking and pottery skills were brought from Europe around 2000 BC by the Bronze Age Beaker people. The Iron Age arrived in the 3rd century BC, followed by the Celts, who established themselves as the dominant culture.

1 Viking longships first reached Ireland in AD 795.

2 Poulnabrone Dolmen, a Neolithic portal tomb.

3 King Henry II at Waterford.

4 Strongbow leads the Siege of Waterford.

Timeline of events

7500 BC
First inhabitants of Ireland

500 BC
First wave of Celtic invaders

432 AD
Start of St Patrick's mission to Ireland

795
First Viking invasion of coastal monasteries

3200 BC
Building of Newgrange passage tomb

Celtic Christianity

Celtic Ireland was divided into as many as 100 chiefdoms, though these often owed allegiance to kings of larger provinces such as Munster or Connaught. At times, there was also a titular High King based at Tara. Ireland became Christian in the 5th Century AD, heralding a golden age of scholarship centred on the new monasteries, while missionaries such as St Columba travelled abroad. At the end of the 8th century, Celtic Ireland was shattered by the arrival of the Vikings.

Anglo-Norman Ireland

Anglo-Norman nobles, led by Richard de Clare (nicknamed Strongbow), were invited to Ireland by the King of Leinster in 1169. They took control of the major towns and Henry II of England proclaimed himself overlord of Ireland. In succeeding centuries, however, English power declined – the Anglo-Norman colonies based around Ireland's ports were worst hit by the 1348 Black Death, for example – until the Crown controlled just a small area around Dublin known as the Pale. Many of the Anglo-Norman barons living outside the Pale opposed English rule just as strongly as did the native clans.

WHERE TO SEE ANGLO-NORMAN IRELAND

The strength of Norman fortifications is best seen in the castles at Limerick, Carrickfergus and Trim, and in Waterford's city walls. Surviving Gothic cathedrals include Dublin's Christ Church and St Patrick's, and St Canice's in Kilkenny. There are impressive ruins of medieval Cistercian abbeys at Jerpoint and Boyle.

1014

High King of Ireland Brian Ború defeats joint army of Vikings and the King of Leinster at the Battle of Clontarf

1169

Strongbow's Anglo-Normans arrive at invitation of exiled King of Leinster, Dermot McMurrough

1260

Powerful Irish Chieftain Brian O'Neill killed at the Battle of Down

1348

The Black Death: one third of population killed in three years

1494

Lord Deputy Edward Poynings forbids Irish Parliament to meet without royal consent

49

Protestant Conquest

England's break with the Catholic Church, the dissolution of the monasteries and Henry VIII's assumption of the title King of Ireland (1541) incensed both the Anglo-Norman dynasties and resurgent clans such as the O'Neills. Resistance to foreign rule was fierce and it took over 150 years of war to establish the English Protestant Ascendancy. Tudor and Stuart monarchs adopted a policy of military persuasion, then Plantation – a programme implemented by James I, in which the native Irish were uprooted and their land given to Protestant settlers from England and Scotland in attempts to stabilize the country with garrisons loyal to the Crown. Irish hopes were raised when the Catholic James II ascended to the English throne, but he was deposed and fled to Ireland, where he was defeated by William of Orange in the 1690 Battle of the Boyne.

Georgian Ireland

The Protestant Ascendancy was a period of great prosperity for the landed gentry, who built grand country houses and furnished them luxuriously. Catholics, meanwhile, were denied even the right to buy land. Towards the end of the 18th century,

THE IRISH ABROAD

The Famine resulted in the growth of an Irish community in the USA. The immigrants rose up America's social scale, becoming rich by Irish Catholic standards. They sent money to causes back home, and lobbied for the US government to influence British policies in Ireland. A more militant group, Clan na Gael, sent Civil War veterans to fight in the Fenian risings of 1865 and 1867.

Timeline of events

1541

Henry VIII declared King of Ireland by Irish Parliament

1689

The Siege of Derry, in which 20,000 Protestants are besieged by James II's forces for 105 days; thousands starve to death before relief comes from English warships

1742

First performance of Handel's *Messiah* given in Dublin

1690

William of Orange defeats James II at the Battle of the Boyne; James's army surrenders the following year in Limerick

radicals – influenced by events in America and France – started to demand independence from the English Crown. Prime Minister Henry Grattan tried a parliamentary route; Wolfe Tone and the United Irishmen opted for armed insurrection. Both approaches ultimately failed.

Famine and Emigration

The history of 19th-century Ireland is dominated by the Great Famine of 1845–48, which was caused by the total failure of the potato crop. Although Irish grain was still being exported to England, more than one million people died from hunger or disease, with even more fleeing to North America. By 1900, the pre-famine population of eight million had fallen by half. Rural hardship fuelled a campaign for tenants' rights which evolved into a campaign for independence from Britain. Daniel O'Connell, known as "The Liberator", organized peaceful "monster rallies" of up to a million people in pursuit of Catholic emancipation. O'Connell was dubbed "the uncrowned King of Ireland", a term later also applied to the charismatic politician Charles Stewart Parnell, who made great strides in Parliament towards "Home Rule".

1. Henry VIII named himself King of Ireland in 1541.

2. The 1690 Battle of the Boyne.

3. The capture of Wolfe Tone in 1798.

4. A Great Famine statue in Dublin's Docklands.

Did You Know?

The blight that caused the Famine was a water mould called *Phytophthora infestans*.

1759
Arthur Guinness buys the St James's Gate Brewery in Dublin

GUINNESS
DUBLIN
973584

1798
Rebellion of Wolfe Tone's United Irishmen quashed

1800
Act of Union: Ireland legally becomes part of Britain

1845
Start of Great Famine, which lasts for four years

1884
Founding of Gaelic Athletic Association, first group to promote Irish traditions

War and Independence

Plans for Irish Home Rule were shelved because of World War I, but the abortive Easter Rising of 1916 – which was intended to be a national uprising, but was ultimately confined to 2,500 armed insurgents in Dublin – inspired new support for the Republican cause. In 1919 an unofficial Irish Parliament was established and a war began against the "occupying" British forces.

The Anglo-Irish Treaty of 1921 divided the island in two, granting a degree of independence to the Irish Free State, while Northern Ireland remained in the United Kingdom. This sparked a bitter civil war in the South between those in favour of the Treaty, and staunch republicans who viewed it as a step backwards due to the concessions it granted to Britain. The anti-Treaty faction launched a campaign of guerrilla warfare against the Free State, with Michael Collins (a hero of the 1919 War of Independence) their most prominent victim, until an unofficial ceasefire was called in May 1923. The war created a long-lasting rift between the Irish nationalist parties, but both sides ultimately entered politics, and in 1937 a new constitution declared southern Ireland's complete independence from Great Britain.

ÉAMON DE VALERA

After escaping execution for his part in the Easter Rising, de Valera went on to dominate Irish politics for almost 60 years. He left his original party, Sinn Féin, formed Fianna Fáil and was *Taoiseach* (Prime Minister) 1932-48, and in the 1950s. He was President of Ireland 1959-73.

Timeline of events

1913
Major industrial dispute leads to strikes in Dublin

1916
Easter Rising quashed

1921
Anglo-Irish Treaty signed; de Valera resigns; southern Ireland plunged into civil war

1922
Irish Free State inaugurated; Michael Collins shot dead in ambush in County Cork

1937
New constitution declares complete independence from Britain; country's name changes to Éire

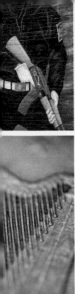

Modern Ireland

Since joining the European Economic Community (now the EU) in 1973, the Irish Republic has done much to modernize its traditional rural-based economy. There have been huge social changes, too; although Ireland was the last country in Europe to legalize divorce (in 1996), in 2015 it became the first country in the world to approve same-sex marriage by a popular vote. In May 2018, Ireland also overwhelmingly voted to repeal the eighth amendment of its constitution, which recognized the equal right to life of mother and unborn child, effectively banning abortion.

Northern Ireland, meanwhile, endured more than 25 years of unrest – widely referred to as the "Troubles". From the late 1960s through to much of the 1990s, Northern Ireland was a battleground, with both Loyalist and Republican paramilitary groups waging bombing campaigns. In 1998 the Good Friday Agreement led to the inauguration of the Northern Ireland Assembly, which brought with it a sustained era of peace, prosperity and hope. Devolved government has at times proved fragile during the ensuing 20 years, however, and Brexit also continues to raise questions over Ireland's future.

1 An Irish newspaper during 1916. ↑

2 Murals in Belfast depict the city's history.

3 Euro coin engraved with a Celtic harp.

4 Irish voters celebrate the gay marriage vote.

Did You Know?

Ireland has won the Eurovision Song Contest seven times, more than any other country.

1956

IRA launches a terrorism campaign along the border of Northern Ireland which lasts until 1962

1972

Bloody Sunday: 14 demonstrators die in Derry after British soldiers open fire; Northern Ireland Parliament suspended and Westminster rule imposed.

1991

Mary Robinson becomes first female President of the Republic, succeeded by Mary McAleese in 1998

2015

Ireland becomes the first country in the world to approve same-sex marriage by popular vote

1998

The Good Friday Agreement sets out proposed framework for self-government in Northern Ireland

EXPERIENCE
DUBLIN

The Old Library's Long Room, Trinity College

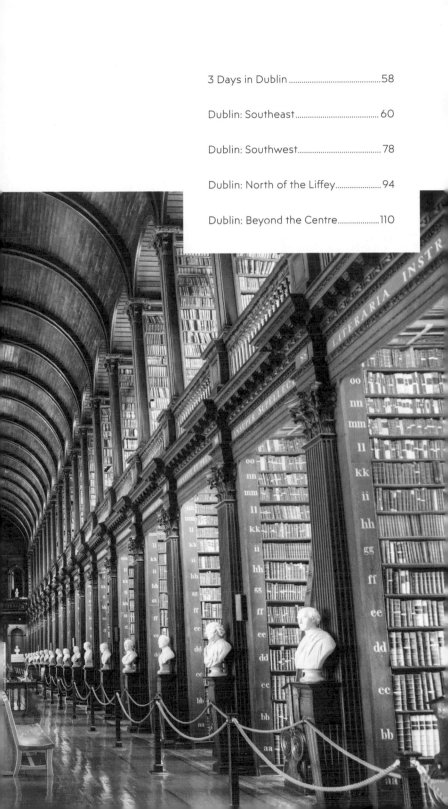

EXPLORE
DUBLIN

This guide divides Dublin into four sight-seeing areas: the three shown on this map and Beyond the Centre. Find out more about each area on the following pages.

STONEYBATTER

Decorative Arts and History Museum

Esplanade

Liffey

King's Inns Park

King's Inns

SMITHFIELD

DUBLIN: NORTH OF THE LIFFEY
p94

Jameson Distillery

St Michan's Church

Four Courts

St Mary's Church

National Leprechaun Museum

Temple Bar

Olympia Theatre

Christ Church Cathedral

City Hall

Dublinia and the Viking World

Dublin Castle

Dubh Linn Garden

Guinness Storehouse

DUBLIN: SOUTHWEST
p78

THE LIBERTIES

St Patrick's Cathedral

Whitefriar St Carmelite Church

Marsh's Library

The Cabbage Garden

St Kevin's Park

IRELAND

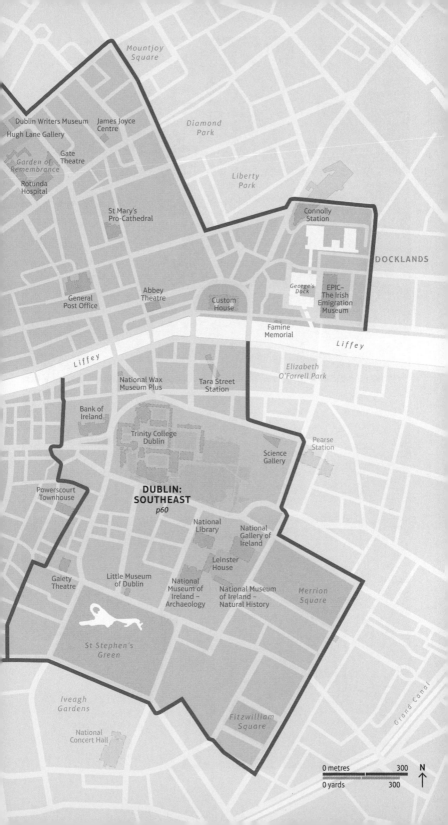

Mountjoy
Square

Dublin Writers Museum
Hugh Lane Gallery
James Joyce
Centre

Diamond
Park

Garden of
Remembrance

Gate
Theatre

Liberty
Park

Rotunda
Hospital

St Mary's
Pro-Cathedral

Connolly
Station

DOCKLANDS

George's
Dock

EPIC–
The Irish
Emigration
Museum

General
Post Office

Abbey
Theatre

Custom
House

Famine
Memorial

Liffey

Liffey

Elizabeth
O'Farrell Park

National Wax
Museum Plus

Tara Street
Station

Bank of
Ireland

Trinity College
Dublin

Science
Gallery

Pearse
Station

Powerscourt
Townhouse

**DUBLIN:
SOUTHEAST**
p60

National
Library

National
Gallery of
Ireland

Gaiety
Theatre

Little Museum
of Dublin

Leinster
House

National
Museum of
Ireland –
Archaeology

National Museum
of Ireland –
Natural History

Merrion
Square

St Stephen's
Green

Iveagh
Gardens

Fitzwilliam
Square

Grand Canal

National
Concert Hall

0 metres   300

0 yards   300

N

←

1 Fallon and Byrne

2 Anne Street South,
off Grafton Street

3 Kilmainham Gaol

4 Irish Museum
of Modern Art

3 DAYS
A Long Weekend in Dublin

Day 1

Morning Split your morning between the magnificent National Museum of Ireland – Archaeology *(p68)* and Trinity College's lovely grounds, making sure to leave time to visit the Book of Kells Exhibition *(p66)*. The university lies right at the heart of the city, so you'll be spoilt for lunch options – try Fallon and Byrne's cavernous food hall (with a candlelit wine bar in the basement) or sample divine pastries at Queen of Tarts *(p88)*.

Afternoon Explore Grafton Street and its offshoots for a little retail therapy; the area offers a huge range, from high street to high-end. Next, stroll the pretty park of St Stephen's Green *(p72)*. If it's a weekend, sign up for the fascinating walking tour, but even a stroll unattended will uncover plenty in this historic city oasis.

Evening Head to Exchequer Street for a cosy dinner at French brasserie The Green Hen. Then finish your night with a pint somewhere on nearby South William Street – try Grogans, one of Dublin's most loved and lively pubs.

Day 2

Morning After a hearty breakfast in the original Brother Hubbard café, stroll across the river for a tour of Dublin Castle *(p82)*. Set aside some time to visit the Chester Beatty Library *(p86)* on site, a one-time winner of the European Museum of the Year. It's also home to The Silk Road Café – a lovely lunch spot offering Middle Eastern and Mediterranean mains and an array of baked goods.

Afternoon Head back north across the Liffey to immerse yourself in Dublin's history at the General Post Office *(p98)*, where the 1916 Rising exhibition is state-of-the-art. Nearby Parnell Square houses both the compact Hugh Lane Gallery *(p104)* and the Dublin Writers Museum *(p105)*, though you may have to choose between the arts in order to do either site justice.

Evening Whatever your decision, end the evening in the Writers Museum basement restaurant, Chapter One. Great Irish ingredients are complemented by knowledgeable staff and lively local customers, resulting in a relaxed gourmet experience.

Day 3

Morning Wander further afield to take a tour of the atmospheric Kilmainham Gaol *(p118)*, before heading across the road to the Irish Museum of Modern Art *(p116)*. A gorgeous museum located in the grounds of the Royal Hospital Kilmainham, this is also the perfect place – Irish weather permitting! – to have a picnic.

Afternoon No trip to Dublin would be complete without a tour of the Guinness Storehouse® *(p114)*, so spend a couple of hours learning all about the history and heritage of the nation's favourite brew. Finish up in the seventh-floor Gravity Bar, which offers panoramic views of the city.

Evening Head towards Portobello for dinner in one of Dublin's best restaurants: the small but sensational Bastible. Hang around for drinks in one of the buzzing bars dotting the neighbourhood, or simply walk off your food with a stroll along the canal.

DUBLIN: SOUTHEAST

Despite its location close to the old walled city, southeast Dublin remained virtually undeveloped until the founding of Trinity College in 1592. Even then, it was almost a hundred years before the ancient common land further south was enclosed to create St Stephen's Green, a spacious city park.

The mid-18th century saw the beginning of a construction boom in the area, with magnificent public buildings such as Trinity College's Old Library and Leinster House being built. The most conspicuous reminders of Georgian Dublin, however, are the beautiful squares and terraces around Merrion Square. Many of these buildings still have their original features, including doorknockers, fanlights and wrought-iron balconies.

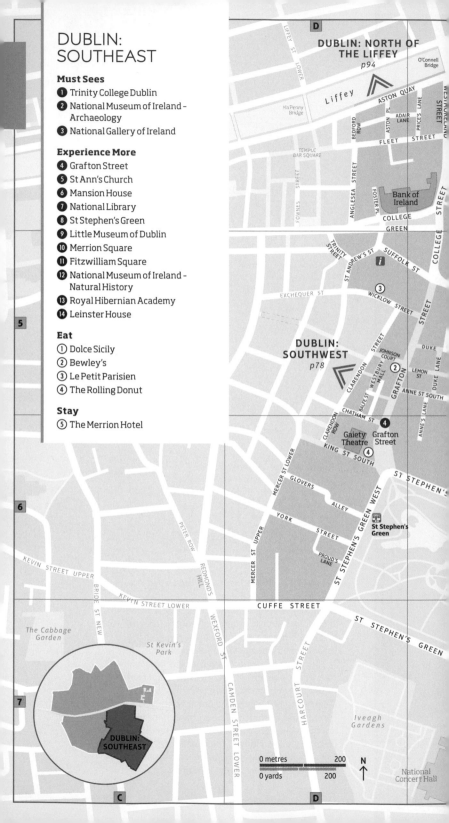

DUBLIN: SOUTHEAST

Must Sees
❶ Trinity College Dublin
❷ National Museum of Ireland – Archaeology
❸ National Gallery of Ireland

Experience More
❹ Grafton Street
❺ St Ann's Church
❻ Mansion House
❼ National Library
❽ St Stephen's Green
❾ Little Museum of Dublin
❿ Merrion Square
⓫ Fitzwilliam Square
⓬ National Museum of Ireland – Natural History
⓭ Royal Hibernian Academy
⓮ Leinster House

Eat
① Dolce Sicily
② Bewley's
③ Le Petit Parisien
④ The Rolling Donut

Stay
⑤ The Merrion Hotel

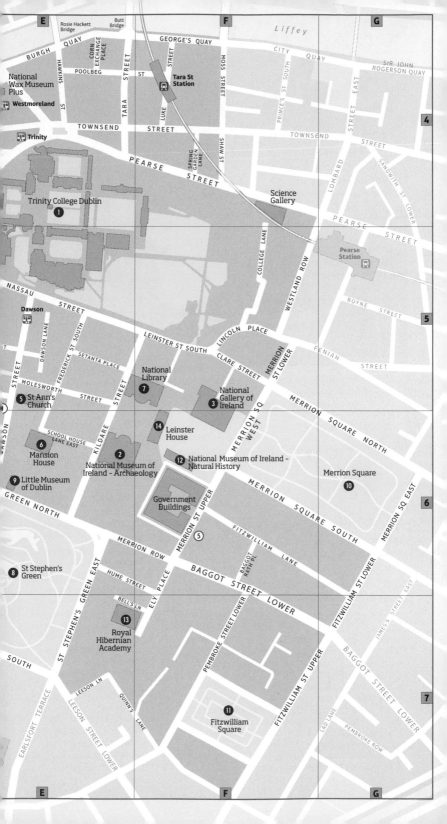

Trinity's Library Square dominated by the campanile, at sunset ↑

TRINITY COLLEGE DUBLIN

E4 🏛 College Green ⏰ Grounds: 7am–midnight Mon–Fri, 8am–6pm Sat & Sun 🌐 tcd.ie

Ireland's most prestigious university, Trinity College Dublin was founded by Queen Elizabeth I in 1592 on the site of an Augustinian monastery.

Originally a Protestant college, it was not until 1793 that Catholics started entering Trinity, although certain restrictions were still applied. Some of these stemmed from the Catholic Church itself, with the threat of excommunication hanging over any Catholic who enrolled until the 1970s. Today, the diverse student population numbers over 17,000, and the college's landscaped lawns and cobbled quads provide a pleasant haven in the heart of the bustling city. The major attractions are the Long Room and the Book of Kells Exhibition, housed in the Old Library (for which there is a small admission fee). At the first hint of warm weather, students and Dubliners alike flock to the Pav – the campus bar – and spill onto the cricket grounds with cans of cold beer.

SCIENCE GALLERY DUBLIN

Bridging the gap between science and art, Trinity's free, innovative museum is full of surprises. Nestled at the very edge of campus, it's packed with thought-provoking exhibitions, from the connection between art and violence to the future of the human race. There's no permanent collection, but rather an ever-changing programme of events, which means there's always a reason to come back.

↑ Arnaldo Pomodoro's *Sphere within Sphere*, one of the many pieces of art that dot the campus

↑ Trinity's main entrance, on College Green

Today, the diverse student population numbers over 17,000, and the college's landscaped lawns and cobbled quads provide a pleasant haven in the heart of the bustling city.

Famous Alumni

1744–8

△ **Edmund Burke**
Political writer Burke founded Trinity's Historical Society, the oldest student society in the world.

1864–70

△ **Bram Stoker**
Best remembered for his Gothic novel *Dracula*, the author was also an exceptionally skilful university athlete.

1871–4

△ **Oscar Wilde**
The legendary playwright graduated with a gold medal and went on to become the darling of London society.

1923–7

△ **Samuel Beckett**
A Nobel Prize-winning playwright, Beckett graduated with a first in Modern Languages and was a keen cricketer.

THE BOOK OF KELLS

Trinity's historic Old Library is home to many magnificent manuscripts, the most famous being the celebrated *Book of Kells*. This contains the four gospels in Latin and is the most richly decorated of Ireland's medieval manuscripts, embellished with intricate spirals and figures. It may have been the work of monks from Iona, who fled to Kells in AD 806 after a Viking raid. The book was moved to Trinity in the 17th century.

Exploring the Campus

Visitors to the college can enter through the dramatic front gate, flanked by two famous alumni in bronze. Inside, three quads branch off cobbled Parliament Square. Turning right leads you to the renowned libraries, while much of New Square and Botany Bay (ahead and to your left, respectively) is taken up with classrooms and student accommodation.

Did You Know?

The annual Trinity Ball is Europe's biggest open-air private party.

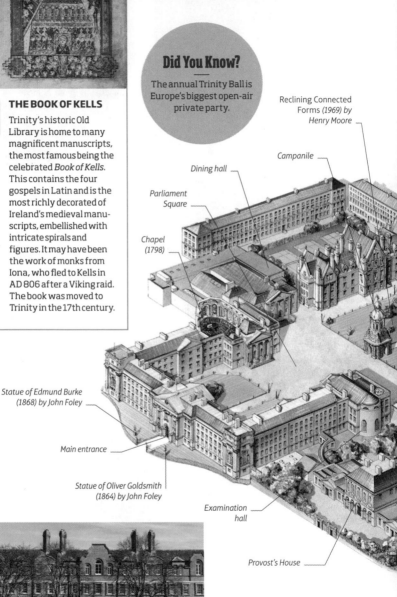

Reclining Connected Forms *(1969)* by Henry Moore

Campanile

Dining hall

Parliament Square

Chapel *(1798)*

Statue of Edmund Burke *(1868) by John Foley*

Main entrance

Statue of Oliver Goldsmith *(1864) by John Foley*

Examination hall

Provost's House

← The Rubrics in Library Square, built around 1700

← The Old Library's spectacular Long Room, home to over 200,000 antiquarian texts

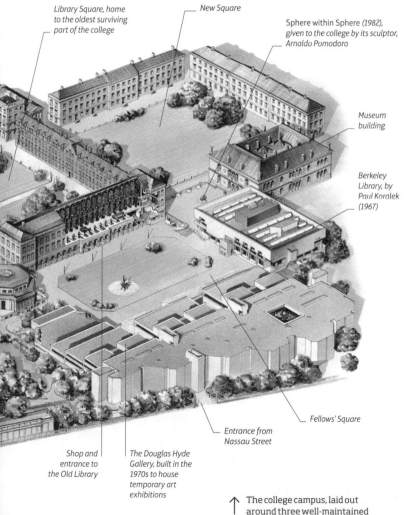

Library Square, home to the oldest surviving part of the college

New Square

Sphere within Sphere *(1982), given to the college by its sculptor, Arnaldo Pornodoro*

Museum building

Berkeley Library, by *Paul Koralek (1967)*

Fellows' Square

Entrance from Nassau Street

Shop and entrance to the Old Library

The Douglas Hyde Gallery, built in the 1970s to house temporary art exhibitions

↑ The college campus, laid out around three well-maintained grass quads

NATIONAL MUSEUM OF IRELAND – ARCHAEOLOGY

📍E6 🏠Kildare St, Dublin 2 🕐10am–5pm Tue-Sat, 1-5pm Mon & Sun
🚫Good Fri & 25 Dec 🌐museum.ie/Archaeology

Opened in 1890, the National Museum of Ireland – Archaeology has a domed rotunda featuring marble pillars and a mosaic floor. The collection is similarly spectacular, and includes some of Ireland's most famous crafted artifacts.

The National Museum of Ireland is housed across four sites, with each specializing in a particular area of science and culture – the others are Decorative Arts and History at Collins Barracks *(p119)*, Country Life in Mayo *(p214)* and Natural History in Merrion Square *(p74)*. The archaeological branch focuses largely on Irish treasures, although there is also a stunning Ancient Egypt display, comprising around 3,000 objects. Other exhibitions here include Viking Ireland; Ór – Ireland's Gold, one of the most extensive collections of Bronze Age gold in Western Europe; and Kingship and Sacrifice, a stand-out collection of Iron Age bog bodies that examines the connection between human sacrifice and sovereignty rituals.

Did You Know?

Bog bodies retain their skin and internal organs because the surrounding peat mummifies them.

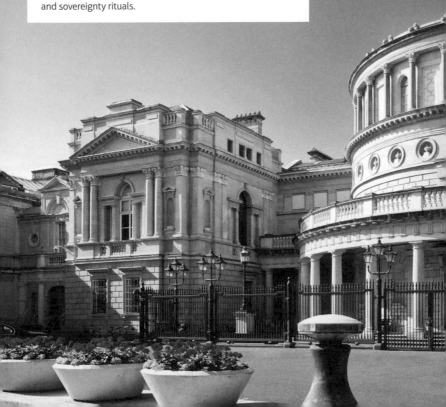

① The National Museum's central atrium, home to its Ór – Ireland's Gold exhibit on the ground floor.

② A 4,500-year-old logboat is part of the Prehistoric Ireland display.

③ This gilt cartonnage case of Egyptian mummy Tentdinebu is thought to date back to c 945–716 BC.

GALLERY GUIDE

The ground floor holds the Treasury, Ór – Ireland's Gold, the Kingship and Sacrifice exhibition, and the Prehistoric Ireland display. On the first floor is the Medieval Ireland exhibition, which illustrates many aspects of life in Ireland during the later Middle Ages. Also on the first floor are artifacts from ancient Egypt and from the Viking settlement of Dublin. Temporary exhibition space is located on both the ground and first floors, with past exhibitions having included Viking Ships and Finds from Irish Wetlands.

←

The National Museum's Kildare Street entrance

NATIONAL GALLERY OF IRELAND

◉ F5 **⌂ Clare Street, Merrion Square W, Dublin 2** **🕐 11am–5:30pm Mon, 9:45am–5:30pm Tue–Sat (to 8:30pm Thu), 11:30am–5:30pm Sun** **🗙 Good Fri & 24–26 Dec** **ⓦ nationalgallery.ie**

This purpose-built gallery was opened to the public in 1864, initially displaying a collection of just 112 pictures. It is now home to over 16,300 European and Irish artworks, including paintings, prints and sculptures.

Ireland's National Gallery houses many excellent exhibits, largely due to generous bequests such as the Milltown collection of works of art from Russborough House (p144) – a gift so large that an extension had to be constructed in order to accommodate it. Playwright George Bernard Shaw was also a benefactor, leaving a third of his estate to the gallery. Although the emphasis is on Irish art such as Jack Yeats' paintings, the major schools of European painting are also well represented, with highlights of the collection including works by Vermeer, Picasso and Velázquez. A magnificent multi-million euro refurbishment of the Dargan and Milltown wings revealed a sleek new interior that deftly marries old and new aspects of the building.

> INSIDER TIP
> **Get Creative**
>
> The gallery has some great online resources for those who have been inspired by their visit. Why not create your own masterpieces from the comfort of your home?

The gallery's rich collection of artworks on display ↓

↑ *The Taking of Christ*, a 1602 composition by Caravaggio that has enhanced the gallery's reputation

↑ *Pierrot*, a 1921 Cubist-style work by Juan Gris, one of many variations that he painted on the theme

→
The gallery's modern Millennium Wing entrance

EXPERIENCE MORE

4

Grafton Street

D6

The spine of Dublin's most popular and stylish shopping district runs south from Trinity College to St Stephen's Green Shopping Centre. This busy pedestrianized strip, cha-racterized by buskers and talented street theatre artists, is home to Brown Thomas, one of Dublin's finest depart-ment stores. There are also many excellent jewellers. Number 78 stands on the site of Samuel Whyte's school, whose illustrious roll included Robert Emmet (p83), leader of the 1803 Rebellion, and the Duke of Wellington. Along many of the side streets are quaint, traditional Irish pubs.

On nearby Suffolk Street, just a short walk away, is a 1988 statue by Jean Rynhart of the celebrated street trader from the traditional song "Molly Malone".

5

St Ann's Church

E5 **Dawson St**
Summer: 10:45am-2:45pm Mon-Fri; winter: 11am-2pm Mon-Fri
stann.dublin.anglican.org

St Ann's, founded in 1707, has a striking Romanesque façade, added in 1868, and colourful stained-glass windows. The church is known for charity work: in 1723 Lord Newton left a bequest to buy bread for the poor. The shelf for the bread still stands next to the altar.

6

Mansion House

E6 **Dawson St**
To the public

Set back from Dawson Street, this Queen Anne-style build-ing was built in 1710 for Joshua Dawson, an aristocrat after whom the street is named. The Dublin Corporation bought it five years later as the official residence of the city's Lord Mayor. The Round Room adjacent to the main building was built in 1821 for the visit of King George IV. The Dáil Éireann (p75) first met here on 21 January 1919.

7

National Library

F5 **Kildare St**
9:30am-7:45pm Mon-Wed, 9:30am-4:45pm Thu & Fri, 9:30am-12:45pm Sat
Public hols **nli.ie**

Designed by Sir Thomas Deane, the National Library opened in 1890. It now contains first editions of every major Irish writer and a copy of almost every book ever published in Ireland. Visitors can view the famous Reading Room where distinguished Irish writers have studied, or explore the award-winning exhibitions.

The Genealogy Advisory Service is available for free to all personal callers. The library also hosts a programme of events, including lectures, poetry and music recitals, theatre, children's storytelling and creative workshops.

8

St Stephen's Green

E6 **Daylight hours all year round**

Originally one of three ancient commons in the old city, St Stephen's Green was enclosed in 1664. The 9-ha (22-acre) green was laid out in its present form in 1880, using a grant given by Lord Ardilaun, a member of the Guinness family. Landscaped with flowerbeds, trees, a fountain and a lake, the green is dotted with memorials to eminent Dubliners, including Ardilaun himself. There is a bust of James Joyce, and a 1967 memorial by Henry Moore dedicated to W B Yeats. At the Merrion Row corner stands a massive monument (1967) by Edward Delaney to 18th-century nationalist leader Wolfe Tone – it is known locally as "Tonehenge". The 1887

← Bronze *Molly Malone* at the top of Suffolk Street

Dubliners relaxing on the sun-dappled grass of St Stephen's Green, with the 1887 bandstand in the background

EAT

Four of the best sweet treats near Grafton Street.

Dolce Sicily

Georgian café with divine Sicilian pastries.

 E5 📍 43 Dawson St 📞 672 9215

€€€

Bewley's

Dublin's most iconic café, with fresh-baked treats.

 D5 📍 78-79 Grafton St 🌐 bewleys.com

€€€

Le Petit Parisien

Parisian-style café with delectable patisserie.

 D5 📍 17 Wicklow St 🌐 lepetitparisien.ie

€€€

The Rolling Donut

Uniquely flavoured doughnuts, including vegan options.

 D6 📍 55 King St South 🌐 therollingdonut.ie

€€€

---

bandstand is the focal point for free concerts in summer.

The imposing Royal College of Surgeons stands on the west side. Built in 1806, it was commandeered by rebel troops under Countess Constance Markievicz in the 1916 Rising *(p99)* and its columns still bear the marks of bullets from the fighting.

The most prominent building on the north side is the venerable Shelbourne hotel. Dating back to 1824, it is well worth popping in for a look at the chandeliered foyer or afternoon tea in the Lord Mayor's Lounge.

Situated on the south side is Newman House, home of the Catholic University of Ireland (now part of University College), named after its first rector John Henry Newman. A complex of two townhouses, the house features some of the city's best surviving Georgian interiors, including intricate Baroque stuccowork (1739) by the Swiss brothers Paolo and Filippo Lafrancini. A part of the building now houses the Museum of Literature Ireland, which celebrates the work of James Joyce, who was a student here, and other titans of Irish literature.

The small University Church (1856) next door has a colourful, marbled Byzantine interior. Also on the south side of St Stephen's Green is Iveagh House – once owned by the Guinness family and now the Department of Foreign Affairs.

Little Museum of Dublin

📍 E6 📍 15 St Stephen's Green 🕚 11am-5pm daily 🌐 littlemuseum.ie

Described as "Dublin's best museum experience" by *The Irish Times*, the Little Museum of Dublin is housed in a beautiful Georgian building on St Stephen's Green. It charts the cultural, social and political history of the capital through a collection of over 5,000 items, including art, photography, letters and postcards, donated by the public. Admission (by guided tour only) includes a 10 per cent discount in Hatch & Sons, the acclaimed restaurant in the basement of the museum.

↑ Artwork by Mick O'Dea, Little Museum of Dublin

↑ Statue of Oscar Wilde lounging on a rock in Merrion Square

 PICTURE PERFECT
Wilde Life

The statue of Oscar Wilde in Merrion Square makes an appropriately colourful photo. The famed playwright can be found reclining on a rock in the square's northern corner, staring back towards his childhood home.

 10

Merrion Square

📍 G6 🌐 merrionsquare.ie

Merrion Square, one of Dublin's largest and grandest Georgian squares, was laid out by John Ensor around 1762.

On the west side of the square are the impressive façades of the Natural History Museum, the National Gallery (p70) and the front garden of Leinster House. There are lovely Georgian townhouses on the other three sides of the square.

Many of the houses – now predominantly used as office space – have plaques detailing the rich and famous who once lived in them. These include the poet W B Yeats, who lived at No 82, while the playwright Oscar Wilde spent his childhood at No 1.

The attractive central park once served as an emergency soup kitchen, feeding the hungry during the Great Famine in the 1840s (p222). On the northwest side of the park stands the restored Rutland Fountain. It was originally erected in 1791 for the sole use of Dublin's poor.

 11

Fitzwilliam Square

📍 F7

This square, which dates from the 1790s, was one of the last Georgian squares to be laid out in central Dublin. Much smaller than Merrion Square, it is a popular location for medical practices. The square still showcases some of the city's finest architecture,

though 16 townhouses on Fitzwilliam Street Lower were torn down in the 1960s to make way for offices. The square's garden is closed to the public.

 12

National Museum of Ireland - Natural History

📍 F6 🏛 Merrion St 🕙 10am-5pm Tue-Sat, 1-5pm Mon & Sun ✖ Good Fri, 25 Dec 🌐 museum.ie

This museum was opened in 1857 with an inaugural lecture by Scottish explorer Dr David Livingstone. Inside the front door are three skeletons of extinct giant deer known as the "Irish elk". The Irish Room on the ground floor is devoted to local wildlife. The upper

GEORGIAN DUBLIN

The 18th century was Dublin's Age of Elegance, when Irish gentry set about remodelling it into one of Europe's most elegant cities. In the 19th century wealth declined and many grand streets deteriorated - but happily much of the surviving architecture can be seen near Merrion Square.

floor illustrates the range of mammals inhabiting our planet. Among the most fascinating exhibits are the primates, a Bengal tiger and skeletons of whales.

13

Royal Hibernian Academy

📍 E7 🏛 15 Ely Place 🕒 11am–5pm Mon–Sat (to 8pm Wed), noon–5pm Sun 🚫 Christmas hols 🌐 rhagallery.ie

The academy is one of the largest exhibition spaces in the city. Through its touring exhibitions of painting, sculpture and other works, the institution challenges the public's understanding of the visual arts. This modern building

does look out of place, however, on Ely Place, an attractive Georgian cul-de-sac.

14

Leinster House

📍 F6 🏛 Kildare St 🕒 Tours temporarily suspended, check website for details 🌐 oireachtas.ie

This stately mansion houses the Dáil and the Seanad – the two chambers of the Irish Parliament. Designed by German-born architect Richard Cassels, the Kildare Street façade resembles that of a large townhouse. However, the rear, looking on to Merrion Square, has the air of a country estate complete with sweeping lawns. Email ahead to book a place on one

of the tours, which include the Seanad chamber with its ornamented ceiling. Tours are available only on days when the parliament is not sitting; photo ID is required to gain entry.

Leinster House, the seat of the Irish government

A SHORT WALK
DUBLIN: SOUTHEAST

Distance 2 km (1.5 miles) **Nearest Luas** Trinity
Time 25 minutes

The area around College Green, dominated by the façades of the Bank of Ireland and Trinity College, is very much the heart of Dublin. Picturesque alleys and side streets cut across the busy pedestrianized Grafton Street, and boast many of Dublin's better shops, hotels and restaurants. Significant buildings along your route include the Irish Parliament, the National Library and the National Museum – Archaeology. At the head of Grafton Street, seek sanctuary in St Stephen's Green, a central oasis that is overlooked by fine Georgian buildings.

Bank of Ireland, a grand Georgian building that was originally built as the Irish Parliament

START

COLLEGE GREEN

SUFFOLK ST

GRAFTON

Grafton Street (p72) *is alive with buskers and pavement artists, while the Brown Thomas department store is a major draw at the foot of the street*

GRAFTON STREET

DUKE ST

St Ann's Church (p72), *an 18th-century church with a striking façade and lovely stained-glass windows inside*

ANNE ST STH

Mansion House (p72), *the official residence of Dublin's Lord Mayor since 1715*

DAWSON ST

Fusiliers' Arch (1907)

ST STEPHEN'S GREEN NORTH

St Stephen's Green (p72), *a relaxing city park that hosts lunchtime concerts in summer*

0 metres 50

0 yards 50

N

DUBLIN: SOUTHEAST

Locator Map
For more detail see p62

Trinity College (p64),
*Dublin's premier university,
with modern artworks
throughout its grounds*

Did You Know?

Up until the 1770s,
most of Dublin's public
executions took
place in St Stephen's
Green.

National Library (p73),
*whose magnificent old
reading room was once a
haunt of novelist James Joyce*

**Leinster
House** (p75),
*home to
the Irish
Parliament
since 1922*

**National Museum of
Ireland – Archaeology**
(p68), *where the collec-
tion of Irish antiquities
includes a remarkable
bronze object known
as the Petrie Crown*

NASSAU STREET

MOLESWORTH ST

KILDARE STREET

*The Shelbourne, an ornate
hotel established in 1824
that overlooks the north
side of St Stephen's Green*

↑ Fusiliers' Arch memorial
at the entrance to
St Stephen's Green

DUBLIN: SOUTHWEST

The area around Dublin Castle was first settled in prehistoric times, and it was from here that the city grew. Dublin gets its name from the dark pool (*Dubh Linn*) that formed where the Liffey and the Poddle – a river that once ran through the site of Dublin Castle – met. Archaeological excavations on the banks of the Liffey reveal that the Vikings established a trading settlement here around AD 841.

Following Strongbow's invasion of Dublin in 1170, a medieval city began to emerge, and the Anglo-Normans built strong defensive walls around the castle. Other conspicuous reminders of the Anglo-Normans are the grand Christ Church Cathedral and Ireland's largest church, St Patrick's Cathedral. When the city expanded to the north and east during the Georgian era, the narrow cobbled streets of Temple Bar became a quarter of skilled craftsmen and merchants. Today, this area is well established on the tourist trail, and is home to a variety of alternative shops and cafés.

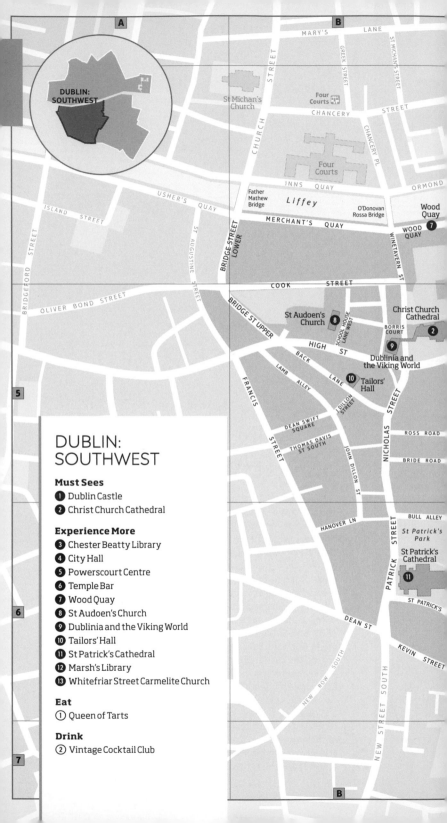

DUBLIN: SOUTHWEST

Must Sees
1. Dublin Castle
2. Christ Church Cathedral

Experience More
3. Chester Beatty Library
4. City Hall
5. Powerscourt Centre
6. Temple Bar
7. Wood Quay
8. St Audoen's Church
9. Dublinia and the Viking World
10. Tailors' Hall
11. St Patrick's Cathedral
12. Marsh's Library
13. Whitefriar Street Carmelite Church

Eat
① Queen of Tarts

Drink
② Vintage Cocktail Club

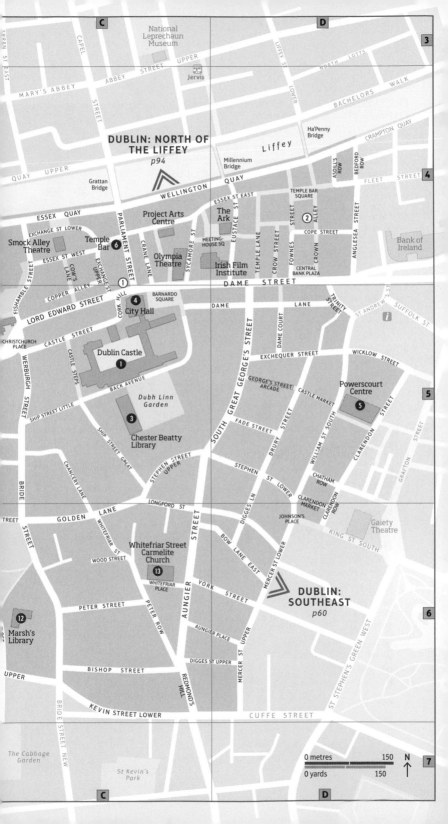

❶ 🏃 Ⓜ 🍽

DUBLIN CASTLE

📍C5 🏠 Off Dame St, Dublin 2 🕘9:45am–5:45pm daily
🚫1 Jan, 25–27 Dec 🌐dublincastle.ie

One of the most important buildings in Irish history, Dublin Castle was built on the site of a Viking fortress in the 13th century and remained the seat of English rule here for seven centuries. Today the castle is both a key visitor attraction and a government complex.

All that remains of the original castle is the southeastern Medieval Tower (also known as the Record Tower), with most of the rest of the building added from the 18th century onwards. Following a fire in 1684, the Surveyor-General, Sir William Robinson, laid down plans for the Upper and Lower Castle Yards in their present form. On the first floor of the south side of the Upper Yard are the luxury State Apartments, including St Patrick's Hall. These magnificent rooms served as home to the British-appointed Viceroys of Ireland. The castle was officially handed over to Ireland in 1922, when the Irish Free State was declared.

↑ Bedford Tower, the centrepiece of the Upper Yard

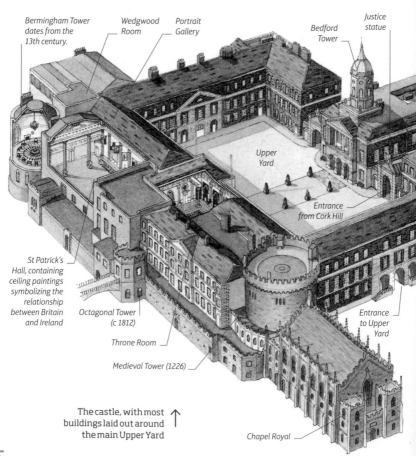

Bermingham Tower dates from the 13th century.

Wedgwood Room

Portrait Gallery

Justice statue

Bedford Tower

Upper Yard

Entrance from Cork Hill

St Patrick's Hall, containing ceiling paintings symbolizing the relationship between Britain and Ireland

Octagonal Tower (c 1812)

Throne Room

Medieval Tower (1226)

Entrance to Upper Yard

The castle, with most buildings laid out around the main Upper Yard ↑

Chapel Royal

1 The figure of Justice faces the Upper Yard above the main entrance from Cork Hill. The statue initially aroused much cynicism among Dubliners, who felt she was turning her back on the city.

2 The Chapel Royal was completed in 1814 by Francis Johnston. The 103 heads on the exterior of this Neo-Gothic church were carved by Edward Smyth.

3 The Throne Room, one of the grandest of the State Apartments, contains a throne first installed for the visit of King George IV in 1821.

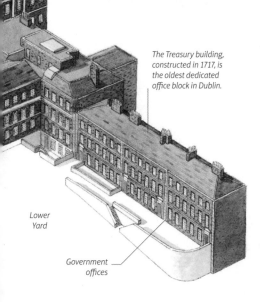

The Treasury building, constructed in 1717, is the oldest dedicated office block in Dublin.

Lower Yard

Government offices

ROBERT EMMET

Leader of the abortive 1803 rebellion, Robert Emmet (1778–1803) is remembered as a heroic champion of Irish liberty. His plan was to capture Dublin Castle as a signal for the country to rise up against the Act of Union. The plan failed; Emmet was detained in the Kilmainham Gaol and hanged, but the defiant, patriotic speech he made from the dock helped to inspire future generations of Irish freedom fighters.

② 🗺 Ⓜ 🖼 🛍

CHRIST CHURCH CATHEDRAL

📍 B5 🏠 Christchurch Place 🕐 Check website for details
🚫 26 Dec 🌐 christchurchcathedral.ie

This is Dublin's oldest building, with earliest manuscripts dating the cathedral to its current hilltop location from the 1030s. Once a place of great medieval pilgrimage, its ornate interiors and fascinating crypt can still be explored today.

Christ Church Cathedral was established by the Hiberno-Norse king of Dublin, Sitric "Silkbeard", and Dunan, the first bishop of Dublin. It has since been rebuilt several times; first by the Anglo-Norman archbishop John Cumin, in 1186. By the 19th century the cathedral had fallen into a bad state of repair, but was remodelled by architect George Street in the 1870s – resulting in the heavily Victorianized exterior seen today. The vast 12th-century crypt was restored in 2000 and contains a number of interesting curios, plus the cathedral café and shop. Today, both Christ Church and its sister cathedral, St Patrick's, are unusual in their Church of Ireland affiliation within a largely Catholic nation.

→

The cathedral, a mix of original medieval architecture and Victorian renovation

Great Nave

Bridge to the Synod Hall, added when the cathedral was being rebuilt in the 1870s

Crypt

Strongbow Monument

←

Christ Church Cathedral in its hilltop location at the end of Dublin's Fishamble Street

Did You Know?
—
After being exposed as a pretender, Lambert Simnel was put to work in Henry VII's royal kitchens.

The Lady Chapel, used to celebrate the daily Eucharist

Stairs to crypt

1 The 25-m- (68-ft-) high Great Nave has some fine early Gothic arches.

2 A mummified cat and rat are two of the crypt's more unexpected residents, affectionately nicknamed Tom and Jerry.

3 This curious monument may be part of the original tomb of Strongbow, who is buried in the cathedral.

Timeline				
1038 Construction of original wooden Viking cathedral	*1240* ▲ Completion of stone cathedral	*1487* ▲ Coronation of 10-year-old Lambert Simnel as King of England	*1742* Choir participates in the first performance of Handel's *Messiah*	*1871* ▲ Major rebuilding of the cathedral begins, including the Synod Hall and bridge

EXPERIENCE MORE

3

Chester Beatty Library

📍 C5 🏛 Dublin Castle
🕐 9:45am-5:30pm Mon-
Sat (to 8pm Wed), noon-
5:30pm Sun 🚫 Nov-Feb:
Mon, 1 Jan, Good Fri, 24-26
Dec & public hols 🌐 chester
beatty.ie

This world-renowned collection of artistic treasures from Asia, the Middle East, North Africa and Europe was donated to Ireland by the American mining magnate and art collector Sir Alfred Chester Beatty. He was consequently named as Ireland's first honorary citizen in 1957.

During his lifetime, Beatty accumulated almost 300 copies of the Koran, representing the works of master calligraphers. Also on display are 6,000-year-old Babylonian stone tablets, Greek papyri and biblical material written in Coptic, the ancient language of Egypt.

← Babylonian stone tablet on display at Chester Beatty Library

Treasures from the Far East include a collection of Chinese jade books – each leaf is made from thinly cut jade, engraved with Chinese characters, which are then filled with gold. Burmese and Siamese art is represented by the collection of 18th- and 19th-century *Parabaiks*, books of folk tales with colourful illustrations on mulberry leaf paper. The Japanese collection includes paintings, woodblock prints, and books and scrolls from the 16th to 19th centuries. One of the most beautiful manuscripts in the western European collection is the *Coëtivy Book of Hours*, an illuminated 15th-century French prayer book.

4

City Hall

📍 C5 🏛 Cork Hill, Dame St
🕐 10am-5:15pm Mon-Sat
🚫 1 Jan, Good Fri & 24-26
Dec & bank hols 🌐 dublin
city.ie/dublincityhall

Designed by Thomas Cooley, this Corinthian-style building was erected between 1769 and 1779 as the Royal Exchange. It was bought by Dublin Corporation in 1851 as a meeting place for the city council.

The building has been sympathetically restored to its original condition and a permanent multimedia exhibition, *Dublin City Hall – The Story of the Capital*, traces the evolution

↑ The Powerscourt Centre's imposing staircase and enclosed courtyard

A bustling pub in Dublin's Temple Bar area

performance art; and the Irish Film Institute on Eustace Street, which shows art-house and independent films, and houses a restaurant/bar and shop.

Nearby Meeting House Square, with its retractable canopy, hosts a programme of outdoor concerts, film screenings and theatre performances. The National Photographic Archive and Gallery of Photography are also on the square and there is an excellent organic food market here on Saturdays.

---

7 Wood Quay

📍 B4

Named after the timber supports used to reclaim the land, Wood Quay underwent controversial excavations in the 1970s, which revealed the remains of one of the earliest Viking villages in Ireland (p89). The artifacts can be seen at the Dublinia exhibition (p88) and at the National Museum (p68).

The site is now occupied by Dublin City Council's civil offices, but parts of the excavated area are open for public viewing.

---

of Dublin, from before the Anglo-Norman invasion of the city in 1170 to the present day.

---

5 Powerscourt Centre

📍 D5 🏛 William St South
🕐 10am-6pm Mon-Fri (8pm Thu), 9am-6pm Sat, noon-6pm Sun
🌐 powerscourtcentre.ie

Completed in 1774 by Robert Mack, this grand mansion was built as the city home of Viscount Powerscourt. Granite from the Powerscourt Estate (p132) was used in its construction. Inside it still features the original grand mahogany staircase, and detailed plasterwork by Michael Stapleton.

Today the building houses one of Dublin's best shopping centres. Major restoration during the 1960s turned it into a centre of specialist galleries, antique shops, jewellery stalls, cafés and other shop units. The enclosed central courtyard, topped by a glass dome, is a popular meeting place with Dubliners. The centre can also be reached from Grafton Street down the Johnson Court alley.

---

6 Temple Bar

📍 C4 🏛 Temple Bar
Information: 677 2255

These narrow, cobbled streets running between the Bank of Ireland and Christ Church Cathedral (p84) are now home to some of the city's best galleries and arts spaces, as well as many lively pubs. In the 18th century the area was home to many insalubrious characters– Fownes Street was noted for its brothels. Skilled craftsmen and artisans lived and worked around Temple Bar until post-war industrialization led to a decline in the area's fortunes.

In the 1970s, some of the retail and warehouse premises were rented out to young artists or to record, clothing and book shops, and the area developed an "alternative" identity. Temple Bar today is a mix of galleries and theatres alongside kitsch tourist pubs, souvenir shops, fast-food restaurants and nightclubs. Highlights include the Project Arts Centre on East Essex Street, a highly respected venue for avant-garde

---

↑ The tower of St Audoen's Church, set among beautifully kept green shrubbery

8

St Audoen's Church

📍 B5 🏠 High St, Cornmarket
🕐 Hours vary, check website
🌐 heritageireland.ie

Designated a national monument, St Audoen's is the earliest surviving medieval church in Dublin.

Inside, the 15th-century nave remains intact and leads to the high altar. There is also a beautiful carved pulpit and canopy. An outstanding organ sits in an elevated position at the rear, atop the wooden entrance. The church's three bells date from 1423.

The building stands in an attractive churchyard with well-kept lawns and shrubs. To the rear of the churchyard, steps lead down to St Audoen's Arch, the only remaining gate-way of the old city. Flanking the gate are restored sections of the 13th-century city walls.

Next door stands a grand Roman Catholic Church of the same name, which was built in the 1840s and designed by Irish architect Patrick Byrne. Two Pacific clam shells by the front door hold holy water.

EAT

Queen of Tarts

Great brunches, savoury dishes and - most importantly - a magnificent array of homemade cakes can be enjoyed at this quaint Dublin institution.

📍 C4 🏠 4 Cork Hill, Dame St
🌐 queenoftarts.ie

9

Dublinia and the Viking World

📍 B5 🏠 St Michael's Hill
🕐 Mar-Sep: 10am-6:30pm daily (last adm 5:30pm); Oct-Feb: 10am-5:30pm daily (last adm 4:30pm)
🗓 24-26 Dec 🌐 dublinia.ie

Relive life in medieval Dublin with this state-of-the-art exhibition. Dublinia, as the town was first recorded on a map around 1540, covers the formative period of Dublin's history from the arrival of the Anglo-Normans in the city in 1170 to the closure of the monasteries in the 1540s. The exhibition is housed in the Neo-Gothic Synod Hall, which, up until 1983, was home to the ruling body of the Church of Ireland. The building and the hump-backed bridge linking it to Christ Church Cathedral (there is a charge to enter the cathedral) date from the 1870s. Before Dublinia was established in 1993, the Synod Hall was used as a nightclub.

The exhibition is interactive, encouraging the visitor to investigate Dublin's past. The Medieval Dublin exhibition brings the city's sights and sounds to life. Crime and pun-ishment, death and disease, and even toothache remedies from 700 years ago are all part of the Dublinia experience. Major events in Dublin's history, such as the Black Death and the rebellion of Silken Thomas, are also portrayed here, and there is a large-scale model of Dublin around 1500. An interactive archaeology room highlights excavations at nearby Wood Quay (p87).

> **Crime and punish-ment, death and disease, and even toothache remedies from 700 years ago are all part of the Dublinia experience.**

Climb the 96 steps of the 60-m- (200-ft-) high medieval St Michael's Tower for one of the best vantage points for views across the city.

Tailors' Hall

☐ B5 ☐ Back Lane ☐ Closed temporarily until further notice, check website ☐ antaisce.org

Dublin's only surviving guildhall preserves a delightful corner of old Dublin in an otherwise busy redevelopment zone. Built in 1706, Tailors' Hall stands behind a limestone arch in a cobbled yard. The building is the oldest guildhall in Ireland and was used by various trade groups including hosiers, saddlers, and barber-surgeons as well as tailors. It also hosted political meetings – Wolfe Tone addressed a public United Irishmen rally here before the 1798 rebellion. The building was closed down in the early 1960s due to neglect, but an appeal by Desmond Guinness saw it refurbished. It is now the headquarters of An Taisce (the National Trust for Ireland).

THE VIKINGS IN DUBLIN

Viking raiders arrived in Ireland in the late 8th century AD and founded Dublin in 841. They built a fort where the River Poddle met the Liffey at a black pool (Dubh Linn), on the site of Dublin Castle. Following their defeat by Brian Ború at the Battle of Clontarf in 1014, the Vikings integrated with the local Irish, adopting Christian beliefs. After Strongbow's Anglo-Norman invasion of Ireland in 1169, the Hiberno-Viking trading community declined, and many were banished to a separate colony called Oxmanstown.

VIKING SHIP

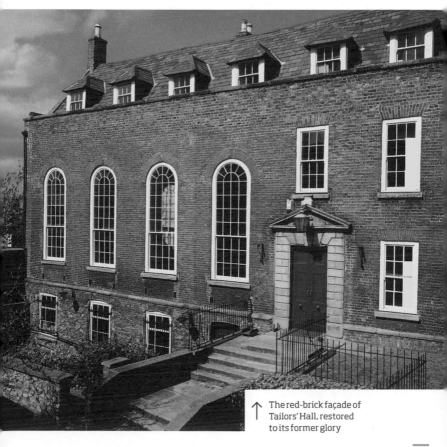

↑ The red-brick façade of Tailors' Hall, restored to its former glory

St Patrick's Cathedral

⑦B6 **⛨St Patrick's Close**
**🕐9:30am-5pm Mon-Fri,
9am-6pm Sat (to 5pm Nov-
Feb), 9-10:30am, 12:30-
2:30pm, 4:30-6pm Sun
(to 2:30pm Nov-Feb)**
🌐stpatrickscathedral.ie

Ireland's largest church was founded beside a sacred well where St Patrick is said to have baptized converts around AD 450. A Celtic stone slab covering the remains of a well was unearthed over a century ago. It is now preserved in the west end of the cathedral's nave. The original building was just a wooden chapel and remained so until 1192, when Archbishop John Cumin rebuilt it in stone.

In the mid-17th century, Huguenot refugees from France arrived in Dublin, and were given the Lady Chapel by the Dean and Chapter as their place of worship. The chapel was separated from the rest of the cathedral and used by the Huguenots until the late 18th century. Today St Patrick's Cathedral is the Anglican/Episcopalian Church of Ireland's national cathedral.

Much of the present building dates back to work completed between 1254 and 1270. The cathedral suffered over the centuries from desecration, fire and neglect but, thanks to the generosity of Sir Benjamin Guinness, it underwent extensive restoration during the 1860s. The building is 91 m (300 ft) long; at the western

end is a 43-m (141-ft) tower, restored by Archbishop Minot in 1370 and now known as Minot's Tower. The spire was added in the 18th century.

The interior is dotted with busts, brasses and monuments, identified through the help of a leaflet available at the front desk. The largest, most colourful and elaborate tomb was dedicated to the Boyle family in the 17th century. Erected by Richard Boyle, Earl of Cork, in memory of his second wife, Catherine, it is decorated with painted figures of his family. Other

famous citizens remembered in the church include the harpist Turlough O'Carolan (1670–1738) and Douglas Hyde (1860–1949), the first president of Ireland.

Many visitors come to see the memorials associated with Jonathan Swift (1667–1745), the satirical writer and Dean of St Patrick's. In the south aisle is "Swift's Corner", containing memorabilia such as an altar table and a bookcase holding his death mask. A self-penned epitaph can be found on the wall on the southwest side of the nave. Close by, brass plates mark his grave and that of his beloved friend (and, some believe, his secret wife) Stella, who died before him in 1728.

At the west end of the nave is an old door with a hole in it – a relic from a feud that took place between the Lords Kildare and Ormonde in 1492. The latter took refuge in the chapter house, but a truce was soon made and a hole was cut in the door by Lord Kildare so the two could shake hands in friendship.

OFF THE BEATEN TRACK

From Christ Church Cathedral it's a 15-minute walk to Dublin's trendy Portobello area - a route lined by fantastic bars and restaurants. Try Gaillot et Gray, a French pizzeria and bakery, or Bastible, one of the neighbourhood's finest bistros. Fallon's Bar has a great buzz, while Leonard's Corner is perfect for a cosy pint.

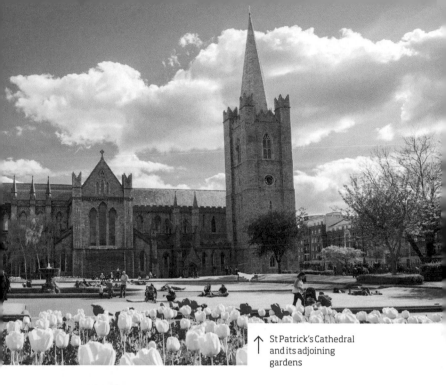

↑ St Patrick's Cathedral and its adjoining gardens

 ←

Volume from the collection at Marsh's Library

Marsh's Library

12

📍 C6 ⏴ St Patrick's Close 🕐 9:30am–5pm Mon & Wed–Fri, 10am–5pm Sat 🔒 10 days at Christmas & public hols 🌐 marshlibrary.ie

The oldest public library in Ireland was built in 1701 for the Archbishop of Dublin, Narcissus Marsh. It was designed by Sir William Robinson, the architect of much of Dublin Castle (p82) and also of the Royal Hospital Kilmainham.

Inside, the bookcases are topped by a mitre and feature carved gables with lettering in gold leaf. To the rear of the library are wired alcoves (or "cages") where readers were locked in with rare books. The collection, from the 16th, 17th and early 18th centuries, includes irreplaceable volumes, such as Bishop Bedell's 1685 translation of the Old Testament into Irish, and Clarendon's *History of the Rebellion*, complete with anti-Scottish margin notes by Jonathan Swift.

Whitefriar Street Carmelite Church

13

📍 C6 ⏴ 56 Aungier St 🕐 7:45am–6pm Mon & Wed–Sat, 8am–7:30pm Tue, 9:30am–7pm Sun & public hols 🌐 whitefriarstreetchurch.ie

Designed by George Papworth, this Catholic church was built in 1827. It stands alongside the site of a medieval Carmelite foundation of which nothing remains.

In contrast to the two cathedrals, St Patrick's and Christ Church, which are usually full of tourists, this church is frequented by city worshippers. Every day they come to light candles to various saints, including St Valentine – the patron saint of lovers. His remains, previously buried in the cemetery of St Hippolytus in Rome, were offered to the church as a gift from Pope Gregory XVI in 1836. Today they rest under the commemorative statue of St Valentine, which stands in the northeast corner of the church beside the high altar.

Nearby is a Flemish oak statue of the Virgin and Child, dating from the late 15th or early 16th century. It may have belonged to St Mary's Abbey (p106) and is believed to be the only wooden statue of its kind to escape destruction when Ireland's monasteries were sacked at the time of the Reformation.

A SHORT WALK
DUBLIN: SOUTHWEST

Distance 2 km (1.5 miles) **Nearest Luas** Westmoreland **Time** 25 minutes

This is Dublin's historic centre, with a wealth of ancient buildings, such as Dublin Castle and Christ Church Cathedral. Some parts lack the sleek appeal of the neighbouring streets around Grafton Street, but redevelopment has helped to rejuvenate the area – especially around Temple Bar, where the attractive cobbled streets are lined with interesting shops, galleries and cafés.

↑ Christ Church Cathedral, with its bridge to Dublinia

Wood Quay (p87), *where the Vikings established their first permanent settlement in Ireland around AD 841*

Sunlight Chambers, *built in 1900 for the Lever Brothers soap-making company and featuring a delightful frieze on the façade*

Christ Church Cathedral (p84), *Ireland's oldest cathedral, has a fascinating crypt*

Dublinia and the Viking World (p88), *an interactive museum, located in the former Synod Hall of the Church of Ireland*

St Werburgh's Church, *built in the 18th century, has an ornate interior hiding behind its somewhat drab exterior*

Dublin Castle (p82), *one of the most important buildings in Irish history, laid out around a wide yard*

City Hall (p86), *originally built as the Royal Exchange in 1779, is fronted by a huge Corinthian portico*

0 metres 50
0 yards 50

Ha'penny Bridge

Temple Bar
(p87), *an arts and entertainments district that occupies a maze of narrow, cobbled streets*

Millennium Bridge

DUBLIN: SOUTHWEST

Locator Map
For more detail see p80

QUAY

TEMPLE BAR

CROWN ALLEY

FOWNES S

▶ START

Central Bank of Ireland

TEMPLE LANE

EUSTACE STREET

EUSTACE ST

SYCAMORE ST

DAME STREET

↑ Cheerful red façade of the iconic Temple Bar Pub

DAME CT

Powerscourt Centre (p87), one of the best places in Dublin to shop for fashion or arts and crafts

EXCHEQUER ST

WILLIAM ST SOUTH

STH GT GEORGE'S ST

DRURY ST

Ⓞ **FINISH**

The Long Hall, a magnificent, old-fashioned pub with a great atmosphere and home to a bewildering array of antique clocks

George's Street Arcade, between Drury Street and South Great George's Street, is a popular spot for buying second-hand clothes and antique jewellery

Did You Know?

The story told along the panels of the Sunlight Chambers is the history of hygiene.

DUBLIN: NORTH OF THE LIFFEY

Dublin's northside was the last part of the city to be developed during the 18th century. The authorities envisioned an area of wide, leafy avenues, but the reality of today's heavy traffic has rather spoiled their original plans. Nonetheless, O'Connell Street – lined with fine statues and monuments – is an impressive thoroughfare.

The area is also home to some of the city's finest public buildings, such as James Gandon's glorious Custom House and the historic General Post Office. Dublin's two most celebrated theatres, the Abbey and the Gate, act as a cultural magnet, as do the Dublin Writers Museum and the James Joyce Centre, two museums dedicated to writers who lived in the city.

Some of Dublin's finest Georgian streetscapes are also found in the north of the city. Many have been neglected for decades, but thankfully some areas, most notably North Great George's Street, have now undergone restoration.

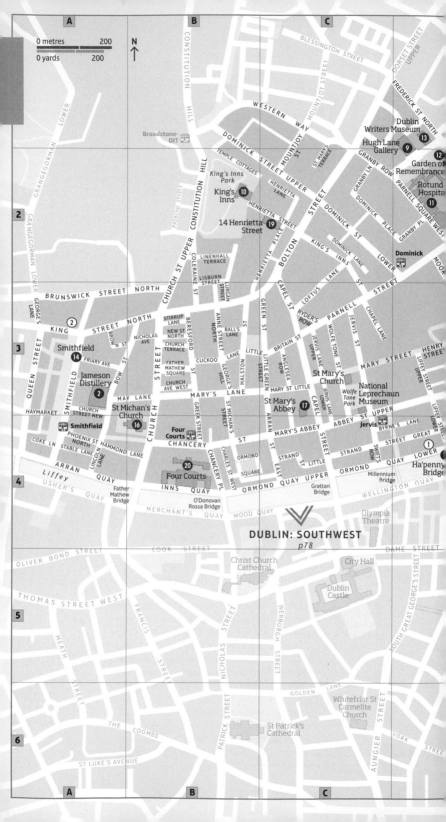

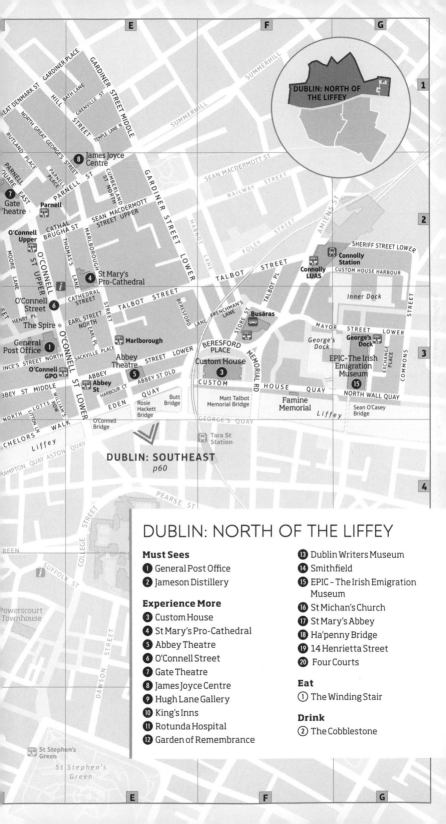

DUBLIN: NORTH OF THE LIFFEY

Must Sees
1 General Post Office
2 Jameson Distillery

Experience More
3 Custom House
4 St Mary's Pro-Cathedral
5 Abbey Theatre
6 O'Connell Street
7 Gate Theatre
8 James Joyce Centre
9 Hugh Lane Gallery
10 King's Inns
11 Rotunda Hospital
12 Garden of Remembrance
13 Dublin Writers Museum
14 Smithfield
15 EPIC – The Irish Emigration Museum
16 St Michan's Church
17 St Mary's Abbey
18 Ha'penny Bridge
19 14 Henrietta Street
20 Four Courts

Eat
① The Winding Stair

Drink
② The Cobblestone

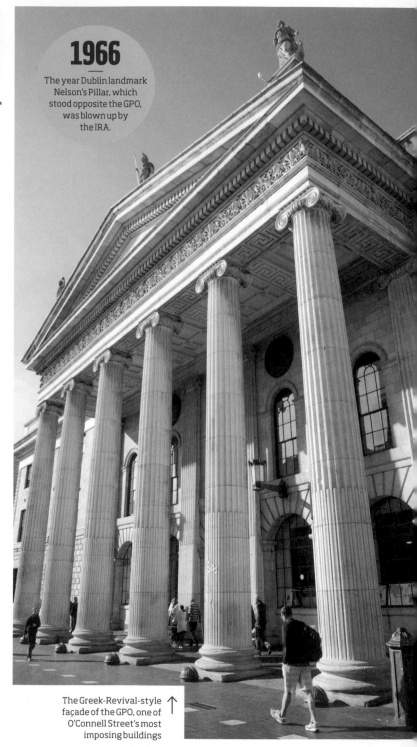

1966
—
The year Dublin landmark Nelson's Pillar, which stood opposite the GPO, was blown up by the IRA.

The Greek-Revival-style ↑ façade of the GPO, one of O'Connell Street's most imposing buildings

① ⊘ Ⓜ ▢ 🏛

GENERAL POST OFFICE

📍 D3 🏠 O'Connell St Lower, Dublin 1 🕐 Post Office: 8:30am–6pm Mon–Sat; Museum: 10am–5:30pm Mon–Sat, noon–5:30pm Sun and public holidays 🚫 1 Jan, 17 Mar, Easter Sunday, 24–26 Dec 🌐 gpowitnesshistory.ie

The General Post Office looms large over Ireland's recent history. Rebels made their headquarters in this building during the 1916 battle for independence, and it has since come to symbolize the Easter Rising more than any other landmark.

Built in the Greek Revival style in 1818, the building still functions as the headquarters of the Irish Post Office. Its imposing façade, with six huge columns of Wicklow granite, makes it one of the most recognizable structures in the country. It suffered heavy damage during the fighting of 1916, and only reopened in 1929 after extensive rebuilding, with the iconic façade all that remains of the original building. Due to its vital role during the Easter Rising, the building's basement now houses a state-of-the-art exhibition called "GPO Witness History", an immersive and interactive attraction that relates the rebellion and its aftermath via eyewitness accounts.

↑ Main hall, where Ireland's declaration of independence is displayed *(right)*

↑ An interactive exhibit, part of "GPO Witness History", the building's basement museum

THE GPO AND THE EASTER RISING

On Easter Monday 1916, members of the Irish Volunteers and Irish Citizen Army seized control of the GPO, and Patrick Pearse read out the Proclamation of the Irish Republic in front of it. The rebels remained inside for a week, but shelling from the British eventually forced them out. Initially many viewed the Rising unfavourably, but as W B Yeats wrote, public opinion "changed utterly" during the following weeks, when 14 of the leaders were caught and shot at Kilmainham Gaol.

JAMESON DISTILLERY

⌖ A3 ⌂ Bow St, Smithfield Village, Dublin 7 ⊕ Hours vary, check website ⌛ 24–26 Dec ⊞ jamesonwhiskey.com

Housed in part of John Jameson's original distillery, a working factory between 1780 and 1971, this beautifully restored building is a worthy monument to the world's leading producer of Irish whiskey. The distillery is based in the heart of Smithfield and offers first-rate tours and whiskey tastings.

A visit here starts with a video, before a 40-minute tour filled with plenty of whiskey-related facts. The displays are set out as a working distillery, with different rooms devoted to the various stages of production. Guides detail how the Irish process differs from that of Scotch whisky distilling: here the barley is dried with clean air, while in Scotland it is smoked over peat. It's claimed that the Irish product is a smoother, less smoky tipple as a result – but you can decide for yourself with a free sample in the bar.

In addition to the tour, visitors can enjoy various other "experiences", including a whiskey cocktail-making class, a whiskey blending class and a cask draw demonstration. The last of these offers visitors the rare opportunity to draw and taste a 14-year-old unblended, pot-still whiskey straight from a Jameson cask.

THE GREAT WHISKEY FIRE OF DUBLIN

On the night of 18 June 1875, a central malt house and warehouse went up in flames, igniting the 5,000 barrels of whiskey within and starting one of the most destructive fires in Dublin's history. Rivers of the ignited liquid spilled through the streets, engulfing everything they touched. By the time the blaze could be brought under control, 13 people were dead. Ironically, none of them died as a direct result of the fire - but rather from alcohol poisoning contracted by drinking the burning hot whiskey flowing through Dublin's dirty gutters.

① A whiskey blending class, where visitors can learn how the experts pull the ingredients together before attempting a blend of their own.

② Huge copper pot stills at the factory in Dublin. Copper is the preferred material to impart flavour into the whiskey.

③ Visitors to the distillery can witness a rare cask draw demonstration.

↑ Bow Street entrance to the distillery, on John Jameson's original site

TOP 5 DISTILLERIES IN IRELAND

Teelings
⌂ 13-17 Newmarket, Dublin
A slick distillery in the heart of Dublin, with great tours and tastings.

Pearse Lyons
⌂ 121-122 James's St, Dublin
One of Ireland's newest distilleries, housed in the refurbished St James' Church.

Tullamore Dew
△ C4 ⌂ Bury Quay, Co Offaly
This legendary Offaly distillery has a restaurant and bar attached *(p258)*.

Kilbeggan Distillery
△ C3 ⌂ Lower Main St, Co Westmeath
The oldest licensed distillery in Ireland, dating back to 1757 *(p258)*.

Dingle Whiskey
△ A5 ⌂ Farranredmond, Dingle
A small, independent distillery on the west coast, representing the new wave of Irish whiskey production.

EXPERIENCE MORE

3 Custom House

F3 **Custom House Quay**
888 2000 **Visitor
centre: 10am–4:30pm daily**

This majestic Neo-Classical
building was designed as the
Custom House by the English
architect James Gandon in
1791. However, just nine years
later, the 1800 Act of Union
transferred the customs and
excise business to London,
rendering the building obso-
lete. It was almost completely
burnt down during the Irish
War of Independence in 1921,
before being restored in 1991,
when the building reopened
as government offices. The
visitor centre houses an exhibition on the building's history.

The main façade, decorated
with allegorical carvings, has
pavilions at each end with a
Doric portico in its centre.

4 St Mary's Pro-Cathedral

E2 **83 Marlborough
St** **Hours vary, check
website** **procathedral.ie**

Dedicated in 1825, before
Catholic emancipation, St
Mary's backstreet site was

↑ The intricately carved
high altar of St Mary's
Pro-Cathedral

the best the city's Anglo-Irish
leaders would allow a Catholic
cathedral. The façade is based
on a Greek temple. Doric columns support a pediment with
statues of St Mary, St Patrick
and St Laurence O'Toole,
12th-century Archbishop of
Dublin and the patron saint
of the city.

5 Abbey Theatre

E3 **26/27 Abbey St
Lower** **Box office: noon–
7pm Mon-Sat; tours: 4pm
Mon, Wed & Fri, 11am Sat**
abbeytheatre.ie

The Abbey staged its first play
in 1904 with W B Yeats and
Lady Gregory as co-directors.

The early years of this
acclaimed national theatre
also witnessed works by J M
Synge and Sean O'Casey. Many
were controversial: nationalist
sensitivities were tested in
1926 during the premiere of
O'Casey's *The Plough and the
Stars* when the flag of the Irish
Free State appeared on stage
in a scene which featured a
pub frequented by prostitutes.

Today, it nurtures new Irish
writing and artistic talent,
and produces an innovative
programme of Irish and
international theatre. The
backstage tour includes the
chance to see the set of the
current production up close.

6 O'Connell Street

D3

O'Connell Street is very
different from the original
plans of Irish aristocrat Luke
Gardiner. When he bought the
land in the mid-18th century,
Gardiner envisioned a grand
residential parade with an
elegant mall running along
its centre. Such plans were
short-lived. The construction
of Carlisle (now O'Connell)
Bridge around 1790 trans-
formed the street into the
city's main north–south route,
and several buildings were
destroyed during the 1916
Easter Rising and the Irish
Civil War. Since the 1960s
many of the old buildings
have been replaced by the
glass and neon of fast-food
joints and chain stores. A few
venerable buildings remain,
such as the General Post Office
(1818) *(p99)*, Gresham Hotel
(1817) and the former Clery's
department store (1822).

At the south end stands a
massive monument to Daniel
O'Connell, after whom the
street is named, unveiled in
1882. Higher up, almost facing

↑ The fine Georgian façade of the Custom
House, as best seen from across the Liffey

O'Connell Bridge stretching across the Liffey, set against a backdrop of illuminated shops at the bottom of O'Connell Street ↑

the General Post Office, is an animated statue of James Larkin, leader of the Dublin general strike in 1913. At the north end of the street is the obelisk-shaped monument to Charles Stewart Parnell (1846–91), who was leader of the Home Rule Party and known as the "uncrowned King of Ireland" (p51). The stainless steel Dublin Spire sits on the site where Nelson's Pillar used to be. It tapers from a 3-m- (10-ft-) diameter base to a 10-cm (4-in) pointed tip of optical glass at a height of 120 m (394 ft).

❼
Gate Theatre

📍 D2 🏠 1 Cavendish Row
🕐 Box office: 10am–7pm Mon–Sat 🌐 gatetheatre.ie

Renowned for its staging of contemporary international drama in Dublin, the Gate Theatre was founded in 1928 by Hilton Edwards and Micheál Mac Liammóir. The latter is now best remembered for *The Importance of Being Oscar*, his long-running one-man show about the writer Oscar Wilde. An early success was Denis Johnston's *The Old Lady Says No*, so-called because of the

margin notes made on one of his scripts by Lady Gregory, founding director of the Abbey Theatre.

Although still noted for staging new plays, the Gate's current output often includes classic Irish plays. Among the young talent to get their first break here were James Mason and a teenage Orson Welles.

---

❽
James Joyce Centre

📍 E2 🏠 35 North Great George's St 🕐 Hours vary, check website 🔒 Good Fri; Oct–Mar: Mon; 21 Dec–1 Jan & public hols 🌐 jamesjoyce.ie

This agreeable stop on the literary tourist trail is primarily a meeting place for Joyce enthusiasts, but is also worth visiting for its Georgian interior. The centre is in a 1784 townhouse that was built for the Earl of Kenmare. Michael Stapleton, one of the greatest stuccoers of his time, contributed to the plasterwork, of which the friezes are particularly noteworthy.

The centre's permanent and temporary exhibitions interpret and illuminate aspects of Joyce's life and work. Among the displays are biographies

of real people on whom Joyce based his characters. Professor Dennis J Maginni, a peripheral character in *Ulysses*, ran a dancing school from this townhouse. Leopold and Molly Bloom, the central characters of *Ulysses*, lived a short walk away at No 7 Eccles Street. The centre organizes walking tours of Joyce's Dublin.

At the top of the road, on Great Denmark Street, is the Jesuit-run Belvedere College attended by Joyce between 1893 and 1898. He recalls his unhappy schooldays there in *A Portrait of the Artist as a Young Man*. The college's interior contains some of Stapleton's best and most colourful plasterwork (1785).

↑ The writer's personal effects on show at the James Joyce Centre

Bright and airy
exhibition space at the
Hugh Lane Gallery ↑

Hugh Lane Gallery

📍 D1-D2 🏛 Charlemont House, Parnell Sq North 🕐 9:45am-6pm Tue-Thu, 9:45am-5pm Fri, 10am-5pm Sat, 11am-5pm Sun 🔒 24-26, 31 Dec 🌐 hughlane.ie

Art collector Sir Hugh Lane donated his collection of 39 Impressionist paintings to the Dublin Corporation in 1908. Thirty-one of these renowned works by Manet, Degas, Renoir, Vuillard and others are housed in the Hugh Lane Gallery. The remaining eight are shared with the National Gallery in London and are loaned back to Dublin every few years.

Besides the Lane bequest of Impressionist paintings, the gallery has a collection of modern and contemporary Irish and international art. This includes stained-glass

windows by Irish artists, such as *The Eve of St Agnes* by Harry Clarke. An exciting addition in 1998 was a bequest by John Edwards of the contents of Francis Bacon's London studio. Sean Scully, who like Francis Bacon was born in Dublin, gifted a series of his abstract Expressionist paintings to the gallery in 2006.

King's Inns

📍 B2 🏛 Henrietta St/ Constitution Hill 🔒 To the public 🌐 kingsinns.ie

This classically proportioned public building was founded in 1800 as a place of residence and study for barristers, and was built by James Gandon. Francis Johnston added the graceful cupola in 1813, and the building was finally completed in 1817. Inside is a fine dining hall, and the Registry of Deeds (formerly the Prerogative Court). The west façade has two doorways flanked by Classical caryatids carved by Edward Smyth. The male figure, with book and quill, represents the law.

Sadly, much of the area around Constitution Hill is less attractive than it was in Georgian times. However, the gardens, which are open to the public, are still pleasing.

Rotunda Hospital

📍 D2 🏛 Parnell Sq

Standing in the middle of Parnell Square is Europe's first purpose-built maternity hospital. Founded in 1745 by Dr Bartholomew Mosse, the design of the hospital is similar to that of Leinster House (*p75*). German-born architect Richard Cassels designed both buildings, as well as Powerscourt House (*p132*) and Russborough House (*p144*).

On the first floor is a beautiful chapel featuring striking stained-glass windows, exuberant Rococo plasterwork and a ceiling (1755) by the stuc-coer Bartholomew Cramillion. The ceiling portrays the symbol of fertility and the virtues of faith, hope and charity.

Nowadays, over 8,000 babies are born every year in the Rotunda Hospital.

Garden of Remembrance

📍 D2 🏛 Parnell Sq 🕐 Apr-Sep: 8:30am-6pm daily; Oct-Mar: 9:30am-4pm daily 🌐 opwdublin commemorative.ie

At the northern end of Parnell Square is a park dedicated to

HIDDEN GEM
The Hungry Tree

When wandering the grounds of King's Inns, look out for this London plane tree ingesting a nearby bench. Dating from the 19th century, it is now a listed tree and shows no sign of giving up the unfortunate seat.

the men and women who have died in the pursuit of Irish freedom. Designed by Daithí Hanly, the garden was opened by President Êamon de Valera *(p52)* in 1966, to mark the 50th anniversary of the 1916 Easter Rising. The Garden of Remembrance marks the spot where several leaders of the Rising were held overnight before being taken to Kilmainham Gaol *(p118)*. The Irish Volunteers movement was formed here in 1913.

In the centre is a cruciform pool. A mosaic on the pool floor depicts abandoned weapons and shields, symbolizing peace. The focal point at one end of the garden is a bronze sculpture by Oisín Kelly, *Children of Lir* (1971). Kelly references the poignant Irish fairy tale in which three children are turned into swans by their wicked stepmother. Queen Elizabeth II laid a commemorative wreath in the gardens during her historic state visit to Ireland in 2011.

13 Dublin Writers Museum

📍 D1 🏠 18 Parnell Sq North
📞 872 2077 🕐 9:45am–5pm Mon–Sat, 11am–5pm Sun & public hols (last adm: 45 mins before closing)
🗓 25 & 26 Dec

Opened in 1991, this absorbing museum occupies a tasteful 18th-century townhouse. There are displays relating to Irish literature in all its forms from 300 years ago to the present day. The captivating exhibits include paintings, manuscripts, letters, rare editions and mementos of many of Ireland's finest authors. Highlights include original letters by the poet Thomas Moore. There are a number of temporary exhibits and a grandly decorated Gallery of Writers upstairs. The museum hosts poetry readings and lectures. A specialist bookstore, providing an out-of-print search service, adds to the relaxed, friendly ambience.

14 Smithfield

📍 A3

Laid out in the 17th century as a marketplace, Smithfield was one of Dublin's oldest residential areas. The space received a makeover in the early 2000s, resulting in this well-designed pedestrian, cobbled plaza surrounded by contemporary architecture, including the fabulous Lighthouse Cinema. The square is used for outdoor civic events, most notably the twice-yearly Dublin Horse Fair.

DRINK

The Cobblestone
One of Dublin's best-loved pubs, popular with visitors and locals alike. It's a cosy spot with a welcoming bar and a long-standing reputation for excellent live trad music.

📍 A3 🏠 77 King St North, Smithfield
🌐 cobblestonepub.ie

←
Painting of George Bernard Shaw, which hangs in the Dublin Writers Museum *(below)*

EAT

The Winding Stair

Overlooking the Ha'penny Bridge, this charming restaurant is the upper half of one of Dublin's oldest bookshops. Expect wholesome Irish cooking with an artisanal touch.

📍D4 🏠40 Lower Ormond Quay
🌐winding-stair.com

€€€

EPIC - The Irish Emigration Museum

📍G3 🏠Custom House Quay
🕐10am-6:45pm daily (last adm 5pm) 📅24-26 Dec
🌐epicchq.com

From the Great Famine to the 2008 financial crash, the history of Ireland has long been punctuated by emigration, sometimes on a massive scale. Through 20 themed galleries, this interactive museum in Dublin's docklands explores why people left, how they influenced the world they found, and the connection to their descendants in Ireland

today. A highlight is being able to retrace the journeys of over 300 significant Irish people, and witnessing their achievements in art, politics, science and sport. Providing valuable insight into the country's past, the exhibition is particularly unmissable for those who claim Irish heritage.

St Michan's Church

📍B4 🏠Church St 📞872 4154 🕐Mid-Mar-Oct: 10am-12:45pm & 2-4:30pm Mon-Fri, 10am-12:45pm Sat; Nov-mid-Mar: 12:30-3:30pm Mon-Fri, 10am-12:45pm Sat

Largely rebuilt in 1685 on the site of an 11th-century Hiberno-Viking church, the dull façade of St Michan's hides a more exciting interior. Deep in its vaults lie a number of bodies preserved because of the dry atmosphere created by the church's magnesian limestone walls. Their wooden caskets, however, have cracked open, revealing the intact bodies, complete with skin and strands of hair. Among those thought to lie here are the brothers Henry and John Sheares, leaders of the 1798 rebellion, who were executed that year.

Other less gory attractions include an organ (1724) on which Handel is said to have

↑ Human skull preserved in the vaults of St Michan's Church

played. It is thought that the churchyard contains the unmarked grave of United Irishman Robert Emmet *(p83)*, leader of the abortive 1803 Rising against British rule.

St Mary's Abbey

📍C3 🏠Meetinghouse Lane 📞833 1618
🕐Until further notice

Founded by Benedictines in 1139, but transferred to the Cistercian order in 1147, this was one of the largest and most important monasteries in medieval Ireland. As well as controlling extensive estates, the abbey acted as state treasury and meeting place for the Council of Ireland. It was during a council meeting in St Mary's that "Silken Thomas" Fitzgerald renounced his allegiance to Henry VIII and marched out to raise the short-lived rebellion of 1534. The monastery was dissolved in 1539 and during the 17th century the site served as a quarry. All that remains today is the vaulted chamber of the chapter house containing a model of how it would have looked 800 years ago.

←

Onlookers absorbed in an exhibit at the Irish Emigration Museum

> **Opened in 1816, the bridge got its better-known nickname from the halfpenny toll that was levied on it up until 1919.**

13 confined to a single room. The extent of the squalor, malnutrition, disease and infant mortality rates is hard to fathom, but exhibits bring it to life in this unique and moving insight into Dublin's urban poverty in the 19th and 20th centuries. Note that visits are by guided tour only, which take place on the hour.

⓴
Four Courts

📍 B4 🏛 Inns Quay

Completed in 1802 by James Gandon, this majestic public building was virtually gutted 120 years later during the Irish Civil War. The Public Records Office, with its irreplaceable collection of documents dating back to the 12th century, was also destroyed by fire. By 1932, the main buildings were sympathetically restored using Gandon's original design. An imposing copper-covered lantern dome rises above the six-columned Corinthian portico, which is crowned with the figures of Moses, Justice, Mercy, Wisdom and Authority. This central section is flanked by two wings containing the four original courts.

↑ Ha'penny Bridge, beloved by Dubliners and considered by many to be an unofficial symbol of the city

⓲
Ha'penny Bridge

📍 D4 🏛 Bachelors Walk

Linking the Temple Bar area (*p87*) and Liffey Street, this high-arched, cast-iron footbridge is used by thousands of people every day, and is one of Dublin's most photographed sights. It was built by John Windsor, an ironworker from Shropshire, England. Originally named the Wellington Bridge, it is now officially called the Liffey Bridge, but is much more widely known as the Ha'penny Bridge. Opened in 1816, the bridge got its better-known nickname from the halfpenny toll that was levied on it up until 1919. Restoration work,

which included the installation of period lanterns, has made the bridge even more attractive.

⓳
14 Henrietta Street

📍 C2 🏛 14 Henrietta St
🕙 10am–4pm Wed–Sat, noon–4pm Sun
🌐 14henriettastreet.ie

Set in a converted Georgian townhouse originally built for a single wealthy family, this museum charts the history of tenement life in the capital. The slums of Dublin were considered to be some of the worst in Europe; over 100 people lived in this house alone, with families of up to

> ### Did You Know?
> The Ha'penny Bridge toll was paid to William Walsh, a ferryman who retired his boats when it was built.

A SHORT WALK
DUBLIN: NORTH OF THE LIFFEY

Distance 3 km (2 miles) **Nearest Luas** O'Connell Upper **Time** 35 minutes

Throughout the Georgian era, O'Connell Street was very much the fashionable part of Dublin to live in. While the 1916 Easter Rising destroyed many of the fine buildings along the street – including much of the General Post Office, of which only the original façade still stands – there are still a number that make the area worth a leisurely stroll. Amid the shops and businesses, look out for St Mary's Pro-Cathedral and James Gandon's Custom House, overlooking the Liffey.

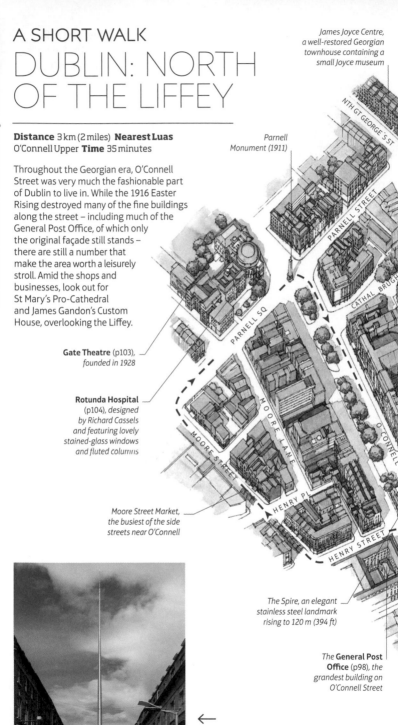

James Joyce Centre, a well-restored Georgian townhouse containing a small Joyce museum

NTH GT GEORGE'S ST

Parnell Monument (1911)

PARNELL STREET

CATHAL BRUGHA ST

PARNELL SQ

Gate Theatre (p103), *founded in 1928*

Rotunda Hospital (p104), *designed by Richard Cassels and featuring lovely stained-glass windows and fluted columns*

MOORE LANE

O'CONNELL STREET

MOORE STREET

Moore Street Market, the busiest of the side streets near O'Connell

HENRY PL

HENRY STREET

The Spire, an elegant stainless steel landmark rising to 120 m (394 ft)

The **General Post Office** (p98), *the grandest building on O'Connell Street*

← The gleaming steel Spire towers above O'Connell Street

| 0 metres | 50 |
| 0 yards | 50 |

N ↑

↑ The richly decorated ceiling of St Mary's Pro-Cathedral

Locator Map
For more detail see p96

DUBLIN:
NORTH OF THE LIFFEY

St Mary's Pro-Cathedral
(p102), *built around 1825 and still Dublin's main place of worship for Catholics*

The statue of James Joyce (1990) by Marjorie Fitzgibbon commemorates one of Ireland's most famous novelists. Born in Dublin in 1882, Joyce catalogued the city's people and streets in Dubliners *and in his most celebrated work,* Ulysses

Did You Know?

The slender tip of the Spire can sway up to 1.5 m (5 ft) from its base in extreme winds.

Custom House
(p102), *adorned with a Classical grotesque head keystone, by Edward Smyth, that symbolizes the River Liffey*

James Larkin Statue (1981)

Abbey Theatre (p102), *Ireland's national theatre, which has a worldwide reputation for its productions by Irish playwrights*

CATHEDRAL ST

EARL STREET NORTH

MARLBOROUGH ST

SACKVILLE PL

ABBEY STREET LR

EDEN QUAY

LIFFEY

CUSTOM HOUSE QUAY

Butt Bridge

FINISH

O'Connell Bridge

START

O'Connell Street
(p102), *at the foot of which is a monument to its namesake, Daniel O'Connell, by John Foley*

Sun setting over Howth harbour, Dublin

Must Sees

1 Phoenix Park
2 Guinness Storehouse®
3 Irish Museum of Modern Art

Experience More

4 Glasnevin Cemetery
5 National Print Museum
6 Kilmainham Gaol
7 National Botanic Gardens
8 Dublin Docklands
9 National Museum of Ireland – Decorative Arts & History
10 Malahide Castle
11 Dún Laoghaire
12 Howth
13 Dalkey
14 Killiney
15 Sandymount

DUBLIN: BEYOND THE CENTRE

Some of Dublin's most interesting sights lie just outside the close-knit streets of the city centre. Phoenix Park, Europe's largest city park, is a great place for a stroll and also home to the popular Dublin Zoo. West of the city is the Irish Museum of Modern Art, and, of course, the iconic Guinness Storehouse®, a visitor centre sited at the original St James's Gate Brewery. There are also a number of coastal towns, worth visiting for their stunning views of Dublin Bay, which can be easily reached by the DART rail network.

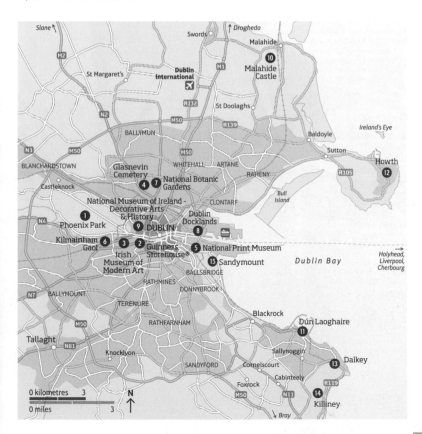

❶ 🚲 🖵

PHOENIX PARK

🏠 Phoenix Park, Dublin 8 🕐 Visitor Centre: 9:30am–6pm daily; Walled Garden: 10am–4pm daily; Dublin Zoo: hours vary, check website 🚫 Visitor Centre: Mon & Tue Jan & Feb 🌐 phoenixpark.ie

Europe's largest enclosed city park, Phoenix Park came into being in 1662, when the Duke of Ormonde turned the land into a deer park. In 1745 it was landscaped and opened to the public, and today remains a verdant oasis both for wildlife and for Dubliners seeking to escape the bustle of the city.

Near the centre of the park is the Phoenix Column, a monument crowned by a statue of the famous mythical bird. However, the park's name likely has nothing to do with a phoenix, but rather results from a mispronunciation of the Gaelic name *Fionn Uisce*, or "clear water". Key attractions in the park include the lakeside People's Garden and the 27-m (90-ft) steel Papal Cross, which marks the spot where Pope John Paul II celebrated Mass in front of more than one million people in 1979. There's also the hugely popular Dublin Zoo (you'll need to purchase a ticket to enter), as well as Áras an Uachtaráin, the Irish president's official residence – 525 tickets are issued every Saturday for a free guided tour of the building.

Beautiful autumnal colours in Phoenix Park, the centre of which is marked by the Phoenix Column *(inset)* ↓

1. The entrance to Dublin Zoo. Established in 1831, it is the third-oldest zoo in the world and is one of Ireland's top family attractions. It is home to approximately 400 animals.

2. Ashtown Castle is a fully restored 17th-century tower that now houses the Phoenix Park Visitor Centre, with the carefully cultivated Victorian Walled Garden nearby.

3. Phoenix Park started as a deer park in 1662, and there is still a herd of around 500 today.

> INSIDER TIP
> **On Your Bike**
>
> The best way to take in the entire sprawling site is by bicycle; these can be rented at the Park Gate entrance on Chesterfield Avenue. Adult, child and tandem bikes are available.

2 🎟️ 🍴 🖥️ 🛍️

GUINNESS STOREHOUSE®

📍 St James's Gate, Dublin 8 🚌 78A, 51B, 123 🕐 Sep–Jun: 9:30am–7pm daily (last adm 5pm); Jul & Aug: 9am–9pm (last adm 7pm) 🚫 Good Fri, 24–26 Dec 🌐 guinness-storehouse.com

Guinness® is a black beer, known as "stout", renowned for its distinctive malty flavour and creamy head. From its humble beginnings over 250 years ago, the Guinness Storehouse® is now the largest brewery in Europe.

↑ The Storehouse's huge glass atrium, stretching seven storeys into the air

The Guinness Storehouse® is a development based in St James's Gate Brewery, the original house of Guinness®, which has been completely remodelled. The 1904 listed building covers nearly four acres of floor space over seven floors, built around a huge glass atrium. The first impression the visitor has is of walking into a large glass pint, with light spilling down from above. Enshrined on the floor is a copy of the original lease signed by Arthur Guinness.

Take the Tour

First up is the Ingredients section, which looks in depth at the beer's components and the initial treatments undertaken during the brewing process. The tour

The imposing factory gates lead into the Storehouse ↓

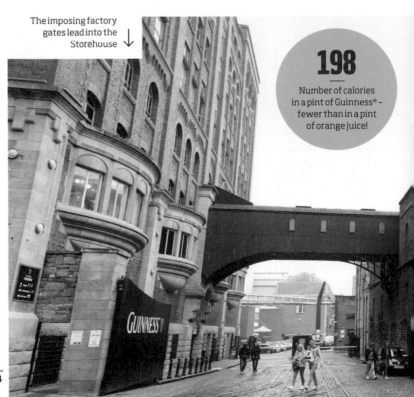

198

Number of calories in a pint of Guinness® – fewer than in a pint of orange juice!

then continues into an authentic Georgian anteroom to "meet" Arthur Guinness and see him at work.

Next up, the Brewing Exhibition is a noisy, steamy and "hoppy" area, which provides a full explanation of the process. The historical development of the Guinness® company and brand is accompanied by video footage of the craft. Models and displays tell the story of the beer's transportation, its worldwide appeal, and the company's popular advertising campaigns. The tour ends with a free pint of draught Guinness® – either learn to pull the perfect six-step pint yourself in the centre's academy, or relax in Arthur's Bar or the glass-walled Gravity Bar.

↑ Visitors enjoying views of Dublin and a drink in the rooftop Gravity Bar at the end of their tour

ARTHUR GUINNESS

In December 1759, 34-year-old Arthur Guinness signed a 9,000-year lease at an annual rent of £45 to take over the vacant St James's Gate Brewery. Dublin's brewing industry was at a low ebb; the standard of ale was much criticized and whiskey, gin and poteen were the more favoured drinks. Guinness started brewing ale, but was also aware of a popular black London ale called porter. Guinness decided to develop his own recipe for porter, and it was so successful that he made his first export shipment in 1769.

3 ✏️ 🎨 💻 🛍️

IRISH MUSEUM OF MODERN ART

📍 **Royal Hospital Kilmainham, Dublin 8** 🕐 **11:30am-5:30pm Tue-Fri, 10am-5:30pm Sat, 12-5:30pm Sun** 🚫 **24-26 Dec** 🌐 **imma.ie**

One of Dublin's finest museums, the Irish Museum of Modern Art is housed in what were previously the residential quarters of the spectacular Royal Hospital Kilmainham. The collection comprises a cross-section of Irish and international modern and contemporary art – some 3,500 works, mainly from the 1940s onwards.

The building alone is worth a visit; it is Ireland's finest surviving 17th-century property, built in 1684 and styled on Les Invalides in Paris. It was designed by Sir William Robinson and used as a home for wounded or retired soldiers – a role it fulfilled until 1927. When it was first completed, many were so impressed by the building's Classical symmetry that it was suggested that it would be better used as a campus for Trinity College.

After the building underwent a major government restoration, IMMA was opened in 1991 and it remains the primary collection of modern art in Ireland. The displays are usually temporary shows, mixed with a small permanent collection that includes heavyweights such as Marina Abramović. New works are added every year, with an emphasis on pieces by living artists.

←

Visitor to Jac Leirner's solo exhibition, Institutional Ghost, at the IMMA

Paul Henry,
1877–1958

A popular Irish artist best known for his Post-impressionist landscapes.

Francis Bacon,
1909–92

▽ Famed for his often-grotesque religious paintings.

Key Irish Artists

Jack Butler Yeats,
1871–1957

▲ Brother of W B Yeats and a significant 20th-century Irish painter, he also won Ireland's first Olympic medal - in the 1924 arts and culture category.

Eileen Gray,
1878–1976

An influential furniture designer, Gray was one of the first women to be accepted into London's Slade School of Fine Art.

Harry Clarke,
1889–1931

▲ An internationally renowned stained-glass artist.

Did You Know?

The hospital took four years to renovate in the 1980s – as long as it took to originally build 300 years earlier.

The hospital's symmetrical façade and stunning formal gardens ↑

FORBIDDEN FRUIT FESTIVAL

First launched in 2011, the Forbidden Fruit music and arts festival has become a staple of Ireland's gig scene. It's held every June Bank Holiday, in Royal Hospital Kilmainham's impressive grounds, which are transformed into a bohemian playground for electronic, house and indie fans. Previous acts have included Bon Iver, Orbital and Elbow. The headliners finish at 10:45pm each evening, when official after-parties get going in the city centre.

EXPERIENCE MORE

4

Glasnevin Cemetery

🚩 Finglas Rd 🚌 13, 19, 19A, 40, 40A from Parnell St ⏰ 10am–5pm Mon–Fri, 10am–6pm Sat & Sun 🚫 24–26 Dec, 1 Jan 🌐 glasnevin museum.ie

The largest cemetery in Ireland, Glasnevin covers more than 50 ha (124 acres) and contains over one million graves. The cemetery was founded in 1828 after Daniel O'Connell campaigned for a burial ground in which both Irish Catholics and Protestants could bury their dead with dignity.

The main part features high walls and watchtowers, intended to keep out body snatchers. The burial plots have a huge variety of monuments, such as the austere high stones used until the 1860s, the elaborate Celtic crosses of the nationalist revival from the 1860s to the 1960s, and the plain marble of the late 20th century.

Glasnevin's museum details the cemetery's history, with information on the people buried here. Daily walking tours offer insights into the people whose final resting place it is, including Daniel O'Connell, Michael Collins, Éamon de Valera, Constance Markievicz and Brendan Behan.

5

National Print Museum

🚩 Garrison Chapel, Beggar's Bush Barracks, Haddington Rd, Dublin 4 🚉 DART to Landsdowne or Grand Canal Dock 🚌 4, 7 ⏰ 9am–5pm Mon–Fri, 2–5pm Sat & Sun 🚫 Public hol weekends, 24 Dec–1 Jan 🌐 national printmuseum.ie

This museum has an extensive collection that depicts the history of print in Ireland. It includes functional printing machinery, printing blocks, pamphlets, periodicals and books. Along with exhibitions and tours, the museum has art and crafts workshops on calligraphy, letterpress printing, traditional bookbinding, origami and card making. The Press Café is housed in the museum's conservatory.

6

Kilmainham Gaol

🚩 Inchicore Rd, Kilmainham, Dublin 8 🚌 51B, 51C, 69, 73, 78A, 79 ⏰ Jun–Aug: 9am–7pm daily (to 6pm Apr, May & Sep); Oct–Mar: 9:30am–5:30pm daily (last adm: 1hr 15min before closing) 🚫 24–26 Dec 🌐 kilmainhamgaol museum.ie

During its 130 years as a jail, Kilmainham – which opened in 1796 – housed many of those involved in the fight for Irish independence.

Visits, which are by guided tour only, include the chapel where Joseph Plunkett married Grace

← Grave monument in Glasnevin Cemetery

↑ Letterpress at the National Print Museum

Gifford hours before he faced the firing squad for his part in the 1916 Rising (p99). Tours end in the prison yard where Plunkett's badly wounded colleague James Connolly was strapped into a chair before being shot. You also pass the dank cells of those involved in the 1798, 1803, 1848 and 1867 uprisings, as well as the punishment cells and hanging room.

7

National Botanic Gardens

🚩 Botanic Ave, Glasnevin, Dublin 9 🚌 4, 13, 19, 19A, 83 ⏰ Mar–Oct: 9am–5pm Mon–Fri, 10am–6pm Sat & Sun; Nov–Feb: 9am–4:30pm Mon–Fri, 10am–4:30pm Sat & Sun 🚫 25 Dec 🌐 botanic gardens.ie

Opened in 1795, the National Botanic Gardens are Ireland's foremost centre of botany and horticulture. They still possess an old-world feel, thanks to the beautiful Palm House and architect Richard Turner's curvilinear glasshouses.

The park contains over 16,000 different plant species. Noteworthy are the colourful Victorian carpet bedding, the rich collections of cacti and orchids, renowned rose garden, and 30-m- (100-ft-) high redwood tree.

The visitor centre houses a café, a display area with exhibits relating to the history and purpose of the gardens, and a lecture hall, which hosts a programme of regular talks and workshops.

Also located in the gardens is the Viking House. Built by local craftsmen using traditional building materials and techniques, it is a faithful replica of a typical Dublin house and garden of 1,000 years ago, similar to buildings excavated in the city centre in the late 1980s.

8

Dublin Docklands

🚇 DART to Pearse Street Station or Grand Canal Dock
🌐 dublindocklands.ie

Over 300 years ago, most of the Docklands was underwater. Redeveloped during the 1990s and 2000s, the area is one of Dublin's most exciting districts. Theatres, museums, numerous cafés and restaurants, watersports and a memorial to those who died in the Great Famine are all draws. The Docklands span both sides of the Liffey to the east of the city, with the two sides joined by the Samuel Beckett Bridge.

9

National Museum of Ireland – Decorative Arts & History

📍 Collins Barracks, Benburb St, Dublin 7
🚌 25, 25A, 66, 67, 90
🕙 10am–5pm Tue–Sat, 1–5pm Mon & Sun 🚫 Good Fri & 25 Dec 🌐 museum.ie

The decorative arts and history annexe of the National Museum (*p68*) is housed in the historic Collins Barracks, a huge complex that was commissioned by King William III in 1700.

In marked contrast to the grey institutional exterior, the museum's interior presents exhibits in an innovative way using the latest technology.

Furniture, silver, glassware, ceramics and scientific instrument collections form the bulk of items on show in the South Block. In the West Block, however, visitors get an insight into the history, work and development of the National Museum. The Out of Storage exhibit brings together a wide array of artifacts from around the world. The North Block holds a permanent exhibition, Soldiers and Chiefs, which explores Irish military history through the eyes of the average Irish soldier from 1550 to the late 1990s.

EAT

Junior's Deli & Café
One of Dublin's best sandwich joints. The Italian-inspired dinner menu has big portions cooked to perfection.

📍 2 Bath Ave
🌐 juniors.ie

€€€

Paulie's Pizza
Sublime pizzas – with classic Neapolitan or New York-inspired toppings – are cooked in a wood-fired oven.

📍 58 Grand Canal St
🌐 paulies.ie

€€€

Farmer Brown's
Hearty Irish food with a nod to the Deep South. Famed for their brunch and burgers, the crispy chicken wings are also amazing.

📍 170 Rathmines Rd Lower
🌐 farmerbrowns.ie

€€€

The Great Palm House, focal point of the National Botanic Gardens ↓

Malahide Castle

⌂ Malahide, Co Dublin
🚋 DART to Malahide
🚌 42 from Beresford Place, near Busáras
🕐 9:30am–5:30pm daily
🚫 24–26 Dec 🌐 malahide castleandgardens.ie

Near the seaside dormitory town of Malahide stands a huge castle set in 100 ha (250 acres) of grounds. The castle's core dates from the 12th century but later additions, such as its rounded towers, have given it a classic fairy-tale appearance. The building served as a stately home for the Talbot family until 1973. They were staunch supporters of James II: on the day of the Battle of the Boyne in 1690 (p251), 14 members of the family breakfasted here; none came back for supper.

The obligatory guided tour takes you round the castle's collection of 18th-century Irish furniture, the oak-beamed Great Hall and

↑ Malahide Castle as seen from the extensive grounds, which were created by Lord Milo Talbot

the impressively carved Oak Room. Part of the Portrait Collection, on loan from the National Gallery of Ireland (p70), can be seen here.

A visitor centre has an exhibition on the fascinating history of the Talbot family. Also worth exploring are the ornamental walled gardens, home to an exotic Butterfly House filled with 20 different species.

Dún Laoghaire

⌂ Co Dublin 🚋 DART
🌐 dunlaoghairetown.ie

Pronounced "Dunleary", Dún Laoghaire was once a key port for passenger ferries between Ireland and Britain. This seaside town, with its brightly painted villas, parks and palm

EAT

Teddy's Ice Cream

This seaside shop has barely changed since it opened in the 1950s. Nostalgia aside, the creamy cones draw crowds of locals and tourists alike.

 1A Windsor Terrace, Dún Laoghaire
 teddys.ie

€€€

Johnnie Fox's

Situated in the Dublin Mountains with live traditional music, an award-winning seafood menu and open turf fires, this is more of an attraction than a pub.

🏠 Glencullen
🌐 johnniefoxs.com

€€€

Bandstand on the waterfront at Dún Laoghaire ↓

trees, can sometimes exude a continental feel. There are some good walks around the harbour and to the lighthouse along the east pier. Sandycove and Dalkey can be reached via "The Metals" footpath.

The **National Maritime Museum** is housed in the 1837 Mariners' Church. Exhibits include a longboat used by French officers during Wolfe Tone's unsuccessful invasion at Bantry in 1796 *(p167)*.

National Maritime Museum

 Haigh Terrace ⏰ 11am–5pm daily 🗓 24–26 & 31 Dec, 1 Jan 🌐 mariner.ie

---

12
Howth

🏠 Co Dublin 🚆 DART ⏰ Howth Castle grounds: 8am–sunset daily 🌐 howthcastle.com

This commercial fishing town is the northern limit of Dublin Bay. Howth Head, a huge rocky mass, has lovely views of the bay. A footpath – known as the "Nose" – runs around its tip.

To the west is Howth Castle, which dates back to Norman times. The grounds are also home to the **National Transport Museum**, which has vintage vehicles on display.

Ireland's Eye, an islet and bird sanctuary where puffins nest, can be reached by a short boat trip from Howth.

National Transport Museum

⏰ 2–5pm Sat, Sun & public hols 🌐 nationaltransport museum.org

---

13
Dalkey

🏠 Co Dublin 🚆 DART 🌐 ilovedalkey.com

Dalkey was once known as the "Town of Seven Castles", but only two of these now remain.

Both are on the main street of this attractive village whose tight, winding roads and villas give it a Mediterranean feel.

A little way offshore is tiny Dalkey Island, a rocky bird sanctuary with a Martello tower and a medieval Benedictine church, both now in a poor state of repair. In summer the island can be reached by a boat ride from the town's Coliemore Harbour.

14
Killiney

🏠 Co Dublin 🚆 DART to Dalkey or Killiney

South of Dalkey, the coastal road climbs uphill before tumbling down into the village of Killiney. The route offers one of the most scenic vistas on this stretch of the east coast. Howth Head is clearly visible to the north, with Bray Head *(p144)* and the foothills of the Wicklow Mountains *(p146)* to the south. There is another exhilarating view from the top of Killiney Hill Park, off Victoria Road – well worth tackling the short steep trail for. Down below is the popular pebbly beach, Killiney Strand.

15
Sandymount

🏠 Co Dublin 🚆 DART

Sandymount is an idyllic coastal suburb with a surprising literary heritage. W B Yeats was born here, while Seamus Heaney lived in Sandymount for many years before his death in 2013; busts of both poets stand in the village park. It was also from the golden sands of Sandymount Strand that Stephen Dedalus, in James Joyce's *Ulysses*, wanders "into eternity". The village consequently is known for great Bloomsday celebrations *(p39)*.

EXPERIENCE
IRELAND

The Giant's Causeway, Northern Ireland

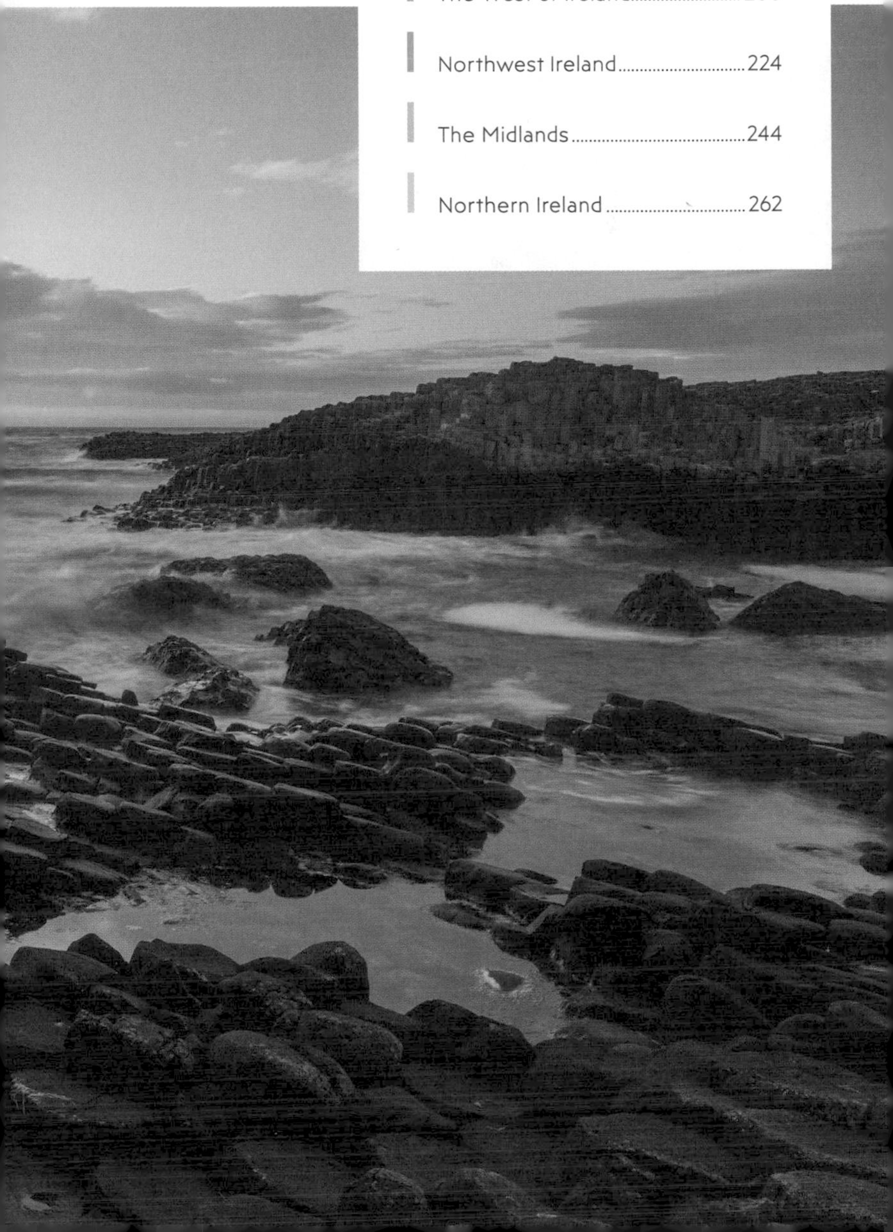

SOUTHEAST IRELAND

The Southeast's proximity to Britain meant that it was often the first port of call for foreign invaders. Viking raiders arrived in the area during the 9th century and went on to establish some of Ireland's earliest towns, including Waterford and Wexford. They were followed in the 12th century by the Anglo-Normans, who shaped the region's subsequent development.

Given its strategic importance, the Southeast was heavily protected, mostly by Anglo-Norman lords loyal to the English Crown. Remains of impressive castles attest to the power of the Fitzgeralds of Kildare and the Butlers of Kilkenny, while wealthy Anglo-Irish families felt confident enough to build fine mansions in the region, such as the Palladian masterpieces of Russborough and Castletown. English rule was not universally accepted, however. The Wicklow Mountains became a popular refuge for opponents to the Crown, and the mountainous terrain is still the only real wilderness in the Southeast – contrasting sharply with Kildare's flat grasslands to the west, and sandy stretches of beach to the east.

SOUTHEAST IRELAND

Must Sees

1. Glendalough
2. Powerscourt Estate
3. Castletown House
4. Kilkenny
5. Waterford

Experience More

6. Kildare
7. Bog of Allen Nature Centre
8. Monasterevin
9. Robertstown
10. Bray
11. Killruddery House and Gardens
12. Russborough House
13. Wicklow Mountains
14. Mount Usher Gardens
15. Avondale House
16. Brownshill Dolmen
17. Hook Peninsula
18. Ardmore
19. Jerpoint Abbey
20. Dunmore East
21. Lismore
22. Enniscorthy
23. New Ross
24. Wexford
25. Saltee Islands
26. Rosslare
27. Johnstown Castle
28. Irish National Heritage Park

1 A valley in Glendalough, County Wicklow

2 A medieval street in Kilkenny

3 The Dunbrody Famine Ship

4 St Canice's Cathedral

3 DAYS

In the Sunny Southeast

Day 1

Morning Starting in Waterford *(p140)*, Ireland's oldest city, spend the morning exploring its ancient, winding streets. Most of your time will be spent in the Viking Triangle, the city's cultural and heritage quarter that is packed with historic buildings and unique museums. When you've had your fill, head to the Granary café on Hanover Street for a light lunch near the river.

Afternoon Next drive 23 km (14 miles) to New Ross *(p150)* to visit the Dunbrody Famine Ship. This reproduction of an 1840s emigrant vessel offers a moving insight into one of the darkest periods in Irish history.

Evening Continue on to Wexford, where centrally located Cistín Eile is a great choice for dinner. Its name means "another kitchen" in English, but such self-deprecation fails to do the well-priced local menu justice.

Day 2

Morning After a hearty breakfast in the Red Kettle, hit the road and drive north to Enniscorthy *(p150)*. This is novelist Colm Tóibín's hometown, and the setting for a number of his books; the film version of *Brooklyn* (perhaps the most well known of his novels) was also shot here. Make time to visit the town's truly remarkable 12th-century Anglo-Norman castle – it's one of the only castles in Ireland to allow visitors onto the roof, so don't miss the chance to climb the steps and take in the glorious view.

Afternoon For lunch try the cosy Bailey Café Bar, before continuing on to Kilkenny *(p136)* to discover this city's fascinating medieval heritage. If you aren't yet castled out, a tour of Kilkenny Castle is an obvious place to start. It's one of Ireland's most famous fortresses, while the Design Centre housed in its stables is also celebrated.

Evening After a few hours of sightseeing and shopping, relax with a pint in the Left Bank, just across the road from the castle. Round off the evening with dinner in Zuni, a slick restaurant in a boutique hotel.

Day 3

Morning Give yourself the full morning to further explore the rest of Kilkenny, taking in St Canice's Cathedral and Round Tower, and Rothe House – a Tudor merchant's house with a small museum inside. Pick up some lunch to go in Blaa Blaa Blaa Sandwiches, a local shop with fresh ingredients and generous servings.

Afternoon Take the 90-minute scenic drive to the stunning Glendalough valley in County Wicklow *(p130)*, eating alfresco at one of the various rest stops along the way. The rest of your afternoon can be spent exploring the monastic settlement and other ruins in the valley.

Evening When you've wandered Glendalough's slopes long enough, head for the seaside village of Greystones, just over 30 minutes away. Enjoy fine Indian cuisine at Chakra in the Meridient Point Centre, before splurging on a night of luxury in the nearby Druid's Glen Hotel and Spa.

① ⑤

GLENDALOUGH

D4 **Bray, Co Wicklow** **Visitor Centre: 9:30am–5pm daily (to 6pm mid-Mar–mid-Oct)** **23–29 Dec** **glendalough.ie**

The steep, wooded slopes of Glendalough – or *Gleann dá Loch*, meaning "Valley of the Two Lakes" – harbour one of Ireland's most atmospheric monastic sites, established by St Kevin in the 6th century.

The age of many of Glendalough's buildings is uncertain, but most date from the 10th to 12th centuries. Many were restored during the 1870s. The main group of ruins lies east of the Lower Lake, but other buildings associated with St Kevin are by the Upper Lake. Here, where the scenery is much wilder, you are better able to enjoy the tranquillity of Glendalough and to escape the crowds that inevitably descend on the site. Try to arrive as early as possible in the day, particularly during the peak tourist season. The monastery is entered through the double stone arch of the Gatehouse, the only surviving example in Ireland of a gateway into an early monastic enclosure.

A short walk leads to a graveyard with a round tower in one corner. Reaching 30 m (100 ft) in height, this is one of the finest of its kind in the country. Its cap was rebuilt in the 1870s, using stones found inside the tower. The nearby roofless cathedral dates mainly from the 10th and 13th centuries and is the valley's largest ruin.

The round tower and cemetery at Glendalough's monastic site ↑

> **Not far from here, on a rocky spur overlooking the Upper Lake, stands St Kevin's Cell, the ruins of a beehive-shaped structure thought to have been the hermit's home.**

At the centre of the churchyard stands the tiny Priests' House, whose name derives from the fact that it was a burial place for local clergy. East of here is St Kevin's Cross, which is made of granite and dates from the 8th century. It is one of the best preserved of Glendalough's High Crosses. Below, nestled in the lush valley, a minuscule oratory with a steeply pitched stone roof is a charming sight; it is popularly known as St Kevin's Kitchen, perhaps because its belfry resembles a chimney. Not far from here, on a rocky spur overlooking the Upper Lake, stands St Kevin's Cell, the ruins of a beehive-shaped structure thought to have been the hermit's home.

There are two sites on the south side of the lake that cannot be reached on foot but are

←

The double-arched gateway at Glendalough, Ireland's only such surviving entry to a monastery

← The roofless cathedral, one of seven churches in Glendalough and the valley's oldest ruin

ST KEVIN AT GLENDALOUGH

St Kevin, born in AD 498, was one of the descendants of the royal house of Leinster. He rejected his life of privilege, however, choosing instead to live as a hermit in a cave at Glendalough. He founded a monastery here, and went on to create a centre of learning devoted to care of the sick and the copying of manuscripts. Many disciples arrived during his lifetime, but the monastery became celebrated as a place of pilgrimage after his death in around AD 618. Colourful legends about the saint make up for the dearth of facts about him – that he lived to the age of 120 is just one of them.

visible from the opposite shore. Teampall-na-Skellig, or the "church of the rock", was supposedly built on the site of the first church that St Kevin founded at Glendalough. To the east of it, carved into the cliff, is St Kevin's Bed – a little rocky ledge above the upper lake that was apparently used as a retreat by St Kevin. It was from here that the saint allegedly rejected the advances of a woman by tossing her into the lake.

2 🏃 🎭 🍽 🍷 💻 🛍

POWERSCOURT ESTATE

🅐 D4 **📍 Enniskerry, Co Wicklow** **🚌 185 from Bray DART station, 44 from Enniskerry**
🕐 Gardens: 9:30am–5:30pm (to dusk Oct–Mar) daily; ballroom and garden rooms:
9:30am–1:30pm Sun (also Mon May–Sep) **🚫 25 & 26 Dec** **🌐 powerscourt.com**

**Nestled in a dramatic setting at the foot of Great Sugar Loaf Mountain,
this sprawling estate is County Wicklow's most visited attraction.**

The 68-room Palladian mansion is stunning, but the manicured gardens, probably the finest in Ireland, are the real draw. Both house and grounds were commissioned in the 1730s by Richard Wingfield, the first Viscount Powerscourt. New ornamental gardens were completed in 1875 by the seventh Viscount, who added gates, urns and statues collected during his travels in Europe. The house was gutted by a fire in 1974, but the ground floor has been beautifully renovated and now houses an upmarket shopping centre with an excellent café. There is a restaurant at the nearby Powerscourt Hotel.

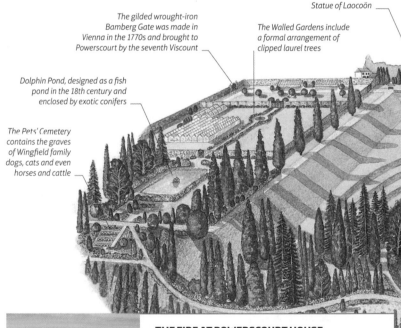

The gilded wrought-iron Bamberg Gate was made in Vienna in the 1770s and brought to Powerscourt by the seventh Viscount

Statue of Laocoön

The Walled Gardens include a formal arrangement of clipped laurel trees

Dolphin Pond, designed as a fish pond in the 18th century and enclosed by exotic conifers

The Pets' Cemetery contains the graves of Wingfield family dogs, cats and even horses and cattle

THE FIRE AT POWERSCOURT HOUSE

One night in November 1974, a fire broke out on the top floor of Powerscourt House. Despite the best efforts of firemen and estate workers, by morning the building was a burnt-out, roofless shell, with many irreplaceable artworks and artifacts destroyed. The Slazenger family – sportswear heirs who bought the house in 1961 – have since worked to restore it, and the building was re-roofed and finally opened to the public in 1997.

1 Leading down to Triton Lake is the Perron, a beautiful Italianate stairway added in 1874 and guarded by two statues of Pegasus.

2 Triton Lake is named for its fountain, which is modelled on Bernini's 17th-century work in Rome.

3 The Edwardian gardens, created out of bogland, contain Chinese conifers and bamboo trees.

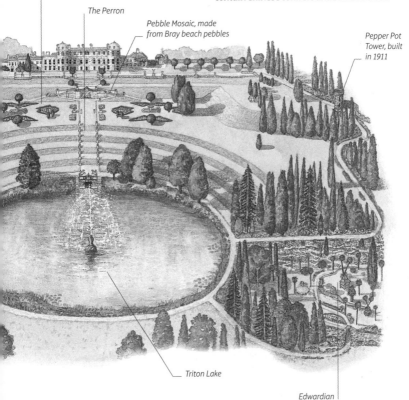

The Italian Garden is laid out on terraces, which were first cut into the steep hillside in the 1730s

The Perron

Pebble Mosaic, made from Bray beach pebbles

Pepper Pot Tower, built in 1911

Triton Lake

Edwardian gardens

Powerscourt Estate, with its impressive mansion and 47 acres (19 hectares) of formal gardens ↑

③ 🗡️ 🏰 💻

CASTLETOWN HOUSE

🔲 D4 🏠 Celbridge, Co Kildare 🕐 House: Mar–Oct: 10am–6pm daily, Nov–mid-Dec: 10am–5:30pm Wed–Sun; Gardens: daily 🚌 67, 67A from Dublin 🌐 castletown.ie

Castletown is Ireland's first and largest Palladian-style house. Built in 1722–9 for William Conolly, who was then Speaker of the Irish Parliament, the imposing estate is a testament to his status as the wealthiest and most powerful politician in Ireland.

The façade was the work of Florentine architect Alessandro Galilei, and gave the country its first taste of Palladianism. Galilei returned to Italy before construction began, so Edward Lovett Pearce, a leading 18th-century Irish architect, took responsibility for the interior, wings and colonnades. The magnificent interiors date from the second half of the 18th century. They were commissioned by Lady Louisa Lennox, wife of William Conolly's great-nephew Tom, who lived here from 1759. Castletown remained in the family until 1965, when it was taken over by the Irish Georgian Society. The house is now owned by the state, and is open to the public.

Did You Know?
When Edward Pakenham inherited the house in 1821, he had to change his name to Conolly.

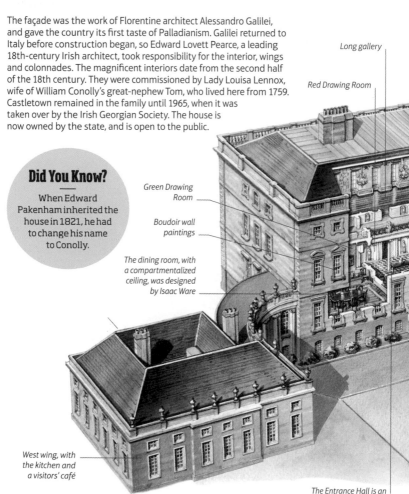

Long gallery

Red Drawing Room

Green Drawing Room

Boudoir wall paintings

The dining room, with a compartmentalized ceiling, was designed by Isaac Ware

West wing, with the kitchen and a visitors' café

The house is built in typical Palladian style, with a central block flanked by two pavilions ↑

The Entrance Hall is an austere Neo-Classical room; its most decorative feature is the delicate carving on the pilasters of the upper gallery

① Castletown House is situated amid beautiful grounds in County Kildare.

② Castletown's iconic staircase hall contains one of the largest cantilevered staircases in Ireland.

③ The Red Drawing Room was named for its most distinctive feature: the 19th-century crimson damask that covers the walls.

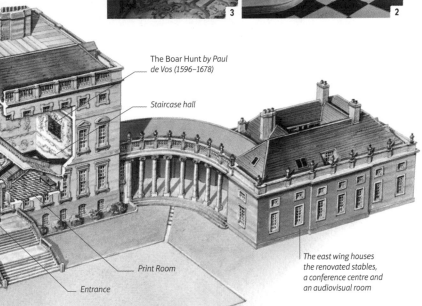

The Boar Hunt *by Paul de Vos (1596–1678)*

Staircase hall

Print Room

Entrance

The east wing houses the renovated stables, a conference centre and an audiovisual room

CONOLLY'S FOLLY

This folly, which lies just beyond the grounds of Castletown House, provides the focus of the view from the Long Gallery. Speaker Conolly's widow, Katherine, commissioned it in 1740 as a memorial to her late husband, and to provide employment after a harsh winter. The unusual structure of superimposed arches crowned by an obelisk is from designs by Richard Cassels, architect of Russborough House *(p144)*.

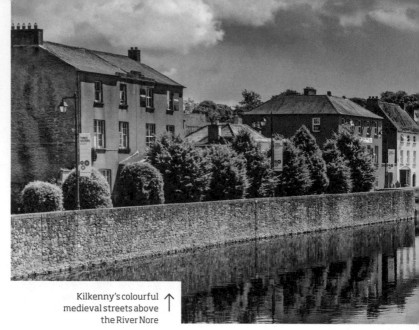

Kilkenny's colourful
medieval streets above
the River Nore ↑

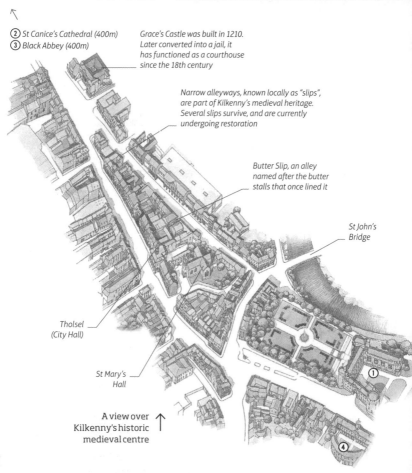

② St Canice's Cathedral (400m)
③ Black Abbey (400m)

*Grace's Castle was built in 1210.
Later converted into a jail, it
has functioned as a courthouse
since the 18th century*

*Narrow alleyways, known locally as "slips",
are part of Kilkenny's medieval heritage.
Several slips survive, and are currently
undergoing restoration*

*Butter Slip, an alley
named after the butter
stalls that once lined it*

*St John's
Bridge*

*Tholsel
(City Hall)*

*St Mary's
Hall*

A view over ↑
Kilkenny's historic
medieval centre

4

KILKENNY

C4 · **Co Kilkenny** · **Dublin Rd (056 772 2024)** · **Bus Éireann (051 317 864)**
Shee Alms House, Rose Inn St; www.visitkilkenny.ie

Kilkenny is undoubtedly Ireland's loveliest inland city. It rose to prominence in the 13th century, becoming the medieval capital of Ireland, and while it is no longer so powerful, its legacy is visible in the city's historic buildings.

Set on a kink in the River Nore, Kilkenny is of great architectural interest, with much use made of the distinctive local black limestone known as Kilkenny marble. A tour of the city's winding lanes reveals many unexpected treasures; a Georgian façade often conceals a Tudor chimney, a Classical interior or some other surprise.

The Anglo-Norman Butler family came to power here in the 1390s and held sway over the city for 500 years. The survival of the city's Irishtown district, now dominated by St Canice's Cathedral, recalls past segregation in Kilkenny. The area once known as Englishtown still boasts the city's grandest public buildings.

Other draws to the city include Ireland's top arts festival and the renowned Cat Laughs Comedy Festival, which Kilkenny hosts annually.

$\rightarrow$

Rothe House - a fine Tudor merchant's townhouse fronted by arcades once typical of Kilkenny's main streets - now has a small museum inside

①

Kilkenny Castle

🏠 The Parade ⏰ Daily
(check website for details)
🚫 Good Fri, 24-26 Dec
🌐 kilkennycastle.ie

Set in a commanding position overlooking the River Nore, this Norman fortress is one of Ireland's most famous castles. It was built in the 1190s and occupied right through until 1935. The powerful Butler family lived in it from the late 14th century, and their descendants eventually signed the castle over to the nation in 1967 for £50. With its drum towers and solid walls, the castle retains its medieval form, but has undergone many alterations. The Victorian changes, made in Gothic Revival style, have had the most enduring impact.

Two wings of the castle have been restored to their 19th-century splendour and include a library, drawing room and the magnificent Long Gallery with its impressive picture collection and a striking hammer-beam and glass roof. The final phase of restoration includes a state-of-the-art conference centre, situated in one of the castle's beautiful 12th-century towers.

The castle grounds have diminished over the centuries, but the French Classical gardens remain, with terraces opening onto a woodland walk and pleasant rolling parkland.

---

②

St Canice's Cathedral

🏠 Irishtown ⏰ Hours vary,
check website 🌐 stcanices
cathedral.ie

The hilltop cathedral, flanked by a round tower, was built in the 13th century in an early English Gothic style. It was sacked by Cromwell's forces in 1650, but has survived as one of Ireland's medieval treasures. Walls made from the local black limestone and pillars of pale limestone combine to create an interior of simple grandeur. An array of splendid 16th-century

Did You Know?

Dame Alice Kyteler, Ireland's first convicted witch, was born in Kilkenny in 1280.

tombs includes the beautiful effigies of the Butler family in the south transept. The cathedral's Round Tower is the oldest standing structure in Kilkenny, thought to date from the mid-9th century. One of only two round towers in Ireland that can be climbed (the other being in Kildare), it is worth doing so for fine views over the town.

---

③

Black Abbey

🏠 Abbey St ⏰ Daily
🌐 visitkilkenny.ie

Lying just west of Parliament Street, outside the original walls of the town, this

Kilkenny Castle, with its striking Victorian crenellations ↑

The interior of St Canice's Cathedral, with its 14th-century stained-glass windows ↑

Dominican abbey was founded in 1225. Part of it was turned into a courthouse in the 16th century, but today it is once again a working monastery. The church has a fine vaulted undercroft, distinctive stonework, some beautiful stained-glass windows and a unique 14th-century alabaster statue of the Holy Trinity.

Kilkenny Design Centre

🅐 Castle Yard 🕘 9am–6pm daily 🆆 kilkenny design.com

Housed in Kilkenny Castle's stable block, this design centre has a nationwide reputation. The sprawling shop floor is packed with handcrafted Irish pieces, offering a selection of jewellery, knitwear, china, pottery and glass. Fittingly – for Kilkenny is often proclaimed as Ireland's craft capital – the National Design and Craft Gallery is also housed here, plus there's a restaurant and food hall to sate the appetites of enthusiastic shoppers.

↑ Boats moored on the River Suir, at the edge of Waterford city

5

WATERFORD

🅰D5 **🅰Co Waterford** **🚉Plunkett Station, The Bridge (051 873401)** **🚌The Quay (051 879000)** **ℹ120 Parade Quay (051 875823)** **✈10 km (6 miles) S** **🌐visit waterford.com**

Ireland's oldest city, Waterford was founded by Vikings in AD 914, and the extensive remains of the city walls clearly define this originally fortified area. Set in a commanding position by the estuary of the River Suir, the city became southeast Ireland's main seaport. From the 18th century, the city's prosperity was consolidated by local industries, including the glassworks for which Waterford is famous. The strong commercial tradition persists today and Waterford's port is still one of Ireland's busiest. Although the city retains its medieval layout, most of Waterford's finest buildings are Georgian, with best examples seen on the Mall and in the lovely Cathedral Square.

①

Reginald's Tower

🅰The Quay **🕐For renovation until further notice, check website** **🌐waterfordtreasures.com**

This three-storey tower was built by the Anglo-Normans in 1185, making it the oldest civic urban structure in Ireland. With walls 3-m- (10-ft-) thick it is said to be the first to use mortar – a primitive concoction of blood, lime, fur and mud. Today, it is home to the Viking Waterford exhibition.

→

Reginald's Tower, the largest structure in the city's ancient fortifications

②

Medieval Museum

🅰Cathedral Square **🕐Hours vary, check website** **🕐25 & 26 Dec, 1 Jan** **🌐waterfordtreasures.com**

Waterford's Medieval Museum showcases many treasures from the Middle Ages. The building incorporates preserved medieval structures within its walls, including the 13th-century Choristers' Hall.

(3)

Bishop's Palace

⌂ The Mall ⊙ Hours vary, check website Ⓦ waterfordtreasures.com

Built in 1741 on the site of a medieval palace, this elegant building was the home of the bishops of the Church of Ireland until the early 20th century. It is now a museum furnished in the style of a fashionable 18th-century townhouse and displays a great collection of Waterford Crystal. A combined ticket can be purchased for entry to the Bishop's Palace and the Medieval Museum.

(4)

House of Waterford Crystal

⌂ The Mall ⊙ Hours vary, check website Ⓦ waterfordvisitorcentre.com

A visit to the Waterford Crystal Visitor Centre, where you can learn about and observe the process of crystal-making, is highly recommended during a stay in the city.

The original glass factory was founded in 1783 by two brothers, George and William Penrose, who chose Waterford because of its port. For many decades their crystal enjoyed an unrivalled reputation, but draconian taxes forced the firm to close in 1851.

A new factory and visitor centre was opened in 1947, just south of the city, and master blowers and engravers were brought from the Continent to train local apprentices. Competition from Tipperary and Galway Crystal had an effect in the early 1990s, but sales revived. Following the 2009 closure of the factories and visitor centre, a deal was brokered to secure the future of the glass in Waterford. While much of the glass manufacturing now happens elsewhere, visitors can still observe the making of prestige pieces in a custom-built facility on the site of the grand old ESB building on the Mall.

SHOP

The Book Centre
Browse the shelves of this unique bookshop, housed in a 1930s Art Deco cinema with the original screen still visible.

⌂ 25 John Roberts Square Ⓦ thebookcentre.ie

The centre offers tours that cover more than 225 years of glass-making and take in master craftsmen at work on individual pieces. You can observe all the stages that go towards creating the crystal objects, including mould making, cutting, sculpting and engraving. A shop with the world's largest display of Waterford Crystal sells fine pieces engraved with the famous Waterford signature.

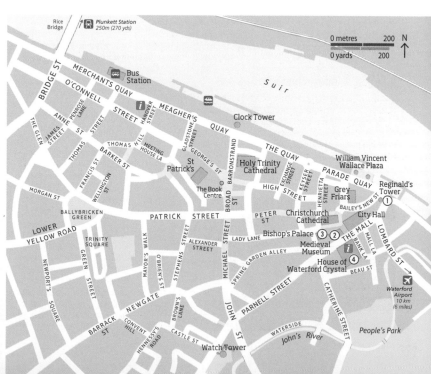

↑ The Bridge of Life in Kildare's attractive Japanese Gardens

EXPERIENCE MORE

 6

Kildare

⚇D4 ⚇Co Kildare
🚌 🚆 𝒊 Market House;
www.kildare.ie

The charming town of Kildare is dominated by **St Brigid's Cathedral**, which commemorates the saint who founded a religious community on this site in AD 480. Unusually, monks and nuns lived here under the same roof, but this was not the only unorthodox practice associated with their community. Curious pagan rituals, including the burning of a perpetual fire, continued until the 16th century. The fire pit is still visible, as is the highest round tower that can be climbed in Ireland, which was probably built in the 12th century and has a Romanesque doorway. The cathedral was rebuilt in the Victorian era, but the restorers largely adhered to the 13th-century design.

Kildare lies at the heart of racing country: the Curragh racecourse is nearby, stables are scattered all around and bloodstock sales take place at Kill, northeast of town.

The **National Stud**, just south of Kildare, was founded in 1900 by an eccentric Anglo-Irish colonel called William Hall-Walker. He sold his foals on the basis of their astrological charts, and put skylights in the stables to allow the horses to be "touched" by sunlight and moonbeams.

Visitors can explore the vast grounds and watch the horses being exercised. There is a special foaling unit where the mare and foal can remain undisturbed after the birth, and also a Horse Museum that illustrates the importance of horses in Irish life. Exhibits include the frail skeleton of Arkle, a famous champion steeplechaser in the 1960s.

Sharing the same estate as the National Stud are the **Japanese Gardens** and **St Fiachra's Garden**. The Japanese Gardens were laid out in 1906–10 by Japanese landscape gardener Tassa Eida, with the help of his son Minoru and 40 assistants. The impressive array of trees and shrubs includes maple, bonsai, mulberry, magnolia, sacred bamboo and cherry. The gardens take the form of an

---

▌ HORSE RACING IN IRELAND

Ireland has a strong racing culture. Much of the thoroughbred industry centres around the Curragh, a grassy plain in County Kildare. The racecourse there hosts many major flat races, including the Irish Derby. Other fixtures are held at nearby Punchestown (most famously the steeplechase festival in April/May), at Leopardstown (which also hosts major National Hunt races), and at Fairyhouse (home to the Irish Grand National).

---

allegorical journey through life, beginning with the Gate of Oblivion and leading to the Gateway of Eternity, a contemplative Zen rock garden.

St Fiachra's Garden covers 1.6 ha (4 acres) of woodland, wetland, lakes and islands, and features a Waterford Crystal Garden in the monastic cells.

St Brigid's Cathedral
 Market Sq 085 120 5920 May–Sep: daily kildare.ie/heritage

National Stud, Japanese Gardens and St Fiachra's Garden
Tully 9am–6pm daily irishnationalstud.ie

7

Bog of Allen Nature Centre

D4 Lullymore, Co Kildare To Newbridge To Allenwood 9am–5pm Mon–Fri, special weekends May–Sep ipcc.ie

Housed in an old farmhouse, the Nature Centre lies at the heart of the Bog of Allen, a vast expanse of raised bogland that extends across the

STAY

Three of the sunny southeast's famed golf resorts.

Carton House
Enjoy sweeping fairways at this restored mansion hotel.

D3 Maynooth, Co Kildare cartonhouse.com

€€€

The K Club
Luxury resort that has hosted the Ryder Cup and Irish Open.

D4 Straffan Demesne, Straffan, Co Kildare kclub.ie

€€€

Mount Juliet Estate
Georgian hotel with a course designed by Jack Nicklaus.

D5 Thomastown, Co Kilkenny mountjuliet.ie

€€€

---

counties of Offaly, Meath, Westmeath, Laois and Kildare. An exhibition of flora, fauna and archaeological finds explores the history and ecology of the bog. Pre-booked guided walks across the peatlands introduce visitors to the bog's delicate ecosystem.

8

Monasterevin

D4 Co Kildare

This Georgian market town lies west of Kildare, where the Grand Canal crosses the River Barrow. Waterborne trade brought prosperity to Monasterevin in the 18th century, but the locks now see little traffic. You can still admire the aqueduct, which is a superb example of canal engineering.

Also of interest is Moore Abbey. Built during the 18th century on the site of a monastic foundation, this grand Gothic mansion owes much to Victorian remodelling. It is now a hospital.

9

Robertstown

D4 Co Kildare

Robertstown is a characteristic 19th-century canalside village, with warehouses and cottages flanking the waterfront. Freight barges plied the route until about 1960, but pleasure boats have now replaced them. Visitors can take barge cruises from the quay. Another landmark is the Robertstown Hotel, built in 1801.

Near Sallins, about 8 km (5 miles) east of Robertstown, the canal is carried over the River Liffey along the Leinster Aqueduct, a fine example of engineering built in 1783.

←

A barge navigating the canal at Robertstown

⑩ Bray

🅰 D4 🏙 Co Wicklow
🚆 DART 🚌 ℹ Civic Offices,
Main St; www.bray.ie

Once a refined Victorian resort, Bray is nowadays a brash holiday town, with amusement arcades and fish-and-chip shops lining the seafront. Its beach attracts large crowds in summer, including young families. A more peaceful option is nearby Bray Head, where there is scope for bracing cliffside walks. Bray also makes a good base from which to explore the Wicklow Mountains and the nearby coastal villages.

⑪ Killruddery House and Gardens

🅰 D4 🏙 Bray, Co Wicklow
🏠 House: tours noon, 1:30pm & 3pm Tue-Sun; Gardens: May-Sep: 9:30am-6pm Tue-Sun, Apr & Oct: 9:30am-5pm Tue-Sun
🌐 killruddery.com

Killruddery House lies south of Bray, in the shadow of Little Sugar Loaf Mountain. Built in 1651, it has been the family seat of the Earls of Meath ever since, although the original mansion was remodelled in an Elizabethan Revival style in the early 19th century. The house contains some good carving and stuccowork, but the real charm of Killruddery lies in the 17th-century formal gardens. They were laid out in the 1680s by a French gardener who also worked at Versailles.

The gardens, planted with great precision, feature romantic parterres, hedges and many fine trees and shrubs. The sylvan theatre, a small enclosure surrounded by a bay hedge, is the only known example of its kind in Ireland.

The Long Ponds, a pair of canals which extend 165 m (542 ft), once stocked fish. Beyond, a pool enclosed by two circular hedges leads to a Victorian arrangement of paths flanked by statues and hedges of yew, beech and lime.

⑫ Russborough House

🅰 D4 🏙 Blessington, Co Wicklow 🚌 65 from Dublin
🕐 Mar-Dec: 10am-6pm daily
🌐 russboroughhouse.ie

This Palladian mansion, built in the 1740s for Joseph Leeson, Earl of Milltown, is one of Ireland's finest houses. Its architect, Richard Cassels, also designed Powerscourt House (p132) and is credited with introducing the Palladian style to Ireland.

Unlike many grand estates in the Pale, Russborough has survived magnificently, both inside and out. The house claims the longest frontage in Ireland, with a façade adorned by heraldic lions and curved colonnades. The interior is even more impressive, and is visited by taking the obligatory guided tour. Many rooms feature superb stucco

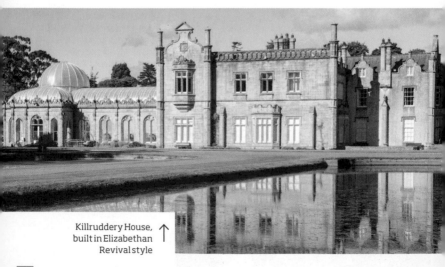

Killruddery House, built in Elizabethan Revival style ↑

↑ This beautiful saloon, enhanced by an Italian marble fireplace, is one of the many highlights seen during a guided tour of Russborough House *(right)*

decoration, which was created largely by the Italian Lafrancini brothers, who also worked on Castletown House *(p134)*. The best examples are found in the music room, saloon and library, which are embellished with exuberant foliage and cherubs. Around the main staircase, a riot of Rococo plasterwork depicts a hunt, with hounds clasping garlands of flowers. The stucco mouldings in the drawing room were designed especially to enclose marine scenes by the French artist Joseph Vernet (1714–89). The paintings were sold in 1926, but recovered over 40 years later and returned to the house.

Russborough has many other treasures to delight in, including finely worked fireplaces made of Italian marble, imposing mahogany doorways and priceless collections of silver, porcelain and Gobelin tapestries.

Such riches aside, one of the principal reasons to visit Russborough is to see the Beit Art Collection, famous for its Flemish, Dutch and Spanish Old Master paintings. Sir Alfred Beit, who bought the house in 1952, inherited the pictures from his uncle – also named Alfred Beit and co-founder of the de Beers diamond-mining empire in South Africa. On four separate occasions (1974, 1986, 2001 and 2002) masterpieces from the collection were stolen, most of which were eventually recovered. Only a selection of paintings is on view in the house at any one time, while others are on permanent loan to the National Gallery in Dublin *(p70)*. A self-guided interactive exhibition in the basement includes 3D photographs taken by Sir Alfred Beit in the 1920s and 1930s, as well as a selection of vinyl records and sheet music from the 1920s.

Away from the house there is much to enjoy, including several pretty parkland trails, a walled garden, a maze and even a bird of prey centre.

Another nearby attraction is the Poulaphouca Reservoir, which was formed by the damming of the River Liffey, and extends southwards from Blessington. It is popular with watersports enthusiasts, while others enjoy the mountain views.

↑ Colourful and remote moorlands of the Wicklow Mountains

 13

Wicklow Mountains

D4 To Rathdrum and Wicklow To Enniskerry, Wicklow, Glendalough, Rathdrum and Avoca Rialto House, Fitzwilliam Sq, Wicklow; 0404 69117 wicklowmountains nationalpark.ie

Standing amid the wilderness of the Wicklow Mountains, it can be hard to believe that Dublin is under an hour's drive away. The inaccessibility of the mountains meant that they once provided a safe hideout for opponents of English rule. When much of the southeast was obedient to the English Crown, within an area known as the Pale (p145), warlords such as the O'Tooles ruled in the Wicklow Mountains. Rebels who took part in the 1798 uprising sought refuge here too. One of their leaders, Michael Dwyer, remained at liberty in the hills around Sally Gap until 1803.

The building of the Military Road, started in 1800, made the area more accessible, but the mountains are still thinly populated. There is little traffic to disturb enjoyment of the beautiful rock-strewn glens, lush forest and bogland where heather gives a purple sheen to the land. Turf-cutting is still a thriving cottage industry, and you often see peat stacked up by the road. Among the numerous walking trails here is Wicklow Way, the oldest established walking route in Ireland, which extends 127 km (79 miles) from Marlay Park in Dublin to Clonegal in County Carlow. It is marked but not always easy to follow, so use a decent map. Although no peak exceeds 915 m (3,000 ft), the Wicklow Mountains can be dangerous in bad weather.

Hiking apart, there is plenty to see and do in this region. A good starting point for exploring the northern area is the estate village of Enniskerry. In summer it is busy with tourists who come to visit the gardens at Powerscourt (p132). From Laragh, to the south, you can reach Glendalough (p130) and the Vale of Avoca, where cherry trees are laden with blossom in the spring. The beauty of this gentle valley was captured in the poetry of Thomas Moore (1779–1852): "There is not in the wide world a valley so sweet as that vale in whose bosom the bright waters meet" – a reference to the confluence of the Avonbeg and Avonmore rivers, the so-called Meeting of the Waters beyond Avondale House. Nestled among wooded hills at the heart of the valley is the hamlet of Avoca, where the Avoca Handweavers produce

1606

This is the year Wicklow is thought to have been formed, the last of Ireland's 32 counties.

colourful tweeds in the oldest hand-weaving mill in Ireland, in operation since 1723.

Further north, towards the coast near Ashford, the River Vartry rushes through the deep chasm of the Devil's Glen. On entering the valley, the river falls 30 m (100 ft) into a pool known as the Devil's Punchbowl. There are good walks around here, with fine views of the coast.

   14

Mount Usher Gardens

D4 Ashford, Co Wicklow To Ashford 10am–5pm daily (to 5:30pm mid-Mar–mid-Oct) mountushergardens.ie

Set beside the River Vartry just east of Ashford are the Mount Usher Gardens. They were designed in 1868 by a Dubliner, Edward Walpole, who imbued them with his strong sense of romanticism.

The gardens contain more than 5,000 species of shrubs and trees, from Chinese conifers and bamboos to Mexican pines. Wander down a tree-lined path – the Maple Walk is glorious in autumn. The river provides the main focus, and amid the vegetation you can glimpse herons.

Avondale House

D4 **Co Wicklow**
To Rathdrum **Park: daily** **House: closed for renovation** **coillte.ie/site/avondale-forest-park/**

Lying just south of Rathdrum, Avondale House is the birthplace of the 19th-century politician and patriot Charles Stewart Parnell *(p51)*. The Georgian mansion is now a museum dedicated to Parnell and the fight for Home Rule; it is currently closed to visitors due to ongoing renovation.

The grounds are open to the public every day. Known as Avondale Forest Park, they include an arboretum planted in the 18th century and much added to since 1900. There are some lovely walks through the woods, with pleasant views along the River Avonmore.

Brownshill Dolmen

D4 **Co Carlow**
To Carlow **Daily**

In a field 5 km (3 miles) outside Carlow stands a dolmen boasting the biggest capstone in Ireland. Weighing a reputed 100 tonnes, this massive stone is embedded in the earth at one end and supported at the other by three much smaller stones. Dating back to 2000 BC, this site is thought to mark the tomb of a local chieftain.

THE MILITARY ROAD

The British built the Military Road through the heart of the Wicklow Mountains during a campaign to flush out Irish rebels after the uprising in 1798. Now known as the R115, this 96-km (60-mile) road takes you through the emptiest and most rugged landscapes of County Wicklow. Fine countryside, in which deer and other wildlife flourish, is characteristic of the whole route. Among the many delights along the way are Glendalough, Great Sugar Loaf Mountain, Lough Tay and Powerscourt Waterfall, which at 121 m (397 ft) is Ireland's highest. There are several pubs and cafés in Enniskerry (including Poppies, an old-fashioned tearoom), and also in Roundwood, but this area is better for picnics. There are several marked picnic spots south of Enniskerry.

17

Hook Peninsula

D5 Co Wexford To Duncannon From Passage East to Ballyhack; 051 382480 Fethard-on-Sea; 051 262995; www.hookpeninsula.com

This tapering headland of gentle landscapes scattered with ancient ruins and quiet villages is perfect for a circular tour. The "Ring of Hook" route begins south of New Ross at **Dunbrody Abbey**, the ruins of a 12th-century Cistercian church, but Ballyhack is another good place to start. Once a fortified crossing point into County Waterford, the town still runs ferries to neighbouring Passage East. **Ballyhack Castle**, built by the Knights Templar in about 1450, contains a small museum. About 4 km (2 miles) beyond is the small resort of Duncannon, with a sandy beach and a star-shaped fort built in 1588 in expectation of an attack by the Spanish Armada.

The coast road continues south to Hook Head. Here, at the tip of the Hook peninsula, is the world's oldest working lighthouse, dating from 1172 with its own visitor centre. Paths skirt the coast famous for its fossils, seals and a variety of sea birds.

Just 2 km (1 mile) east is the village of Slade. A ruined 15th-century tower house, Slade Castle, presides over the harbour where fishing boats cluster around the slipways. The road proceeds along the rugged coastline, past the resort of Fethard-on-Sea and Saltmills to the dramatic ruin of **Tintern Abbey**. This 13th-century Cistercian foundation was built by William Marshall, Earl of Pembroke.

↑ A Norman lighthouse at Hook Head, standing at the very tip of the peninsula

Dunbrody Abbey

Campile
May-Sep: 11am-5:30pm daily (to 6pm Jul & Aug)
dunbrodyabbey.com

Ballyhack Castle

Ballyhack Mid-May-Aug: 9:30am-5pm Sat-Wed
heritageireland.ie

Tintern Abbey

051 562650
Mar-May & Sep-Oct: 9:30am-5pm daily; Jun-Aug: 10am-5:30pm daily

18

Ardmore

C5 Co Waterford ardmorewaterford.com

Ardmore is a popular seaside resort with a splendid beach, lively pubs, good cliff walks and interesting architecture. The hill beside the village is the site of a monastery established in the 5th century by St Declan, the area's first missionary.

Most of the buildings, including the ruined St Declan's Cathedral, one of Ireland's earliest ecclesiastical sites, date from the 12th century. The cathedral's west wall has fine Romanesque sculptures, arranged in a series of arcades. The scenes include the Archangel Michael Weighing Souls in the upper row, and below this the Adoration of the Magi and the Judgment of Solomon.

The adjacent round tower is one of the best-preserved examples in Ireland, and rises to a height of 30 m (98 ft). An oratory nearby is said to mark the site of St Declan's grave.

← Remains of St Declan's Cathedral, Ardmore

STAY

Cliff House Hotel

Luxury hotel in a cliffside setting, with all rooms offering views of the bay. Borrow some wellies for a wander along the headland before relaxing in the on-site spa.

C5 Ardmore cliffhousehotel.ie

€€€

Jerpoint Abbey

A D5 **A** Thomastown, Co Kilkenny **A** **To** Thomastown **O** Mar–Sep: 9am–5:30pm daily; Oct: 9am–5pm daily; Nov: 9:30am–4pm daily **C** 25 Dec; Dec–Feb: pre-booked tours only **W** heritageireland.ie

On the banks of the Little Arrigle is Jerpoint Abbey, one of the finest Cistercian ruins in Ireland. Founded in 1160, the fortified medieval complex rivalled Duiske Abbey *(p150)* in prestige. Jerpoint flourished until the Dissolution of the Monasteries, when it passed to the Earl of Ormonde.

The 15th-century cloisters have not survived as well as some earlier parts of the abbey. Despite this, they are the highlight, with amusing sculptures of knights, courtly ladies, bishops and dragons. The church itself is well preserved. The Irish-Romanesque transepts date back to the earliest period of the abbey's development and contain 16th-century tombs with exquisite stylized carvings. The north side of the nave has a rich array of decorated Romanesque capitals and throughout the abbey are

↑ Ornate stone cross inside Jerpoint Abbey's medieval ruins

tombs and effigies of bishops. The battlemented crossing tower was added in the 1400s.

Dunmore East

A D5 **A** Co Waterford **W** discoverdunmore.com

The appeal of this pretty village lies chiefly in its red sandstone cliffs and bustling harbour. Paths run along the foot of the cliffs, but for the best views take the road that winds uphill from the beach, past cottages and the ivy-clad Azzurro to the Haven Hotel. A gate nearby leads to delightful gardens

overlooking the fishing boats below. Climb the steps cut into the rock and you are rewarded by the views and noisy kittiwake colonies.

Lismore

A C5 **A** Co Waterford **W** **i** Lismore Heritage Centre, Main St; www.discoverlismore.com

This riverside town is dwarfed by **Lismore Castle**. Built in 1185 but remodelled in the 19th century, the castle is the Irish seat of the Duke of Devonshire and is closed to the public, but you can visit the gardens. Lismore Heritage Centre tells the story of St Carthage, who founded a monastic centre here in the 7th century. The town has two cathedrals dedicated to him. The Protestant cathedral dates from 1633 but was later altered to suit the Neo-Gothic tastes of the Victorians. It has a beautiful stained-glass window by the Pre-Raphaelite artist Sir Edward Burne-Jones.

Lismore Castle
⊗ **O** Mid-Mar–mid-Oct: 10:30am–5:30pm daily **W** lismorecastlegardens.com

↑ A bustling fishing harbour at the heart of Dunmore East

22
Enniscorthy

🅐 D5 🅐 Co Wexford 🚌 🚃

The streets of Enniscorthy, on the banks of the River Slaney, are full of character and redolent of its turbulent past. In 1798, the town witnessed the last stand of the Wexford pikemen, when a fierce battle was fought against a British force of 20,000 on nearby Vinegar Hill. The events of that year are told in depth at the multimedia **National 1798 Visitor Centre**. The Neo-Gothic **St Aidan's Cathedral**, designed in the 1840s by A W N Pugin (1812–52), is also worth a visit, as is **Enniscorthy Castle**; built in the 12th century, it offers panoramic views from its roof.

Granaries, potteries and mills overlook the Slaney, including Carley's Bridge, which was established in 1654 and is still operational. The town's historic pubs are also a key attraction.

National 1798 Visitor Centre

⊘ ⊘ ⊚ 🅐 Millpark Rd 🕒 9:30am–5pm Mon–Fri, noon–5pm Sat, Sun & bank hols 🌐 1798centre.ie

St Aidan's Cathedral

🅐 Main St 🕒 8:30am–6pm daily 🌐 staidanscathedral.ie

Enniscorthy Castle

🅐 Castle Hill 🕒 9:30am–5pm Mon–Fri, noon–5pm Sat & Sun 🌐 enniscorthycastle.ie

23
New Ross

🅐 D5 🅐 Co Wexford 🚃 🅘 South Quay; 051 421857

Lying on the banks of the River Barrow, New Ross is one of the oldest towns in the county. Its importance, now as in the past, stems from its status as a port. In summer cruises plying the Barrow, Nore and Suir rivers. Docked at South Quay is the **Dunbrody**

Famine Ship Experience, a full-scale reconstruction of a cargo ship that carried emigrants to the US and Canada during the Famine. Traditional shopfronts line the streets, which rise steeply from the quayside. The Tholsel, now the town hall but originally a tollhouse, was occupied by the British during the 1798 rebellion. Opposite, a monument to a Wexford pikeman commemorates the bravery of the Irish rebels who faced the British.

Nearby is St Mary's, which, when founded in the 13th century, was the largest parish church in Ireland. A modern church occupies the site, but the original (now roofless) south transept remains, as do many medieval tombstones.

A popular trip from New Ross up the meandering Barrow goes 16 km (10 miles) north to Graiguenamanagh. The main attraction of this market town is **Duiske Abbey**, the largest Cistercian church in Ireland. Founded in 1207, it has been extensively restored and now acts as the parish church. The most striking features include a Romanesque door in the south transept and a cross-legged statue of the Knight of Duiske, which is one of the finest medieval effigies in Ireland.

On a hill 12 km (7 miles) south of New Ross, a large area of woodland is enclosed within the **JFK Memorial Park**. Founded in 1968, near the late president's ancestral home in Dunganstown (now the Kennedy Homestead), the 162-ha (400-acre) park boasts more than 4,500 types of tree and provides panoramic views.

DRINK

Holohan's
This traditional Irish pub has a friendly atmosphere with good live music and an unusual location – it's built right into the base of an old quarry.

🅐 D5 🅐 Slaney Place, Enniscorthy 📞 053 923 5743

Dunbrody Famine Ship Experience

⊘ ⊘ ⊕ ⊘ 🅐 South Quay 🕒 9am–6pm daily 🌐 dunbrody.com

Duiske Abbey

🅐 Graiguenamanagh 📞 059 972 4238 🕒 Mon–Fri

JFK Memorial Park

⊘ ⊘ ⊘ 🕒 Dawn–dusk 🌐 heritageireland.ie

24
Wexford

🅐 D5 🅐 Co Wexford 🚌 🚃 🅘 Quay Front; www.visitwexford.ie

Wexford's name derives from *Waesfjord*, a Norse word

↑ The long and narrow South Main Street in Wexford town centre, busy with shoppers

meaning "estuary of the mud flats". It thrived as a port for centuries but the silting of the harbour in the Victorian era put an end to most sea traffic. Wexford's quays, from where ships once sailed to Bristol, Tenby and Liverpool, are now used mainly by a fleet of humble mussel dredgers.

Wexford is a vibrant place, packed with fine pubs and boasting a varied arts scene. The town's singular style is often linked to its linguistic heritage. The *yola* dialect, which was spoken by early settlers, survives in the local pronunciation of certain words.

Wexford retains few traces of its past, but the Viking fish-bone street pattern still exists, with narrow alleys fanning off the meandering Main Street. Keyser's Lane, linking

South Main Street with the Crescent, is a tiny tunnel-like Viking alley that once led to the Norse waterfront. The Normans were responsible for Wexford's town walls, remnants of which include one of the original gateways. Behind it lies Selskar Abbey, the ruin of a 12th-century Augustinian monastery. King Henry II is said to have done penance here for the murder of Thomas à Becket in 1170.

Wexford also has several handsome buildings, including the 18th-century market house on Main Street. Nearby is the Bull Ring, a square used for bull-baiting in Norman times and the scene of a massacre by Cromwell's men in 1649.

Wexford Opera Festival, held from mid-October to early November, is the leading operatic event in the country. The modern **National Opera House** – on the site of the old Theatre Royal – is a fitting home for one of the world's finest opera festivals. Its varied programme includes revivals of forgotten masterpieces, talks and recitals. The event sees the town's restaurants, pubs and bars fill with festival-goers.

Skirting the shore just east of the town is **Wexford Wildfowl Reserve**. It covers 100 ha (250 acres) of reclaimed land and is noted for its geese: over a third of the world's entire population of Greenland white-fronted geese winter here from October to April. The mudflats also attract large numbers of swans and waders. The birds can be viewed from hides and an observation tower.

National Opera House
☺ 🏠High St 🅦national operahouse.ie

Wexford Wildfowl Reserve
🅧 🏠Wexford 🕒9am–5pm daily 🅦wexfordwildfowl reserve.ie

← The port of New Ross, seen from the west bank of the River Barrow

㉕ Saltee Islands

D5 **Co Wexford** **From Wexford to Kilmore Quay: Wed & Sat** **From Kilmore Quay: Apr–Sep (weather permitting); 053 912 9637** **salteeislands.info**

These islands off the south coast of Wexford are a haven for sea birds. Great and Little Saltee together form Ireland's largest bird sanctuary, and are very popular with bird-watchers. The islands nurture an impressive array, from gannets and gulls to puffins and Manx shearwaters. Great Saltee particularly is famous for its colonies of cormorants. It also has more than 1,000 pairs of guillemots and is a popular stopping-off place for spring and autumn migrations. A bird-monitoring programme is in progress, and a close watch is also kept on the colony of more than 100 grey seals.

The two uninhabited islands are privately owned, but visitors are welcome to Great Saltee between 11:30am and 4:30pm. Boat trips are run in fine weather from Kilmore Quay, leaving in late morning and returning mid-afternoon. Kilmore Quay is a quaint little fishing village built on Precambrian gneiss rock – the oldest rock in Ireland. Pretty thatched cottages and friendly pubs nestle above a fine sandy beach and a stone harbour wall.

㉖ Rosslare

D5 **Co Wexford** **053 912 3111**

Rosslare replaced Wexford as the area's main port after the decline of the original Viking city harbour. The port is so active today that people tend to associate the name Rosslare more with the ferry terminal for France and Wales than with the town lying 8 km (5 miles) further north.

Rosslare town prides itself on being the sunniest place in Ireland and draws many holiday-makers. It boasts a fine beach stretching the whole length of the southern peninsula, some 9 km (6 miles). There are a few lively pubs and an excellent golf course fringed by sand dunes, plus some great trails and walks north to Rosslare Point.

The **International Outdoor Adventure Centre** rents kayaks and windsurfing equipment, and runs summer camps for children in July and August.

International Outdoor Adventure Centre
Tagoat **ioac.ie**

㉗ Johnstown Castle

D5 **Co Wexford** **To Wexford** **Gardens & Irish Agriculture Museum: 9am–5:30pm daily** **24 & 25 Dec** **johnstowncastle.ie**

Johnstown Castle, a splendid Gothic Revival mansion, lies amid gardens and woodland 6 km (4 miles) southwest of Wexford. In state hands since 1945, the refurbished castle is is open for pre-booked guided tours. The Irish Agriculture Museum, which is housed in the castle's farm buildings, features reconstructions that illustrate country scenes and traditional trades from the last 200 years or more. There

Hikers exploring the Saltee Islands for their stunning views and wildlife *(inset)*

→ The evocative Johnstown Castle and a statue in its beautiful grounds

> **The real glory of Johnstown Castle is its 20 ha (50 acres) of beautiful grounds, from the Italian garden to the ornamental lakes.**

is an excellent exhibition on the Famine, which puts this national tragedy of the 1840s in perspective, explaining the role of the potato and the changes that followed in the wake of the disastrous blight. Another fascinating exhibition of country kitchens compares the domestic lifestyles of 1800, 1900 and 1950.

The real glory of Johnstown Castle is its 20 ha (50 acres) of beautiful grounds, from the Italian garden to the ornamental lakes. Azaleas and camellias flourish alongside an array of trees including Japanese cedars and redwoods. The lakes are home to a wide range of waterfowl – mute swans, water hens, little grebes and heron. There is also a 1.5-km (1-mile) fully accessible lower lake walk and children's woodland play area.

Hidden among the dense woods west of the house lurk the ruins of Rathlannon Castle, a medieval tower house thought to have been built in the 15th century.

EAT

Mary Barry's Bar & Restaurant

Traditional Irish pub serving fresh seafood caught at Kilmore Quay. In summer oysters and lobster can be chosen from the restaurant's sea tank. Children will enjoy the walled garden's play area.

🅰D5 🏠Ballask, Kilmore

Ⓦmarybarrys.ie

€€€

28

Irish National Heritage Park

🅰D5 🏠Ferrycarrig, Co Wexford ⓇMay-Aug: 9:30am–6:30pm (to 5:30pm Sep–Apr) Ⓣ24–26 Dec Ⓦirish heritage.ie

Built on former marshland near Ferrycarrig, northwest of Wexford, the Irish National Heritage Park is a bold open-air museum. Trails lead through woods to full-scale replicas of homesteads, places of worship and burial sites, providing a fascinating lesson on the country's ancient history.

Highlights include the Viking boatyard and raiding ship, a 7th-century horizontal watermill and interactive experiences such as panning for gold, drawing rock art, archery and rowing a coracle boat. In summer, actors in costume add extra authenticity to the setting. On site there is a craft shop with unique gifts, and a self-service restaurant.

← Reconstructed painted Celtic cross at the Irish National Heritage Park

CORK AND KERRY

Killarney and its romantic lakes are a powerful magnet for tourists, as are Cork's attractive coastal towns and villages. Yet the region remains remarkably unspoiled, with a friendly atmosphere and authentic culture still alive in Irish-speaking pockets.

This corner of Ireland used to be the main point of contact with the wider world; in the 17th century, in response to the threat of invasions from France and Spain, the English built a line of forts along the Cork coast, including the massive Charles Fort at Kinsale. In the 19th century, the city of Cork was an important departure point for people fleeing the hardship of the Great Famine, with Cobh the main port for emigrants to the New World. Cork's importance as a port has since diminished, but it remains the Republic's second city, with a lively cultural scene.

Kerry, meanwhile, is known as "the Kingdom" on account of its tradition of independence and disregard for Dublin rule. The Irish recognize a distinctive Kerry character, with a boisterous sense of living life to the full.

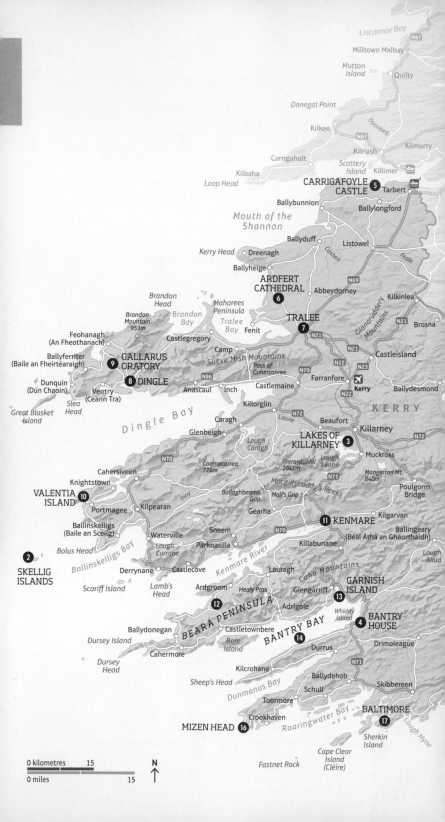

CORK AND KERRY

Must Sees

1. Cork
2. Skellig Islands
3. Lakes of Killarney
4. Bantry House

Experience More

5. Carrigafoyle Castle
6. Ardfert Cathedral
7. Tralee
8. Dingle
9. Gallarus Oratory
10. Valentia Island
11. Kenmare
12. Beara Peninsula
13. Garnish Island
14. Bantry Bay
15. Drombeg Stone Circle
16. Mizen Head
17. Baltimore
18. Clonakilty
19. Timoleague Abbey
20. River Lee
21. Blarney Castle
22. Jameson Distillery Midleton
23. River Blackwater
24. Cobh
25. Youghal
26. Kinsale

THE LOWER SHANNON p184

SOUTHEAST IRELAND p124

Colourful shops and restaurants lining the banks of the River Lee ↑

1

CORK

⬛C5 🏠Co Cork ✈Cork Airport 🚉Kent Station 🚌Parnell Place ℹ125 St Patrick's Street; 021 425 5100; www.purecork.ie

Cork city sits on the banks of the River Lee, where St Finbarr founded a monastery around AD 650. Since the 19th century, when Cork was a base for the National Fenian movement, the city has had a reputation for political rebelliousness. Today this mood is reflected in the city's attitude to the arts and its creative spirit, much in evidence at the lively October jazz festival.

①

St Anne's Shandon

🏠Church St 🕐Daily 🕐2 weeks at Christmas 🌐shandonbells.ie

This famous Cork landmark stands on the hilly slopes of the city, north of the River Lee. Built in 1722, the church has a façade made of limestone on two sides, and of red sand-stone on the other two. The steeple is topped by a weather vane in the shape of a salmon. The clock face is known by the locals as the "four-faced liar" because, up until 1986 when it was repaired, each face showed slightly different times. Visitors can climb the tower and, for a small fee, ring the famous Shandon bells to a variety of different tunes, among them "Hey Jude" and the *Game of Thrones* soundtrack.

②

Cork Butter Museum

🏠O'Connell Square 🕐Mar-Oct: 10am-5pm Mon-Sat, 11am-4pm Sun 🌐thebutter museum.com

This museum tells the story of Ireland's most important food export and the world's largest butter market. The exchange opened in 1770 and was where butter was graded before it was exported to the rest of the world. By 1892 it was exporting around 500,000 casks of butter a year. The exchange shut in 1924. Exhibits at the museum, including a 1,000-year-old keg of butter unearthed from a turf bog, explain the story of a culture where social standing was determined by the number of cattle owned.

③

Crawford Art Gallery

🏠Emmet Place 🕐10am-5pm Mon-Sat (to 8pm Thu), 11am-4pm Sun 🕐Good Fri, 25 Dec 🌐crawfordart gallery.ie

The building that houses Cork's main art gallery dates back to 1724. Built as the city's original custom house, it became a school of design in 1850, before William Horatio Crawford, a noted art patron, extended the building to accommodate studios, and sculpture and picture galleries in 1884.

The gallery houses late 19th- and early 20th-century Irish art, including paintings by Jack Yeats and three windows

④ ✈ Ⓜ 🛍

St Fin Barre's Cathedral

🏠 Bishop Street
🕐 Apr-Nov: daily; Dec-Mar: Mon-Sat 🕐 24 Dec-2 Jan (except for services)
🌐 corkcathedral.webs.com

Found just south of the river, St Fin Barre's Cathedral is the most distinctive landmark of St Fin Barre's Quarter, a quiet part of Cork surrounding Proby's Quay. Dedicated to the city's founder and patron saint, this exuberant edifice – built in the Gothic Revival style from Cork limestone and marble – was completed in 1870 to the design of English architect William Burges.

Inside the cathedral, the painted and gilded apse ceiling shows Christ in Glory surrounded by angels, while the magnificent stained-glass windows depict scenes from both the Old and New Testaments. The cathedral also contains over 1,000 sculptures, as well as a hefty cannonball that was once

DRINK

Mutton Lane Inn
Tucked away near the English Market, this tiny pub is an old-school watering hole. Dimly lit, with no TV, it's the perfect spot for a pint and a chat - get there early to grab a seat.

🏠 3 Mutton Lane, Cork
📞 021 427 3471

used during the 1690 Siege of Cork. Perched atop the cathedral's roof is a beautiful gilded statue of an angel.

Nearby is the ivy-clad Elizabeth Fort, a 16th-century structure that was converted into a prison in 1835 and later into a Garda (police) station. A short walk to the east lies the Red Abbey, a 13th-century relic from an Augustinian abbey – the oldest building in Cork.

by stained-glass artist Harry Clarke *(p116)*. A small collection of works by artists such as Joán Miró and Georges Rouault also feature here.

The gallery is well known for its café, which serves delicious lunches and teas. The room is decorated with works of art from the collection.

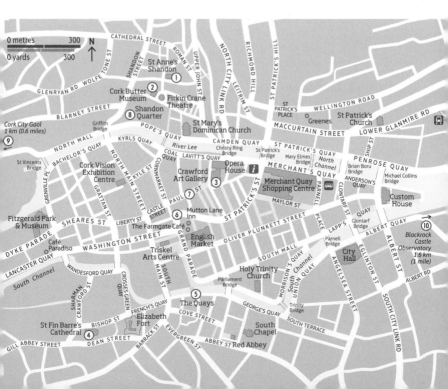

⑤ The Quays

Although the river now plays a minor part in the city's economy, much of Cork's commercial activity still takes place around the bustling Quays (pronounced "kays" in the musical Cork accent). The South Mall, which covers an arm of the River Lee, was a waterway until the late 18th century. Boats were once moored at the foot of a series of stone steps, some of which are still intact today. These led to merchants' domestic quarters above. The arches below led to warehouses.

Close to South Mall is Parliament Bridge, built in 1806 to commemorate the Act of Union. It is an elegant, single-arched bridge made mainly from limestone. Designed by William Hargrave, it replaced a bridge on the same site that was damaged by a flood in 1804. On nearby Sullivan's Quay is the Quay Co-Op, a popular vegetarian restaurant.

⑥ Grand Parade and St Patrick's Street

On the bustling Grand Parade, also once a waterway, stands the grand National Monument, commemorating the Irish patriots who died between 1798 and 1867. The charming Bishop Lucey Park, off Grand Parade, has a section of city walls and a fine gateway from the old cornmarket. Between St Patrick's Street and Grand Parade is the vibrant English Market, a covered fruit and vegetable market established in 1610 – it is the perfect place to pick up delicious local produce. Bustling St Patrick's Street, the backbone of the city, was a waterway until 1800, with boats moored under the steps of gracious houses such as the Chateau Bar. At the top of the street, near St Patrick's Bridge, is the Father Matthew Statue, a monument to the founder of the Temperance Movement.

⑦ Paul Street

Noted for its ethnic restaurants, chic bars, bookshops and trendy boutiques, Paul Street is the hub of the liveliest district in town. Just off Paul Street are the busy back-streets of Carey's Lane and French Church Street. In the early 18th century, Huguenots (French Protestants) settled

in these streets and set themselves up as butter exporters, brewers and wholesale merchants. This area is Cork's equivalent to Dublin's Temple Bar (p87).

⑧ Shandon Quarter

 Pope's Quay

Shandon was originally one of 28 settlements found in and around ancient Cork. Crossing the Christy Ring Bridge to Pope's Quay, you will see St Mary's Dominican Church to your left, with its portico of Ionic columns topped by a huge pediment. John Redmond Street leads to the northern slopes of Cork, which are dominated by the spire of St Anne's Shandon (p158), with its fine views of the city. To the northeast lies the lofty Montenotte district, once the epitome of Victorian gentility.

←

Blackrock Castle on the banks of the River Lee, now home to an observatory

Cork's historic English Market, filled with fruit and vegetable stalls

Cork City Gaol

📍 Convent Avenue, Sunday's Well ⏰ Apr-Sep: 9:30am-5pm daily; Oct-Mar: 10am-4pm daily 🚫 22-26 Dec 🌐 corkcitygaol.com

A pretty 20-minute walk west of the city centre leads to the restored City Gaol, which was designed in 1818. The Gaol closed in 1923 following the release of Republican leaders after the Civil War. Today visitors can explore the Gaol with help of an audio-guide, touring well-preserved cells which document the lives of those imprisoned here – often in miserable conditions. One punishment was making prisoners run on a treadmill normally used to grind grain.

Did You Know?

Cork's Gaelic name is *Corcaigh*, meaning 'a marsh' - the city was founded on a swampy estuary.

The Radio Museum is also housed in this building, as it was once home to Radio Éireann (now RTE). Exhibits include material pertaining to the pioneers of modern radio as well as a re-creation of the old studio.

Blackrock Castle Observatory

📍 Castle Road, Blackrock ⏰ 10am-5pm Thu-Sun 🚫 1 Jan & 24-26 Dec 🌐 bco.ie

On the banks of the River Lee, 1.6 km (1 mile) downstream from the city centre, stands Blackrock Castle. Built in 1582 by Lord Mountjoy as a harbour fortification, the castle was reconstructed in 1829 – following a fire which broke out two years earlier. The restored castle now houses an observatory featuring two exciting and interactive exhibitions called "Cosmos at the Castle" and the "Journeys of Exploration". The castle also has an excellent programme of hosting visiting exhibitions throughout the year.

EAT

Café Paradiso

An iconic Cork dining institution and arguably Ireland's most famous vegetarian restaurant, Café Paradiso has been serving inventive dishes since 1993.

📍 16 Lancaster Quay, Cork City 🌐 paradiso.restaurant

€€€

The Farmgate Café

Perched on a balcony above the bustling stalls of the English Market, this little café uses locally-sourced, seasonal produce. Expect dishes like pea and goat's cheese risotto, as well as pistachio meringues with strawberries and cream.

📍 The English Market, Princes St, Centre 🌐 farmgatecork.ie

€€€

Greenes

This charming restaurant is nestled in the heart of the city's atmospheric Victorian Quarter. All dishes are prepared with organic, seasonal ingredients, many of which have been foraged from the surrounding area. Try the pan-seared hake with sea vegetables or the indulgent wild mushroom risotto.

📍 48 MacCurtain Street, Cork City 🌐 greenes restaurant.com

€€€

2

SKELLIG ISLANDS

A6 **Co Kerry** **Mid-Apr-early Oct: from Portmagee** **skelligislands.com**

Unique for both their historical significance and jagged natural beauty, these inhospitable islands lie off Ireland's southwest coast. The larger – Skellig Michael – is a UNESCO World Heritage Site long known for its magnificent early Christian monastery, but a stint as Luke Skywalker's Jedi temple in the 2015 and 2017 Star Wars films has propelled the island to new levels of fame.

Skellig Michael

Also known as Great Skellig, this is one of the most stunning places to visit in the whole of Ireland. Monks settled for solitude here during the 6th century, building a cluster of stone beehive huts and two boat-shaped oratories, all of which are still standing. Their isolated monastery perches on a ledge 218 m (715 ft) above sea level, reached only by a perilous 1,000-year-old stairway. The monks were self-sufficient, trading eggs, feathers and seal meat with passing boats in return for cereals, tools and animal skin. They remained on this bleak island until the 12th century, when they retreated to the Augustinian priory at Ballinskelligs on the mainland.

Little Skellig

Closer to the mainland, and about 10 ha (25 acres) smaller, lies Little Skellig. Home to a variety of sea birds, the island has one of the world's largest colonies of gannets (about 22,000 breeding pairs). While most boats circle Little Skellig so that the birds can be observed, the island is a sanctuary and no landing is permitted.

> 💬 **INSIDER TIP**
> **Getting Tickets**
>
> Cancellations and no-shows are more common than you might expect. If you're having trouble booking a ticket, try ringing the night before or the morning of the day on which you'd like to go.

The remaining beehive huts on Skellig Michael *(inset)*, with Little Skellig visible in the distance ↑

SKELLIG WILDLIFE

Today the only residents of the Skellig Islands are the thousands of sea birds that nest and breed on the high cliffs, protected from predators by the sea and rocky shore. As well as gannets, Ireland's largest sea bird, there are puffins, arctic terns and fulmars. Larger wildlife, such as basking sharks, dolphins, seals and turtles, may also be seen in the waters around the islands.

Visiting the Islands

For those keen to see the Skellig Islands up close, there are two types of tour that can be booked. Running from mid-April to early October, eco tours circle the islands, focusing on their wildlife – which can include basking seals – and offering fantastic views. Landing tours run only from mid-May to September, but these allow passengers to disembark on Skellig Michael and explore the island. Since the filming of Star Wars, it has become necessary to book well in advance, and both tours are dependent on sea conditions.

The Gap of Dunloe, a dramatic mountain pass carved by glaciers and popular with walkers and cyclists due to its great views

→

3 ⊛ 🍴 ☕ 🛍

LAKES OF KILLARNEY

🅰 B5 🅰 Killarney, Co Kerry 🆆 killarneynationalpark.ie
🄲 Muckross House: Apr-Jun & Sep-Oct: 9am-6pm daily;
Jul-Aug: 9am-7pm daily; Nov-Mar: 9am-5pm daily
🆆 muckross-house.ie

Renowned for its scenery, this is one of Ireland's most popular attractions. The three lakes – Upper, Leane and Muckross – are contained within Killarney National Park, and make up around a quarter of the park's area.

Although the landscape is liberally dotted with ruined castles and abbeys, the lakes are the focus of attention. Their moody water scenery is subject to subtle shifts of light and colour, allowing the area to entrance many artists and writers – such as Thackeray, who praised "a precipice covered with a thousand trees … and other mountains rising as far as we could see". In autumn, the bright red fruits of strawberry trees colour the shores of the lakes.

←

A boat moored by Upper Lake, the smallest of the three lakes

↑ Muckross House, an elegant 19th-century manor that overlooks the lakes and is now the location of the Museum of Kerry Folklife

Killarney National Park, as glimpsed from Ladies' View, a renowned viewpoint ↑

KILLARNEY

Though often derided as a "tourist town", this has not dented Killarney's cheerful atmosphere. It's at its busiest during summer but also has much to offer then, with late-opening shops. Home to a number of excellent restaurants and a few prestigious hotels, it's the perfect base from which to explore the region's lakes.

BANTRY HOUSE

B6 **Bantry, Co Cork** **Apr-May & Sep-Oct: 10am-5pm Tue-Sun; Jun-Aug: 10am-5pm daily** **Cork to Bantry daily** **bantryhouse.com**

Situated on the Wild Atlantic Way, this stately home offers spectacular views of Bantry Bay and has been open to the public since 1946.

Bantry House has been the home of the White family, formerly Earls of Bantry, since 1739, and they still live in and manage the estate today. The original Queen Anne house was built around 1700, but the north façade overlooking the bay was a later addition. Inside is an eclectic collection of art and furnishings brought from Europe by the 2nd Earl of Bantry, with highlights including the Aubusson tapestries made for Marie Antoinette on her marriage to the future Louis XVI. For those keen to extend their stay, guest rooms are available here on a bed-and-breakfast basis.

The accompanying grounds are also magnificent; the Italian Garden, designed in the early 1850s, was inspired by the Boboli Gardens of Florence, while the steps furthest from the house are known as the "Staircase to the Sky", and lead to a series of terraces with fabulous views.

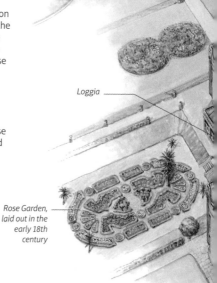

Loggia

Rose Garden, laid out in the early 18th century

① Bantry House enjoys an enviable location overlooking Bantry Bay, with Whiddy Island beyond.

② The rose-coloured tapestries hanging in this drawing room are thought to have been made for Marie Antoinette and date from c 1770.

③ The Blue Dining Room is dominated by portraits of King George III and Queen Charlotte.

Did You Know?
Whiddy Island, in Bantry Bay, became a US Naval Air Station during the final months of WWI.

North façade

Gobelin Drawing Room

Rose Dawing Room

The Anteroom contains family mementos, china and a collection of 18th-century prints

Statue of Diana (1840)

Entrance Hall

Italian Garden

Library

Blue Dining Room

"Staircase to the Sky"

The house, surrounded by formal gardens stretching down to Bantry Bay ↑

1ST EARL OF BANTRY (1767-1851)

Richard White, 1st Earl of Bantry, played a leading role in defending Ireland against Wolfe Tone's attempted invasion. On 16 December 1796, Tone sailed for Ireland from Brittany with a fleet of 43 French ships. White chose strategic spots around Bantry Bay and mustered volunteers to fight. His efforts proved unnecessary as the fleet was forced back by bad weather, but White was nevertheless given a peerage by George III for his "spirited conduct and important services". In 1800 he was made Viscount Bantry, then Earl of Bantry in 1816.

EXPERIENCE MORE

5
Carrigafoyle Castle

B5 ⬛ Co Kerry ⬛ May–Sep: 10am–5pm daily ⬛ To Listowel

High above the Shannon estuary, 3 km (2 miles) from Ballylongford, this 15th-century castle belonged to the O'Connor clan, who ruled much of northern Kerry. The English besieged or sacked it repeatedly but the body blow was delivered in 1649 by Cromwellian forces. The ruins include a keep and stone bawn, with romantic views of the estuary from the top of the tower.

6
Ardfert Cathedral

A5 ⬛ Co Kerry ⬛ Apr–Sep: 10am–6pm daily ⬛ heritageireland.ie

This complex of churches is linked to the cult of St Brendan the Navigator (*p221*), who was born nearby in AD 484 and founded a monastery here in the 6th century. The ruined cathedral dates back to the 12th century and retains a delicate Romanesque doorway and blind arcading. The battlements were added in the 15th century. The south transept houses an exhibition of the history of the site. In the graveyard stand the remains of a Romanesque nave-and-chancel church, Teampall na Hoe, and a late Gothic chapel, Teampall na Griffin. The latter is named after the curious griffins carved beside an interior window.

A short walk away are the ruins of a Franciscan friary. It was founded by Thomas Fitzmaurice in 1253, but the cloisters and south chapel date from the 15th century.

Just northwest of Ardfert is Banna Strand. Irish patriot Roger Casement landed here in 1916 on a German U-boat, bringing in rifles for the Easter Rising. He was arrested as soon as he landed and a memorial stands on the site of his capture.

7
Tralee

B5 ⬛ Co Kerry ⬛ ⬛ ⬛ Ashe Memorial Hall, Denny St; www.tralee.ie

Host of the renowned Rose of Tralee International Festival, which takes place in August, Tralee has a long and proud history as a market town. Its main attraction **Kerry County Museum** offers a great insight into the area's rich history from prehistoric times to the 20th century. Highlights include archaeological finds as well as a recreation of a medieval street, complete with authentic smells.

Siamsa Tíre is home to the National Folk Theatre of Ireland and is a great ambassador for Irish culture. Traditional song and dance performances take place here throughout the summer.

Just outside Tralee is the authentic **Blennerville Windmill**, Ireland's largest working windmill, where

STAY

Ballyseede Castle
Housed in a 16th-century castle and ideally located for touring the Ring of Kerry, this stunning hotel effortlessly fuses old-world elegance with modern comforts.

B5 ⬛ Ballyseede, Tralee ⬛ ballyseedecastle.com

€€€

Ruins that make up the Ardfert Cathedral complex ↑

Fishing trawlers moored alongside the quay at Dingle

underwater tunnels that bring visitors face to face with the local sea life.

Gallarus Oratory

A5 ⬛ **Co Kerry**
🚌 **To Dingle** ⬛ **Gallarus Oratory: daily; visitor centre: Apr–Oct**
🌐 **gallarusoratory.ie**

Shaped like an upturned boat, this miniature church overlooks Smerwick Harbour. It was built some time between the 6th and 9th centuries and is the best-preserved early Christian church in Ireland. It represents the apogee of dry-stone corbelling, using techniques first developed by Neolithic tomb-makers. The stones were laid at a slight angle, allowing water to run off.

> **Dingle is the starting point for harbour tours to see marine wildlife and the beauty of the stunning Dingle peninsula coastline.**

visitors can climb to the top. Among other attractions inside the mill is a model of the old Tralee to Dingle narrow-gauge railway, plus displays on emigration and vintage equipment.

Kerry County Museum
⬛ **Ashe Memorial Hall, Denny St** 🕐 **9:30am–5pm Tue–Sat** 🔒 **Week at Christmas & bank hols** 🌐 **kerrymuseum.ie**

Siamsa Tíre
⬛ **Town Park, Denny St** 🕐 **For performances May–Sep** 🌐 **siamsatire.com**

Blennerville Windmill
⬛ **Windmill Lane** 🕐 **Apr & May, Sep & Oct: 9:30am–5:30pm daily; Jun–Aug: 9am–6pm daily** 🌐 **blennerville-windmill.ie**

Dingle

A5 ⬛ **Co Kerry**
🚌 **Apr–Oct** ℹ️ **Strand St; www.dingle-peninsula.ie**

This once remote Irish-speaking town, which started out as the site of a fort and trading post, is today a thriving fishing port and popular tourist centre. Brightly painted craft shops and cafés abound, often with slightly hippy overtones.

Dingle Bay is attractive, with a ramshackle harbour lined with fishing trawlers. Along the quayside are lively bars offering music and seafood. Dingle is the starting point for harbour tours to see marine wildlife and the beauty of the stunning Dingle peninsula coastline (pp180–81). Other sea creatures can be seen at Oceanworld Aquarium, one of Ireland's foremost aquariums, with

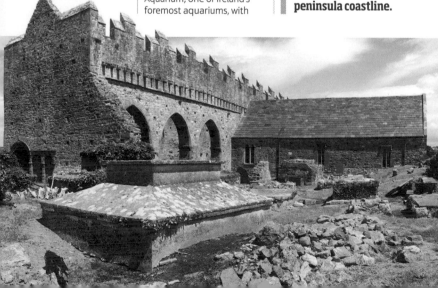

The sprawling landscape of Valentia Island, perfect for coastal walks

EAT

The Chart House
One of Dingle's best restaurants, the Chart House uses local ingredients in inventive dishes.

🅰A5 🏠 The Mall, Dingle 🅦 thechart housedingle.com

€€€

 10

Valentia Island

🅰A5 🏠 Co Kerry 🚌 To Cahersiveen 🚹 Watchhouse Cottages, Knightstown; www.valentiaisland.ie

Although it feels like the mainland, Valentia is an island, albeit linked by a causeway to Portmagee. It is 11 km (7 miles) long and noted for its seascapes, watersports and archaeological sites. Valentia is also popular for its proximity to the Skellig Islands.

The **Skellig Experience Centre**, near the causeway, houses an audiovisual display about the monastery on Skellig Michael (p162). Other subjects include the marine life around the islands, a reminder that the Skellig cliffs lie underwater for a depth of 50 m (165 ft). The centre also operates cruises around the islands.

The village of Knightstown has varied accommodation, pubs and superb views – especially from **Geokaun Mountain and Fogher Cliffs**, the island's highest point. It's ideal for picnics and accessible for cars and walkers.

Skellig Experience Centre
 🏠 Valentia Island 🕐 Mar–Nov: daily (hours vary check website) 🅦 skelligexperience.com

Geokaun Mountain and Fogher Cliffs
⊘ 🏠 Valentia Island 🅦 geokaun.com

11

Kenmare

🅰B5 🏠 Co Kerry 🚌 🚹 The Square; Apr–Oct; www.kenmare.ie

Cromwell's surveyor general, Sir William Petty, founded this town on the mouth of the River Sheen in 1670. However, Kenmare's appearance owes more to the first Marquess of Lansdowne who, in 1775, made it a model landlord's town of neat stone façades with decorative plasterwork.

Today Kenmare is renowned for its traditional lace. During the Famine years, local nuns introduced lace-making to create work for the women and girls. It is also an excellent base for exploring the idyllic scenery of the Beara Peninsula and the Ring of Kerry.

Set in a riverside glade off Market Street is the Druid's Circle, a prehistoric ring of 15 stones associated with human sacrifice.

 12

Beara Peninsula

🅰A6 🏠 Co Cork & Co Kerry 🚌 To Glengarriff (daily) & Castletownbere (Mon, Wed, Fri & Sun) 🚹 Kenmare; www.destinationbeara.ie

Dotted with sparsely populated fishing villages surrounded by bleak moorland, this peninsula is remote. It used to be a refuge for smugglers, with the Irish exchanging pilchards for contraband French brandy.

The peninsula offers some spectacular scenery and wonderful walking country. From the Healy Pass, which cuts a jagged path across the spine of the Caha Mountains, there are some fine views of Bantry Bay and the rugged landscape of West Cork. To the west of the pass is Hungry Hill, the highest mountain in the Caha range and popular with hill walkers.

Encircled by the Caha and Slieve Miskish Mountains is Castletownbere, the main town on the peninsula. This sheltered port is awash with foreign fishing trawlers. The charming McCarthy's Bar on Town Square features an authentic matchmaking booth, where local families previously used to agree marriage terms.

West of Castletownbere stands the shell of Puxley Mansion, home of the Puxley family who owned the mines at Allihies. Centre of the copper-mining district until the 1930s, it is an interesting place, with tall Cornish-style chimneys and piles of

ochre-coloured spoil. It is home to the **Allihies Copper Mine Museum**, covering the history of this local industry.

From the tip of the Beara Peninsula a cable car travels across to Dursey Island, with its ruined castle and colonies of sea birds. Licensed to carry six passengers or one large animal at a time, the cable car offers views of Bull, Cow and Calf islands.

From the headland the R757 road back to Kenmare passes through the pretty villages of Eyeries, noted for its brightly painted cottages and crafts, and Ardgroom, a base for exploring the scenic glacial valley around Glenbeg Lough.

Allihies Copper Mine Museum

 ♿ Allihies ⏰ Easter-Oct: 10:30am–5pm daily
🌐 acmm.ie

---

13 ⊘ 💻

Garnish Island

🅰 B6 📍 Co Cork 🚢 From Glengarriff (027 63116)
📅 Apr–Oct: daily
🌐 garnishisland.com

Also known as Ilnacullin, this small island, located in the harbour of Glengarriff, was turned into an exotic garden in 1910 by Harold Peto for Annan Bryce, a Belfast businessman. Framed by views of Bantry Bay, the gardens are landscaped with Neo-Classical follies and planted with subtropical flora. The microclimate and peaty soil provide the damp, warm conditions needed for these ornamental plants to flourish.

Exotic shrubberies abound, especially during the summer. In May and June, there are beautiful displays of camellias, azaleas and rhododendrons. There is also a New Zealand fernery, a Japanese rockery and a rare collection of Bonsai trees. A Martello tower, thought to be the first ever built, crowns the island and among the follies are a clock tower and a Grecian temple.

The centrepiece is a colonnaded Italianate garden, featuring a Classical folly and ornamental lily pool. Much of its charm resides in the contrast between the cultivated lushness of the garden and the glimpses of wild seascape and barren mountains beyond. An added attraction of the boat trip across to this Gulf Stream paradise is the chance to see seals basking on the rocks and cavorting in Bantry Bay.

→
Italianate garden with lily pond and folly on Garnish Island

↑ Pastel shopfronts line the harbour in Bantry Bay

⑭ Bantry Bay

Ⓐ B6 Ⓜ Co Cork 🚌 To Bantry and Glengarriff ⓘ The Square, Bantry; Apr-Oct ⓦ visitbantry.ie

Bantry Bay encompasses the resorts of Bantry and Glengarriff. It is also a springboard for trips to Mizen Head and the Beara Peninsula.

Bantry nestles beneath the hills that run down to the bay. Just offshore is Whiddy Island, the home of the White family, who moved to Bantry House (p166) in the early 18th century. Further along is Bere Island, a British base until World War II.

Glengarriff exudes an air of Victorian gentility with its neatly painted shopfronts and craft shops. On the coast is the Eccles Hotel, a haunt of Queen Victoria and where George Bernard Shaw supposedly wrote *Saint Joan*. Glengarriff's **Bamboo Park** is an exotic garden with 30 different species of bamboo and tropical plants.

Bamboo Park
♿🚻🅿 Ⓐ Glengarriff
🕙 9am–7pm daily
ⓦ bamboo-park.com

⑮ Drombeg Stone Circle

Ⓐ B6 Ⓜ Co Cork 🚌 To Skibbereen or Clonakilty

Drombeg is the finest of the many stone circles in County Cork. Dating back to about 150 BC, this circle of 17 standing stones is 9.5 m (31 ft) in diameter. At the winter solstice, the rays of the setting sun fall on the flat altar stone that faces the entrance to the circle, marked by two upright stones.

Nearby is a small stream with a Stone Age cooking pit *(fulacht fiadh)*. A fire was made in the hearth, from which hot stones were dropped into the cooking pit to heat the water. Once the water boiled, the meat, usually venison, was added.

⑯ Mizen Head

Ⓐ A6 Ⓜ Co Cork 🚌 To Goleen ⓘ Town Hall, North St, Skibbereen; 028 21489

Mizen Head, the most southwesterly tip of Ireland, has steep cliffs, often lashed by

→ The rocky cliffs at Mizen Head, linked by a bridge *(inset)* to a lighthouse

EAT

Rolf's

This fine-dining restaurant overlooking Roaringwater Bay serves fresh local produce and home-baked breads, desserts and pastries.

 B6 📍 The Hill, Baltimore 🌐 rolfs countryhouse.com

€€€

storms. In a lighthouse, **Mizen Head Visitor Centre** is reached by a bridge. From the car park, a headland walk takes in views of cliffs and Atlantic breakers. The sandy beaches of nearby Barley Cove attract bathers and walkers, and to the east is Crookhaven, a pretty yachting harbour.

Mizen Head can be reached either from Bantry via Durrus or from the market town of Skibbereen, on the R592, via the charming crafts centre of Ballydehob and the village of Schull. Trips to Cape Clear Island leave from Schull in the summer months.

Mizen Head Visitor Centre

♿🚻👶 📍 Mizen Head 🕐 Mid-Mar–Oct: daily; Nov–mid-Mar: Sat & Sun 🌐 mizenhead.ie

 17

Baltimore

🅰 B6 📍 Co Cork 🚌 ⛴ To Sherkin Island (087 911 7377); to Cape Clear Island (028 39159) 🌐 baltimore.ie

Baltimore's most bizarre claim to fame dates back to 1631 when more than 100 citizens were carried off as slaves by Algerian pirates. Now that the threat of being kidnapped has gone, this village appeals to the yachting fraternity and island-hoppers.

Overlooking the harbour is a ruined 15th-century castle, once the stronghold of the O'Driscoll clan. Also worth a visit are the seafood pubs, including the atmospheric Bushe's Bar. Behind the village, cliff walks lead to the Baltimore beacon with its views of Carbery's Hundred Isles – mere specks on Roaringwater Bay.

A short ferry ride away is Sherkin Island with its sandy beaches in the west, ruined 15th-century abbey, marine station and pubs. The ferry ride to Cape Clear Island is more dramatic, as the boat weaves between sharp black rocks to this remote, Irish-speaking island, noted for its bird observatory in the North Harbour. There are spectacular views of the mainland.

18

Clonakilty

🅰 B6 📍 Co Cork 🚌 ℹ 25 Ashe Street; www.clonakilty.ie

Founded as an English outpost around 1588, this market town has a typically hearty West Cork atmosphere. The **West Cork Regional Museum**, set in an old schoolhouse, remembers the town's industrial heritage. Quayside buildings, linked to the town's industrial past, have been restored. Particularly pleasant is the Georgian nucleus of Emmet Square.

Until the 19th century Clonakilty was a noted linen producer. Today, it is known for its rich black puddings, hand-painted Irish signs and traditional music pubs. Near the town centre is a model village, depicting the town as it was in the 1940s.

West Cork Regional Museum

♿ 📍 Western Rd 📞 023 883 3115 🕐 May–Oct, call for times

DRINK

De Barra's Folk Club

This is one of West Cork's best-known pubs, with instruments lining the walls and a traditional folk club. Although it regularly hosts prominent bands, De Barra's remains true to its low-key roots.

 B6 55 Pearse St, Clonakilty debarra.ie

 19

Timoleague Abbey

B6 Co Cork
To Clonakilty or Courtmacsherry
Daily timoleague.ie

Timoleague Abbey enjoys a waterside setting overlooking an inlet where the Argideen estuary opens into Courtmacsherry Bay. The abbey, which was founded around the late 13th century, is a ruined Franciscan friary. The buildings have been extended at various times. The earliest section is the chancel of the Gothic church, while the most recent addition, the 16th-century tower, was added by the Franciscan Bishop of Ross. The friary was ransacked by the English in 1642 but much of significance remains, including the church, infirmary, fine lancet windows, refectory and a walled courtyard. There are also sections of cloisters and wine cellars. In keeping with Franciscan tradition, the complex is plain to the point of austerity. Yet such restraint belied the friars' strong inclination for high living:

→

Battlemented keep and ruined towers of Blarney Castle

the friary prospered on their trade in smuggled Spanish wines, easily delivered thanks to its position on the then navigable creek.

20

River Lee

B6 Co Cork To Cork Cork; 021 425 5100

Carving a course through farm and woodland to Cork city *(p158)*, the River Lee begins its journey in the lake of the enchanting Gougane Barra Park. The shores of the lake are linked by a causeway to Holy Island, where St Finbarr, the patron saint of Cork, founded a monastery. The Feast of St Finbarr, on 25 September, signals celebrations that climax in a pilgrimage to the island on the following Sunday.

The Lee flows through many Irish-speaking market towns and villages. Some, such as Ballingeary, with its fine lakeside views, have good angling. The town is also noted for its Irish-language college. Further east, near the town of Inchigeelagh, stand the ruins of Carrignacurra Castle. Further downstream

lies the Gearagh, an alluvial stretch of marsh and woods that has been designated a wildlife sanctuary.

The river then passes through the Sullane valley, home of the thriving market town of Macroom. The hulk of a medieval castle lies just off the main square. In 1654, Cromwell granted this castle to Sir William Penn. His son, who was later responsible for founding the American state of Pennsylvania, also lived here for a time.

Between Macroom and Cork, the Lee Valley passes through a hydroelectric power scheme, which is surrounded by artificial lakes, water meadows and wooded banks. Just outside Cork, on the south bank of the river, is charming Ballincollig, home to the fascinating former Royal Gunpowder Mills.

Did You Know?

Built into the castle's east wall, the Blarney Stone sits 26 m (85 ft) above the ground.

21

Blarney Castle

B5 **Blarney, Co Cork**
To Cork **Hours vary, check website** **24 & 25 Dec** **blarneycastle.ie**

Visitors from all over the world flock to this ruined castle to see the legendary Blarney Stone. Kissing the stone, which is set in the wall below the castle battlements and reached by climbing to the top of a steep spiral staircase, is a long-standing tradition; according to legend, it confers a magical eloquence. The climb is worthwhile for the magnificent view from the battlements.

Little remains of the castle today except the keep, built in 1446 by Dermot McCarthy. Its design is typical of a 15th-century tower house. The vaulted first floor was once the Great Hall. To reach the battlements you need to climb the vertigo-inducing 127 steps to the top of the keep.

The castle's beautiful parkland, featuring a fern garden and arboretum, 18th-century grottoes, standing stones, a grove of ancient yew trees, limestone rock formations at Rock Close and a lake, offer some wonderful walks. Blarney House, a Scottish baronial mansion and the residence of the Colthurst family since the 18th century, is open to the public only from June to August.

A short walk from the castle, Blarney has a pretty village green with welcoming pubs and some craft shops. The village's second-biggest attraction is the Blarney Woollen Mills, which sells garments and souvenirs.

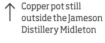

↑ Copper pot still outside the Jameson Distillery Midleton

22

Jameson Distillery Midleton

C5 **Distillery Walk, Midleton, Co Cork** **To Midleton** **10am–6pm daily (last tour: 4:15pm)** **Good Fri & 24–26 Dec** **jamesonwhiskey.com**

A sensitively restored 18th-century distillery, Jameson Distillery Midleton is part of the vast Irish Distillers group at Midleton. Bushmills (p285) is the oldest distillery in Ireland but Midleton is the largest, with a series of units, each producing a different whiskey, including Jameson.

The story of Irish whiskey is presented through audiovisual displays, working models and authentic machinery. A tour (obligatory) of the old distillery takes in the mills, maltings, still-houses, kilns, granaries and warehouses. Visitors can take part in whiskey tasting and try to distinguish between various brands of Irish, Scotch and bourbon whiskies. Highlights of the visit include the world's largest pot still, with an incredible capacity of over 30,000 gallons, and the working waterwheel.

IRISH EMIGRATION

Between 1848 and 1950 more than six million people emigrated from Ireland – with two and a half million of them leaving from Cobh. The Famine years of 1845–48 (p222) triggered mass emigration as the impoverished made the horrific transatlantic journey in cramped, insanitary conditions. Many headed for the United States and Canada, and a few risked the long journey to Australia. Up until the early 20th century, emigrants waiting to board the ships were a familiar sight in Cobh. By the 1930s, however, world recession and immigration restrictions in the United States and Canada led to a fall in the numbers leaving Ireland.

Following a visit by Queen Victoria in 1849, Cobh was renamed Queenstown, but it reverted to its original name in 1922.

fishing, golf and horse racing. Detours along the tributaries include Kanturk, a pleasant market town with a castle.

23 River Blackwater

B5 **Co Cork** **To Mallow** **To Fermoy, Mallow or Kanturk**

The second-longest river in Ireland after the Shannon (p196), the Blackwater rises in high bogland in County Kerry. It then flows eastwards through County Cork until it reaches Cappoquin, County Waterford, where it changes course south through wooded sandstone gorges to the sea at Youghal. The river passes some magnificent country houses and pastoral views. However, the region is best known for its fishing – the Blackwater's tributaries are filled with fine brown trout.

The best way to see the valley is to take the scenic Blackwater Valley Drive from Youghal to Mallow. The route passes through Fermoy, a town founded by Scottish merchant John Anderson in 1789. Angling is the town's main appeal, especially for roach, rudd, perch and pike. Further west is Mallow, a prosperous town noted for its

24 Cobh

C6 **Co Cork** **** **Market House, Casement Sq; www.visitcobh.com**

Cobh (pronounced "cove") lies on Great Island, one of the three islands in Cork Harbour, which are now linked by causeways. Its Victorian seafront has rows of steeply terraced houses overlooked by the impressive St Colman's Cathedral, built in the Gothic Revival style.

The town has one of the world's largest natural

harbours, hence its rise to prominence as a naval base in the 18th century. It was a major port for merchant ships and the main port from which Irish emigrants set out for America. Cobh was also a port of call for luxury passenger liners. In 1838, the *Sirius* made the first transatlantic crossing under steam power from here. Cobh was also the last stop for the *Titanic*, before its doomed Atlantic crossing in 1912. Three years later, the *Lusitania* was sunk by a German submarine just off Kinsale, southwest of Cobh. A memorial on the promenade is dedicated to all those who died in the attack.

North of Cobh is Fota Island, with its glorious Regency mansion and a wildlife park.

25
Youghal

C5 Co Cork 🚌 ℹ️Market Sq; www.youghal.ie

Youghal (pronounced "yawl") is a historic walled town and thriving fishing port. The town was granted to Sir Walter

→
The Red House, a distinctive sight on Youghal's North Main Street

Raleigh by Queen Elizabeth I but later sold to the Earl of Cork.

The picturesque, four-storey clock tower was originally the city gate, but was recast as a prison. Steps beside the tower lead up to a well-preserved section of the medieval town wall and fine views across the Blackwater estuary. In nearby North Main Street is the Red House, a Dutch mansion built in 1710. Virtually next door are some grim Elizabethan alms-houses and a 15th-century tower, known as Tynte's Castle. Just uphill from here is the Gothic Church of St Mary. Inside are tomb effigies and stained-glass windows depicting the coats of arms of local families.

26
Kinsale

B6 Co Cork 🚌 From Cork city ℹ️Pier Rd; www.kinsale.ie

Kinsale, with its yacht-filled harbour and narrow medieval streets, is one of the prettiest towns on Ireland's southwest coast. One of its best sights is **Desmond Castle**, which was built by Maurice Bacach Fitzgerald, the ninth Earl of Desmond, in around 1500. A good example of an urban tower house, this charming castle is closed due to renovations. It has spent time as an ordnance store, workhouse, customs house and prison. The castle also houses the International Museum of Wine, which focuses on Kinsale's links to Ireland's wine trade and charts the

←
Cobh Harbour with the cathedral's steeple rising above the town

journeys of Irishmen who left for France, Spain and California, and became wine producers.

Just east of the town is the impressive Charles Fort, a 1670s star fort that is one of the finest such examples remaining in Europe today. Guided tours are available all year round.

Desmond Castle
🏠Cork Street, Kinsale
🔒For renovation
🌐heritageireland.ie

STAY

Fota Island Resort
This resort hotel provides the perfect base for those who wish to explore Fota Island further. There are extensive recreational activities, including nature walks, tennis courts and a 27-hole golf course.

C6 🏠Fota Island
🌐fotaisland.ie

€€€

A SHORT WALK
KINSALE

Distance 1 km (0.6 miles) **Nearest Station** Kinsale Bus and Coach Station **Time** 15 minutes

For many visitors to Ireland, Kinsale (p177) tops the list of places to see. One of the country's prettiest small towns, it has had a long and chequered history – the defeat of the Irish forces and their Spanish allies in the Battle of Kinsale in 1601, for example, signified the end of the old Gaelic order. Today Kinsale is a popular seaside town, home to pleasant medieval streets. It is also famous for the quality of its cuisine – the town's annual Gourmet Festival in October is one of Ireland's premier events – and there are plenty of wonderful pubs, cafés and restaurants in which you can break up your stroll.

Desmond Castle, built around 1500 and known locally as the "French Prison"

Old Market House, a museum that incorporates the old courthouse and includes a toll board listing local taxes for 1788

St Multose Church, a much-altered Norman church named after an obscure 6th-century saint, which marks the centre of the medieval town

Market Square

CHAIRMAN'S LANE

CORK STREET

MARKET LANE

CHURCH PL

MARKET STREET

GUARDWELL

0 metres 50   N ↑
0 yards 50

← Old tombstones in the graveyard of St Multose Church

↑ The welcoming façade of Mother Hubbards café

↑ Cottages lining the mouth of Kinsale Harbour

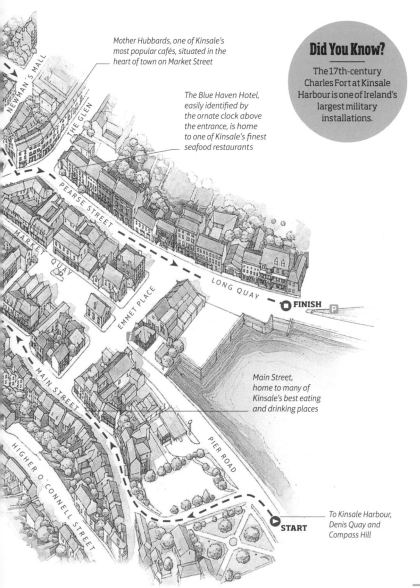

Mother Hubbards, one of Kinsale's most popular cafés, situated in the heart of town on Market Street

The Blue Haven Hotel, easily identified by the ornate clock above the entrance, is home to one of Kinsale's finest seafood restaurants

Did You Know?

The 17th-century Charles Fort at Kinsale Harbour is one of Ireland's largest military installations.

NEWMAN'S MALL

THE GLEN

PEARSE STREET

MARKET QUAY

EMMET PLACE

LONG QUAY

🚩 FINISH P

MAIN STREET

Main Street, home to many of Kinsale's best eating and drinking places

PIER ROAD

HIGHER O'CONNELL STREET

🚩 START

To Kinsale Harbour, Denis Quay and Compass Hill

A DRIVING TOUR
THE DINGLE PENINSULA

Length 40 km (25 miles) **Stopping-off points** Slea Head; Dunquin; Ballyferriter **Terrain** Some winding coastal roads

The Dingle Peninsula offers some of Ireland's most beautiful scenery. To the north rises the towering Brandon Mountain, while the west coast has some spectacular seascapes. A drive around the area, which takes at least half a day, reveals fascinating antiquities ranging from Iron Age stone forts to inscribed stones, early Christian oratories and beehive huts. These are sometimes found on private land, so you may be asked for a small fee by the farmer to see them. Some parts of the peninsula – especially the more remote areas – are still Gaelic speaking, so many road signs are written only in Irish.

The little village of **Ballyferriter (Baile an Fheirtéaraigh)** *is known for its pastel-coloured cottages, Louis Mulcahy's pottery and museum of local cultural heritage.*

Smerwick

Sybil Head

Sybil Point Ballyoughteragh

The **Blasket Centre (Ionad an Bhlascaoid)** *explains the literature, language and way of life of the inhabitants of the Blasket Islands. The islanders moved to the mainland in 1953.*

Ballyferriter

Teeravane

Clogher Head

Croaghmarhin 457 m (1,499 ft)

R559

Inishooskert

Blasket Island Centre

Dunmore Head (Ceann an Dúin Mhoir), *mainland Ireland's most westerly point, offers dramatic views of the Blasket Islands.*

Dunquin

Monte Eagle 516 m (1,692 ft)

Coumeenoole

Fahan

Dunmore Head

Blasket Sound

Coumeenoole Bay

Slea Head

Great Blasket Island

As you round **Slea Head (Ceann Sléibe)** *the Blasket Islands come into full view. The sculpture of the Crucifixion beside the road is known locally as the Cross (An Cros).*

Locator Map
For more detail see p156

The excavated monastic settlement of **Riasc (An Riasc)** dates from the 6th century, and includes remains of an oratory, inscribed slabs and a pillar stone.

↑ The curving sandy beach of Ventry Bay, framed by rippling green hills

Once a pagan centre of worship, **Kilmalkedar (Cill Maolchéadair)** is home to a ruined Irish Romanesque church with stone carvings. The graveyard still contains primitive pagan stones, a cross and a sundial.

The tiny, dry-stone church of **Gallarus Oratory (Séipéilín Ghallrois)** is a relic of early Irish Christianity (p169).

Start at the busy seaside town of **Dingle (An Daingean)** (p169).

Leaving Dingle, make **Ventry Bay** your next port of call. This stunning crescent of fine sand is backed by a succession of low dunes.

Dating from the Iron Age, **Dunbeg Fort (An Dún Beag)** is one of the best-preserved promontory forts in Ireland. Just beyond are the Fahan beehive huts, early Christian huts thought to have been built for pilgrims visiting the area.

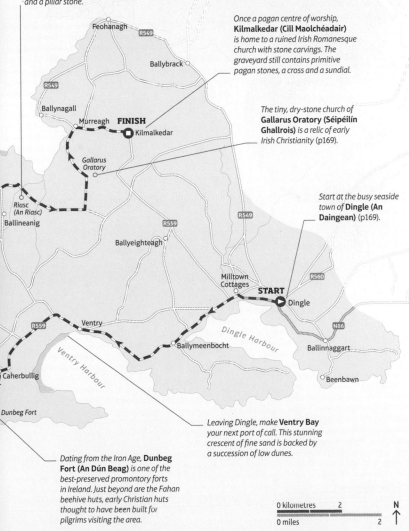

0 kilometres 2

0 miles 2

N ↑

A DRIVING TOUR
THE RING OF KERRY

Length 180 km (112 miles) **Stopping-off points** Killorglin; Cahirciveen; Kenmare **Terrain** Narrow, winding coastal roads

This long-established route around the Iveragh Peninsula, which can be taken in either direction, is always referred to as the Ring of Kerry. Allow a day to see its captivating mountain and coastal scenery, dotted with slate-roofed fishing villages. Set out early to avoid the mass of coach tours which converge on the towns for lunch and tea. There are interesting detours across the spine of the peninsula.

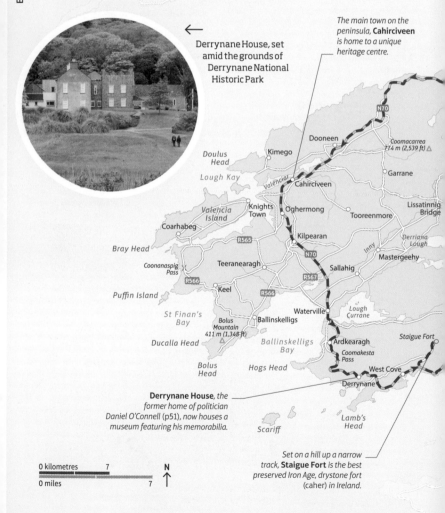

← Derrynane House, set amid the grounds of Derrynane National Historic Park

The main town on the peninsula, **Cahirciveen** *is home to a unique heritage centre.*

Doulus Head

Kimego

Dooneen

Coomacarrea 774 m (2,539 ft) △

Garrane

Lough Kay

Valencia

Cahirciveen

N70

Knights Town

Oghermore

Tooreenmore

Lissatinnig Bridge

Valencia Island

Coarhabeg

R565

Kilpearan

Derriana Lough

Bray Head

N70

Inny

Mastergeehy

Coonanaspig Pass

R566

Teeranearagh

Sallahig

R567

Puffin Island

Keel

R566

Waterville

Lough Currane

St Finan's Bay

Bolus Mountain 411 m (1,348 ft) △

Ballinskelligs

Ballinskelligs Bay

Ardkearagh

Staigue Fort

Ducalla Head

Coomakesta Pass

West Cove

Bolus Head

Hogs Head

Derrynane

Derrynane House, *the former home of politician Daniel O'Connell (p51), now houses a museum featuring his memorabilia.*

Scariff

Lamb's Head

Set on a hill up a narrow track, **Staigue Fort** *is the best preserved Iron Age, drystone fort (caher) in Ireland.*

0 kilometres   7
0 miles   7

N ↑

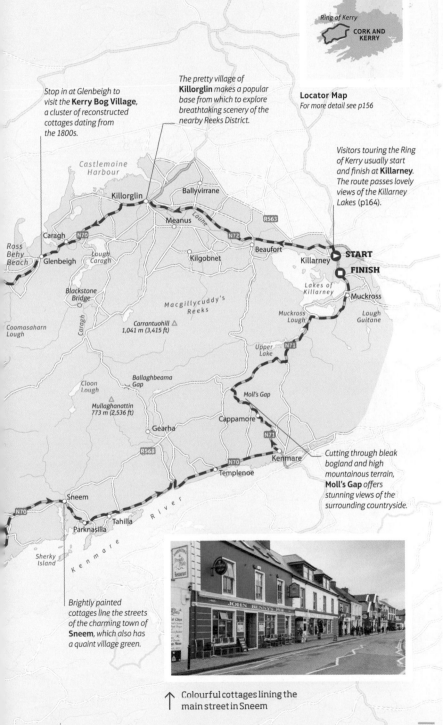

Stop in at Glenbeigh to visit the **Kerry Bog Village**, a cluster of reconstructed cottages dating from the 1800s.

The pretty village of **Killorglin** makes a popular base from which to explore breathtaking scenery of the nearby Reeks District.

Locator Map
For more detail see p156

Ring of Kerry

CORK AND KERRY

Visitors touring the Ring of Kerry usually start and finish at **Killarney**. The route passes lovely views of the Killarney Lakes (p164).

Castlemaine Harbour

Killorglin

Ballyvirrane

Meanus

R563

Caragh

N70

Lough Caragh

Ross Behy Beach

Glenbeigh

Kilgobnet

N72

Beaufort

Killarney

START
FINISH

Lakes of Killarney

Muckross

Blackstone Bridge

Macgillycuddy's Reeks

Muckross Lough

Lough Guitane

Coomasaharn Lough

Caragh

Carrantuohill △
1,041 m (3,415 ft)

Upper Lake

N71

Cloon Lough

Ballaghbeama Gap

Mullaghanattin △
773 m (2,536 ft)

Moll's Gap

Gearha

Cappamore

R568

N71

N70

Kenmare

Templenoe

Cutting through bleak bogland and high mountainous terrain, **Moll's Gap** offers stunning views of the surrounding countryside.

N70

Sneem

Tahilla

Kenmare River

Parknasilla

Sherky Island

Brightly painted cottages line the streets of the charming town of **Sneem**, which also has a quaint village green.

↑ Colourful cottages lining the main street in Sneem

THE LOWER SHANNON

The River Shannon has long made this area an attractive prospect for settlers. There are several important Stone Age sites, and from the 5th century the region lay at the heart of Munster, one of Ireland's four Celtic provinces. Tipperary's Rock of Cashel served as the seat of the Kings of Munster for more than 700 years.

The Vikings penetrated the Shannon in the 10th century, but Gaelic clans put up a stern resistance. During the Norman period, the chieftains of these clans built Bunratty Castle and other fortresses impressive enough to rival Anglo-Irish strongholds. During the Middle Ages, Limerick was often at the centre of events in the Lower Shannon, such as when the 1691 Treaty of Limerick triggered the Catholic nobility's departure for Europe – the so-called "Flight of the Wild Geese".

Lush grassland, which has turned the Lower Shannon into prime dairy country, is typical of the region. In places this gives way to picturesque glens and mountains, such as the Galty range in southern Tipperary, but the region's most dramatic scenery is found along the coast of Clare.

THE LOWER SHANNON

Must Sees

1 🗝 💻 🛍

THE BURREN

🅰B4 🏠Co Clare 🚹The Burren Centre, Kilfenora;
Mar-May & Sep-Oct: 10am-5pm daily; Jun-Aug:
9:30am-5:30pm daily; www.theburrencentre.ie

The word "burren" derives from *boireann*, which means "rocky land" in Gaelic – an apt name for this vast limestone plateau in northwest County Clare.

In the 1640s, Cromwell's surveyor described it as "a savage land, yielding neither water enough to drown a man, nor tree to hang him, nor soil enough to bury". While few trees manage to grow, other plants thrive; the Burren is a unique botanical environment in which Mediterranean and Alpine plants rare to Ireland grow side by side.

From May to August, an astonishing array of flowers adds splashes of colour to the austere landscape, taking root in the crevices of the limestone pavements that are the most striking geological feature of the rocky plateau. In the southern part of the Burren, limestone gives way to the black shale and sandstone that form the dramatic Cliffs of Moher *(p190)*.

The spectacular limestone landscape of the Burren, in northwest County Clare ↑

① A quirk in the local climate means that the hills are warmer in winter than the valleys - so Burren cattle graze on high ground during the cold season.

② Glaciation and wind and rain erosion have formed limestone pavements with deep crevices known as "grykes".

③ Ruined forts and prehistoric sites dot the landscape. In the heart of the limestone plateau is the famed Poulnabrone Dolmen, a portal tomb dating back to 2500–2000 BC.

FAUNA OF THE BURREN

The Burren is one of the best places in Ireland for butterflies, with 28 species found in the area. The birdlife is also varied. Skylarks and cuckoos are common on the hills and in the meadows, while the coast is a good place for razorbills, guillemots, puffins and other sea birds. Mammals are harder to spot; badgers, foxes and stoats all live here, but you are much more likely to see a herd of shaggy-coated wild goats or an Irish hare. The Burren Centre in Kilfenora offers an excellent exhibition on the fauna and geology of the area, as well as man's impact on the landscape.

② ⊘ ▭ ⛾

CLIFFS OF MOHER

🅐 B4 🅐 Lislorkan North, Co Clare 🕐 Jan-Feb & Nov-Dec: 9am-5pm daily; Mar-Apr & Sep-Oct: 8am-7pm daily; May-Aug: 8am-9pm daily 🔒 24-26 Dec 🌐 cliffsofmoher.ie

Ireland's most-visited natural attraction, the Cliffs of Moher are nothing short of majestic. These completely vertical sea cliffs jut out into the blustery Atlantic, creating a dramatic stretch along the country's west coast.

Even when shrouded in mist or buffeted by Atlantic gales, the Cliffs of Moher are breathtaking, rising to a height of 214 m (690 ft) and extending for over 8 km (5 miles). The sheer rock face, with its layers of black shale and sandstone, provides sheltered ledges where guillemots, puffins and other

←

Sightseers entering the eco-friendly visitors' centre, built into the surrounding landscape

Did You Know?

Film buffs will recognize the cliffs as the Horcrux cave from *Harry Potter and the Half-Blood Prince*.

O'BRIEN'S TOWER

Built in 1835, O'Brien's Tower was the brainchild of Cornelius O'Brien, a local landlord with a vision. The tower was constructed as a viewing platform for the cliffs, which even in the 19th century were attracting scores of visitors. It was a huge success, and encouraged the innovative O'Brien to begin further projects – leading locals to joke that he built everything in the area except the cliffs.

sea birds nest. There is a subterranean visitors' centre onsite, carved into the landscape in order to minimize its visual impact on this area of natural beauty. Interactive exhibits here include an audiovisual theatre. Outside, well-worn paths lead along the cliffs. You can walk south to Hag's Head – named because the rock formation is said to resemble a woman looking out to sea – in an hour, or head north for a 3-hour coastal walk between O'Brien's Tower and the charming village of Doolin.

→

A hiker at Hag's Head, the most southerly point of the cliffs

←

The Cliffs of Moher at the edge of County Clare, stretching into the Atlantic Ocean

3 🎿 🍴 🖥 🛍

BUNRATTY CASTLE AND FOLK PARK

📍 B4 🏰 Bunratty, Co Clare 🕐 9am–5pm daily (last admission 4pm)
📅 24–26 Dec 🚌 From Ennis, Limerick, Shannon 🌐 bunrattycastle.ie

This formidable castle was built in the 15th century by the MacNamaras. Its most important residents were the O'Briens, Earls of Thomond, who lived here from the early 16th century until the 1640s.

Abandoned in the 19th century, the castle was derelict when Lord Gort bought it in the 1950s, but it has been beautifully restored to its original state. The present interior looks much as it did under the so-called "Great Earl", who died in 1624. Outside of normal opening hours, visitors can book tickets for a four-course medieval banquet, held nightly at 5:30pm and 8:30pm. The adjacent Folk Park reflects 19th-century Irish rural and village life.

1 The exterior of Bunratty Castle, which is Ireland's most complete medieval fortress.

2 Bunratty Castle is unusual for the high arches on both sides of the keep. The first-floor entrance – designed to deter invaders – is more typical of castles of the period.

3 The South Solar, or upper chamber, housed guest apartments and features an elaborately carved ceiling.

Entrance

The Murder Hole, designed for pouring boiling water or pitch on to the heads of attackers

BUNRATTY FOLK PARK

A meticulous recreation of rural life in Ireland at the end of the 19th century, this Folk Park began with the reconstruction of a farmhouse that was saved during the building of nearby Shannon Airport. It now consists of a complete village, incorporating shops and a whole range of domestic architecture, from a labourer's cottage to an elegant Georgian house. Other buildings include a farmhouse typical of the Moher region in the Burren *(p186)* and a working corn mill. During the main summer season, visitors can meet with various costumed characters from the period. The park also has a gift shop and a café.

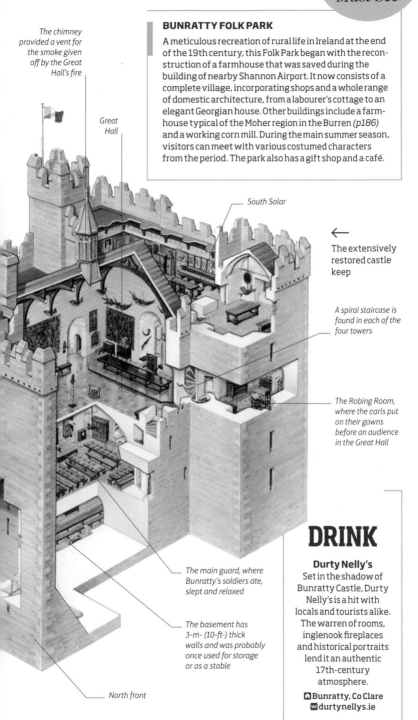

The chimney provided a vent for the smoke given off by the Great Hall's fire

Great Hall

South Solar

←
The extensively restored castle keep

A spiral staircase is found in each of the four towers

The Robing Room, where the earls put on their gowns before an audience in the Great Hall

The main guard, where Bunratty's soldiers ate, slept and relaxed

The basement has 3-m- (10-ft-) thick walls and was probably once used for storage or as a stable

North front

DRINK

Durty Nelly's
Set in the shadow of Bunratty Castle, Durty Nelly's is a hit with locals and tourists alike. The warren of rooms, inglenook fireplaces and historical portraits lend it an authentic 17th-century atmosphere.

🅐 Bunratty, Co Clare
🆆 durtynellys.ie

ROCK OF CASHEL

🅐 C5 🏠 Cashel, Co Tipperary 🚂 To Thurles 🚌 To Cashel
🕐 Daily, check website for times 🚫 24–26 Dec 🌐 cashel.ie

This rocky stronghold, which rises dramatically out of the Tipperary plain, was a symbol of royal and priestly power for more than a millennium. Today it remains one of Ireland's most spectacular historic sites, with a striking meld of architecture from various periods.

From the 4th or 5th century, Cashel was the seat of the Kings of Munster, whose kingdom extended over much of southern Ireland. In 1101, they handed the castle over to the Church, and it flourished as a religious centre until a siege by a Cromwellian army in 1647 culminated in the massacre of its 3,000 occupants. The cathedral, which is subject to ongoing renovation, was finally abandoned in the late 18th century. A good proportion of the medieval complex is still standing, and Cormac's Chapel is one of the most outstanding examples of Romanesque architecture in the country.

←

The buildings on the Rock, including the 28-m (92-ft) round tower

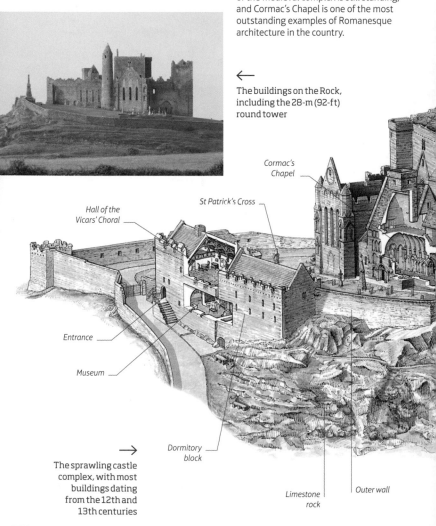

Cormac's Chapel

St Patrick's Cross

Hall of the Vicars' Choral

Entrance

Museum

Dormitory block

Limestone rock

Outer wall

→

The sprawling castle complex, with most buildings dating from the 12th and 13th centuries

↑ Superb Romanesque carvings adorn Cormac's Chapel, the jewel of Cashel

CASHEL

Although the magnificent medieval Rock of Cashel is the area's greatest attraction, there's still plenty to see in the town of Cashel itself. At the foot of the castle is a 13th-century Dominican Friary, an austere sandstone church with a fine west door, a 15th-century tower and lancet windows, while the scant remains of Hore Abbey – a 13th-century Cistercian foundation – lie on farmland just outside the town. Traditional Irish culture can be sampled at the Brú Ború Cultural Centre. Named after Brian Ború, the 11th-century High King of Ireland, the centre offers folk theatre, traditional music, banquets and a craft shop.

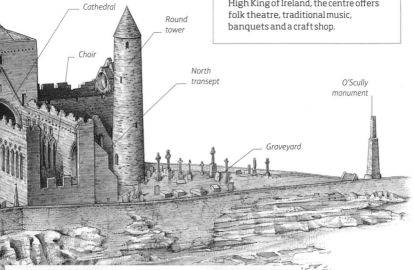

Cathedral

Round tower

Choir

North transept

O'Scully monument

Graveyard

← The roofless Gothic cathedral, whose thick walls are riddled with hidden passages

EXPERIENCE MORE

⑤ Foynes

B5 Co Limerick
From Limerick

Foynes enjoyed fame in the 1930s and 1940s as the eastern terminus of the first airline passenger route across the Atlantic. **Foynes Flying Boat and Maritime Museum**, one of a kind in the world, presents a detailed history of the seaplane service. The original Radio and Weather Rooms have transmitters, receivers and Morse code equipment as well as a full-sized replica of a B314 flying boat and a simulator. Afterwards, you can enjoy refreshments in the 1940s-style tearoom.

Askeaton, a historic town 11 km (7 miles) south east of Foynes, has a castle and a particularly interesting Franciscan friary. Set beside the River Deel, the impressive **Askeaton Friary** features a 15th-century cloister of black marble.

Foynes Flying Boat and Maritime Museum

⊘😊🅰 Aras Ide, Foynes
Mid-Mar-mid-Nov: 9:30am–5pm (Jun–Sep to 6pm) daily
flyingboatmuseum.com

Askeaton Friary

1–5 The Quay 086 086 0174 Daily

↑ A neglected boat in dry dock at Kilrush boatyard, a reminder of the town's rich maritime tradition

⑥ Kilrush

B4 Co Clare
clare.ie

With the addition of a marina and the promotion of Kilrush as a heritage town, the fortunes of this 18th-century estate town have been greatly revived.

Follow the well-marked walking trail starting from Market Square, which highlights the town's historic sights. From Kilrush Marina, boats take visitors dolphin-spotting – the chances of seeing one of the 100 bottle-nosed dolphins identified in the estuary are high. Boats also run to uninhabited Scattery Island, site of a medieval monastery. The ruins include five churches and one of the tallest round towers in the country.

The Loop Head Drive is a 27-km (17-mile) route which begins at the resort of Kilkee, west of Kilrush. It winds south past dramatic coastal scenery to Loop Head, from where you can enjoy superb views.

⑦ River Shannon

B4 To Limerick or Athlone To Carrick-on-Shannon, Athlone or Limerick 20 O'Connell St, Limerick; www.limerick.ie

The Shannon is the longest river in Ireland, rising in County Cavan and meandering down to the Atlantic. Flowing through the heart of the island, it has traditionally marked the border between the provinces of Leinster and Connaught. In medieval times, castles guarded the major fords from Limerick to Portumna, and numerous monasteries were built along the riverbanks, including the celebrated Clonmacnoise (p261). Work began on the Shannon navigation system in the 1750s, but it fell into disuse with the advent of the railways.

There are subtle changes of landscape along the length of the river. South of Lough Allen, the countryside is covered with low hills typical of the northern Midlands. Towards Lough Ree, islands stud the river in an area of ecological importance which is home to otters, geese, grey herons and whooper swans. Continuing south beyond Athlone (p258), the river flows through flood plains and bog before reaching Lough Derg, the biggest of the lakes on

> INSIDER TIP
> ### Irish Coffee Lounge
>
> Foynes and its flying boats are connected to another famous Irish export: Irish coffee. The museum's Irish Coffee Lounge relates the story - and offers samples - of this much-loved tipple.

the Shannon. The scenery is more dramatic here, with the lough's southern end edged by wooded mountains. Walkers can enjoy the Lough Derg Way, a signposted route around the lake. The woods by Lough Key (p223) also provide good walking territory.

From Killaloe (p200), the river gains speed on its rush towards Limerick (p201) and the sea. The mudflats of the Shannon estuary attract a great variety of birdlife. The port of Carrick-on-Shannon (p241) is the cruising centre of Ireland, but there are bases all along the river. Water-buses connect most ports south of Athlone.

Glin

B5 ⚑Co Limerick
🚌From Limerick

This village on the banks of the Shannon is the seat of the Knights of Glin, a branch of the Fitzgeralds who have lived in the district for seven centuries. Their first medieval castle is a ruin, but west of the village stands their newer home, Glin Castle. Built in 1780, the castle acquired both battlements and lodges in the 1820s. To this day it remains the ancestral home of the Fitzgerald family, and is also available for private rental accommodation and events.

9

Ennis

🅱B4 ⚑Co Clare 🚌
🛈Arthur's Row; www.visitennis.com

Clare's county town, on the banks of the River Fergus, is a charming place with winding lanes that recall its medieval beginnings. The town is also renowned for its painted shopfronts and folk music festivals (known as *fleadh* in Gaelic). It abounds in "singing" pubs and traditional music shops.

Ennis can trace its origins to the 13th century and to the O'Briens, Kings of Thomond, who were the area's feudal overlords in the Middle Ages. The Franciscan friary that they founded here in the 1240s is

now the town's main attraction. Dating from the 14th and 15th centuries, the ruined **Ennis Friary** is famous for its rich carvings and decorated tombs in the chancel – above all the 15th-century MacMahon tomb with its finely carved alabaster panels. Extensive conservation work is ongoing here.

Next door to the friary is a delightful 17th-century house, now Cruise's restaurant, and on the corner of nearby Francis Street is the Queen's Hotel – featured in James Joyce's *Ulysses*. To the south, O'Connell Square has a monument to Daniel O'Connell, who was elected MP for Clare in 1828. He also gave his name to the town's main street, where you can spot a medieval tower, a Jacobean chimney stack and an 18th-century arch.

The area around Ennis is rich in monastic ruins. Clare Abbey, 3 km (2 miles) south of the town, is an Augustinian foundation set up by the O'Briens in 1189 but dating mainly from the 1400s. Quin Franciscan Friary, southeast of Ennis, was also built in the 15th century, and incorporates the ruins of a Norman castle. The well-preserved cloister is one of the finest of its kind in Ireland.

Ennis Friary
♿ ⚑Abbey St 🕐Apr-Sep: 10am-6pm daily (to 5pm Oct) 🌐heritageireland.ie

Glin Castle, set on the banks of the River Shannon

↑ Knappogue Castle, a 15th-century medieval tower house

 ⑩ ⟨⟩

Knappogue Castle

🅰B4 🏛Quin, Co Clare
🕐Except for accommodation and banquets, check website for details
🌐knappoguecastle.ie

A powerful local clan called the MacNamaras erected Knappogue Castle in 1467. Apart from a ten-year spell in Cromwellian times, it stayed in their hands until 1815. During the War of Independence, the castle was used by the revolutionary forces.

Knappogue is one of the most charmingly furnished castles in Ireland. The central tower house is original, but the rest of the castle is Neo-Gothic. Although Knappogue is closed to the public, you can spend a night here or attend medieval banquets held between April and October; travel back in time and join a night of storytelling and singing.

---

⑪ ⟨⟩ 🖥 🛍

Craggaunowen

🅰B4 🏛Kilmurry, Co Clare 🕐Easter–early-Sep: 10am–5pm daily
🌐craggaunowen.ie

The Craggaunowen Project, known as "Craggaunowen: the Living Past" and designed to bring Bronze Age and Celtic culture to life, is a shining example of a recreated prehistoric site. The centre was established in the grounds of Craggaunowen Castle in the 1960s by John Hunt, a noted archaeologist who had been inspired by his excavations at Lough Gur *(p200)*. The "Living Past" experience is about the arrival of the Celts in Ireland and the farming and hunting methods they used.

In summer, people in costume act out particular trades, such as spinning or potting, or serve as guides. In addition there is a description of how communities lived in the ring fort, a typical early Christian homestead. You can also see a *fulacht fiadh*, a traditional hunter's cooking hole where meat was prepared.

The complex includes part of a *togher*, an original Iron Age timber road that was discovered in Longford. The most eye-catching sight, however, is the crannog, a man-made island dwelling enclosing wattle-and-daub houses – a style of defensive homestead that survived to the early 1600s.

Another exhibit is a leather-hulled boat built in the 1970s by Tim Severin. He used it to retrace the route which, legend says, St Brendan took in a similar vessel across the Atlantic in the 6th century to discover America centuries before Columbus.

↑ Replica of a wattle-and-daub house, Craggaunowen

12

Dysert O'Dea

🅰B4 🏠Corrofin, Co Clare
🚌From Ennis 🕐May-
Sep: 10am–4pm daily
🌐dysertcastle.com

Dysert O'Dea Castle stands on a rocky outcrop 9 km (6 miles) north of Ennis. This tower house, erected in the 15th century, is home to the Archaeology Centre, which includes a small museum and also marks the start of a trail around nearby historic sights. A map of the path, designed for both walkers and cyclists, is available in the castle.

Across a field from the castle is a monastic site that is said to have been founded by the obscure St Tola in the 8th century. The ruins are overgrown and rather worn, but the Romanesque carving above one doorway is still clear. There is also an impressive 12th-century High Cross, with a bishop sculpted on the east side.

Further south, the trail leads past the remains of two stone forts, a ruined castle and the site where a 14th-century battle took place.

13

Mountshannon

🅰C4 🏠Co Clare
ℹEast Clare Heritage; www.mountshannon.ie

This village on the banks of Lough Derg seems to have its back turned to the lake but is nevertheless a major angling centre. Solid 18th-century stone houses and churches, along with some pubs, cluster in an elevated position around the harbour.

Mountshannon is well placed for exploring the lake's western shores, with plenty of scope for walks and bicycle rides. Fishing boats are available for hire, and in summer you can go by boat to Holy Island, the site of a 7th-century monastery. The ruins include four chapels and a graveyard of medieval tombs.

EAT

Town Hall Bistro

Part of the Old Ground Hotel, this bistro offers delicious afternoon teas and creative dishes for lunch and dinner, all made with locally sourced ingredients.

🅰B4 🏠St Ennis
🌐oldgroundhotel ennis.com

€€€

The Wild Geese

A picture-perfect cottage with several small and tastefully decorated dining rooms. Run by a husband-and-wife duo, the food is flavoursome and the service impeccable.

🅰B5 🏠Rose Cottage, Adare 🌐thewild-geese.com

€€€

↑ Mountshannon, stretching back from the banks of Lough Derg

Lough Gur

B5 **Co Limerick**
**Heritage centre:
Mar–Oct: 10am–6pm
daily; Nov–Feb: 10am–
4pm daily; www.
loughgur.com**

This Stone Age settlement, 21 km (13 miles) south of Limerick, was extensively inhabited in 3000 BC. Today the horseshoe-shaped lough and surrounding hills enclose an archaeological park. All around Lough Gur are standing stones and burial mounds, including mega-lithic tombs. One of the most impressive sights is the Grange Stone Circle, dating back to 2200 BC, just outside the park, by the Limerick–Kilmallock road. Excavations in the 1970s unearthed rec-tangular, oval and rounded Stone Age huts with stone foundations. The interpretive centre, housed in mock Stone Age huts on the site of the original settlement, offers a range of audiovisual dis-plays, models of stone circles, burial chambers and tools and weapons.

As well as the various prehistoric sites scattered all over the Knockadoon Peninsula, there are two castle ruins from more recent times beside the lough – the 15th-century Bourchier's Castle (also known as Castle Doon) and Black Castle, a 13th-century seat of the Earls of Desmond.

Lough Gur, County Limerick, the site of a Stone Age settlement ↑

HIDDEN GEM
A Fairy Trail

Lough Gur is supposedly home to Fer Fí, King of the Fairies. His throne sits beside the site's heritage centre, and a trail made of 110 stone steps will lead children to a fairy village (and stunning lough views).

Killaloe

C4 **Co Clare**
www.clare.ie

Killaloe, birthplace of Brian Ború (940–1014), High King of Ireland, lies close to where the Shannon emerges from Lough Derg, and is the lake's most prosperous pleasure port. A 17th-century bridge separates Killaloe from its twin town of Ballina on the opposite bank. Ballina has better pubs, such as Goosers on the waterfront, which is also the departure point for **Killaloe River Cruises**, but Killaloe offers more of historical interest.

Killaloe's grandest building is St Flannan's Cathedral, built around 1182, and one of Ireland's oldest surviv-ing churches built in the Romanesque style. Its richly carved doorway was once part of an earlier chapel. The church also has an ancient Ogham Stone, unusual because the inscription is carved in both Nordic runes and Ogham (the earliest Irish script). Outside of the church stands St Flannan's Oratory, built around the same time as the cathedral.

Killaloe River Cruises
Lakeside Drive Ballina, Killaloe **Mar–Oct: daily 1-hr cruises on River Shannon and Lough Derg** **killaloerivercruises.com**

→

Limerick viewed from the Shannon, with King John's Castle in the distance

EXPERIENCE The Lower Shannon

Limerick

🅰B4 🏠Co Limerick
✈Shannon 🚉 🚌
ℹ20 O'Connell St; www. limerick.ie

Limerick was founded by the Vikings. Given its strategic point on the River Shannon, it thrived under the Normans, but later bore the brunt of English oppression. After the Battle of the Boyne *(p251)*, the rump of the defeated Jacobite army withdrew here. The siege that followed has entered Irish folklore as a heroic defeat, sealed by the Treaty of Limerick in 1691. English treachery in reneging on most of the terms of the treaty still rankles.

The city centre consists of three historic districts. King's Island was the first area to be settled by the Vikings and was later the heart of the medieval city, when it was known as Englishtown. It boasts Limerick's two main landmarks, **King John's Castle** and **St Mary's Cathedral**.

Founded by King John in 1200, not long after the Normans arrived, King John's Castle has five drum towers and solid curtain walls. Inside, the castle is less interesting architecturally, but it houses a good audiovisual exhibition on the history of the city. Ongoing excavations have unearthed pots and jewellery, and you can also see Viking houses and later fortifications.

Built in 1172, St Mary's Cathedral is the oldest structure in the city. Except for a fine Romanesque doorway and the nave, however, little remains of the early church. The 15th-century misericords in the choir stalls are the pride of St Mary's, with superb carvings in black oak of angels, griffins and other creatures both real and imaginary.

Nearby, George's Quay is a pleasant street with restaurants, outdoor cafés and good views across the river.

The old Irishtown, south of the Abbey River, has its fair share of drab houses and shops, but there is a sprinkling of historic buildings and a pocket of Georgian elegance in St John's Square. Near here is Limerick's most conspicuous sight, St John's Cathedral, built in 1861. Its 85-m (280-ft) spire is the tallest in the country.

Just across the bridge in the Old Customs House, the **Hunt Museum** has one of the greatest collections of antiquities in Ireland, gathered by the archaeologist John Hunt. The best exhibits, dating from the Bronze Age, include gold jewellery and a magnificent shield. Also of interest, the **Limerick Museum** has displays on the city's history and traditions, from lace- and silver-making to rugby.

The most pleasant part of Limerick in which to stroll is Newtown Pery – a grid of gracious Georgian terraces focused on O'Connell Street.

King John's Castle
♿☺ 🏠Nicholas St
🕐9:30am–5pm (Apr–Sep to 6pm) daily 🚫23–26 Dec
🌐kingjohnscastle.com

St Mary's Cathedral
♿ 🏠Bridge St 🕐9am–5pm Mon–Thu, 9am–4pm Fri & Sat, 1:30–4pm Sun
🚫26–27 Dec & 1 Jan
🌐saintmaryscathedral.ie

Hunt Museum
♿♿☺☺ 🏠Rutland St
🕐10am–5pm Mon–Sat, 11am–5pm Sun & public hols; two for one on Sun
🚫1 Jan, Good Fri, 25 & 26 Dec
🌐huntmuseum.com

Limerick Museum
🏠Old Franciscan Friary, Henry St 📞061 557740
🕐10am–5pm Mon–Fri
🚫Public hols & 7 days at Christmas

Did You Know?

Roscrea is home to Sean Ross Abbey, the convent featured in bestselling novel and film *Philomena*.

⑰ Roscrea

🅰C4 🅰Co Tipperary
🚆 🚌 *i* Heritage centre, Castle St; www.heritage ireland.ie

Located on the banks of the River Bunnow, this monastic town has an interesting historic centre. The 13th-century Anglo-Norman **Roscrea Castle** consists of a gate tower, curtain walls and two corner towers. In the courtyard stands Damer House, a Queen Anne-style residence with a magnificent staircase and Georgian garden. Just over the river lies St Cronan's Monastery, with a High Cross, a truncated round tower, and a Romanesque church gable. There are remains of a 15th-century Franciscan friary on Abbey Street and the renovated Blackmills now houses the St Cronan's High Cross and the Roscrea Pillar.

Roscrea Castle and Gardens

🎫🎟 🅰Castle Street
🕐Apr–Sep: 10am–6pm daily
🌐heritageireland.ie

⑱ Glen of Aherlow

🅰C5 🅰Co Tipperary
🚌To Bansha or Tipperary
i Coach Rd, on R663 8 km (5 miles) E of Galbally; www.aherlow.com

The lush valley of the River Aherlow runs between the Galty Mountains and the wooded ridge of Slievenamuck. Bounded by the villages of Galbally and Bansha, the glen was historically an important pass between Limerick and Tipperary and a notorious hideout for outlaws.

Today there are excellent opportunities for riding, cycling, rambling and fishing. Lowland walks follow the trout-filled river along the valley floor. There are many marked trails but more adventurous walkers will be tempted by the Galty range, which offers more rugged hill walking, past wooded foothills, mountain streams, tiny corrie lakes and splendid sandstone peaks.

The Glen of Aherlow leads to Kilfinane at the heart of the Galty and Ballyhoura Mountains. Its main feature, the Kilfinane Moat, is an ancient, flat-topped mound encircled by three ramparts.

⑲ Adare

🅰B5 🅰Co Limerick 🚌
i Heritage centre, Main St; 9am–6pm daily; www.adareheritagecentre.ie

Adare is billed as Ireland's prettiest village. Cynics call it the prettiest "English" village since its manicured perfection is at odds with normal notions of national beauty. Originally a fief of the Fitzgeralds, the Earls of Kildare, Adare owes its present appearance more to the Earls of Dunraven, who restored the village in the 1820s and 1830s. The village is a picture of neat stonework and thatched roofs punctuated by pretty ruins, all in a woodland setting.

The tourist office is housed in the heritage centre, which includes a good exhibition on Adare's monastic history and a model of medieval Adare. Next door is the Trinitarian priory, founded in 1230 by the Fitzgeralds and restored by the first Earl of Dunraven; it is now a Catholic church and convent. Opposite, by a stone bridge, is the Washing Pool, previously a wash-house site.

The 14-arch bridge on the Limerick road dates from medieval times and leads to the Augustinian priory, which was founded by the Fitzgeralds in 1316. Also known as Black Abbey, this priory has a central tower, subtle carvings, delightful

One of Adare village's many pretty thatched cottages

cloisters and a graceful sedilia – a carved triple seat. Just over the bridge, from where it is best viewed, is Desmond Castle, a 13th-century feudal castle on the banks of the River Maigue – tickets are available from the heritage centre (Jun–end Sep).

Nearby stands the main gate to Adare Manor, now a luxury hotel and golf course.

Roscrea Castle complex, fronted by a formal walled garden

Within its 900 ha (2,220 acres) of parkland lie St Nicholas Church and Chantry Chapel, two evocative 12th-century ruins. The graceful 15th-century Franciscan friary, however, is surrounded by the golf course, though it can be seen clearly from the pathway.

In the heart of the village is the elegant Dunraven Arms Hotel, whose award-winning Maigue Restaurant serves delicious Irish cuisine. Some of the nearby cottages, originally built by the Earl of Dunraven in 1828 for his estate workers, have been converted into pleasant cafés and restaurants.

20 🖇 Ⓜ 🛍

Holy Cross Abbey

🅰C4 🄰Thurles, Co Tipperary 🄰 🚌To Thurles 🄰Hours vary, check website 🅦holycrossabbey.ie

In a landscape dotted with ruined abbeys, Holy Cross is a pleasant surprise, and remains in action today. Founded in 1169 by the Benedictines, Holy Cross was supposedly endowed with a splinter from the True Cross, hence its name. It was Ireland's top pilgrimage site, untill the effects of the Dissolution took their toll in the 16th century and it was abandoned. Now it has been restored, and the church is once again a popular place of worship and pilgrimage. Most of the present structure dates from the 15th century. It was built by the Cistercians, who took over the abbey in 1180. This gracious cruciform church, embellished with mullioned windows and sculpted pillars, is one of Ireland's finest examples of late Gothic architecture.

Nearby, Farney Castle is the only round tower in the country that is occupied as a family home. Built in 1495, it also houses the design studio and retail outlet of Irish international designer Cyril Cullen.

→ High Cross at Holy Cross Abbey

21

Cahir

🅰 C5 🏠 Co Tipperary 🚌 🚆
ℹ️ Castle St; Apr–Sep; www.
discoverireland.ie

Once a garrison and mill town, Cahir is today a busy market town. The pub-lined Castle Street is the most appealing area, which leads to the Suir River. On the edge of town lies the ruined Cahir Abbey, a 13th-century Augustinian priory. Its fine windows are decorated with carved heads.

Built on a rocky island in the River Suir, **Cahir Castle** is a formidable sight. This well-preserved fortress dates from the 13th century but is mainly linked to its later owners, the Butlers. A powerful family in Ireland since the Anglo-Norman invasion, they were considered trusty lieges of the English Crown and were granted the Cahir barony in 1375. Under their command, the castle was renovated and extended throughout the 15th and 16th centuries. It remained in the Butler family until 1964.

The castle is divided into outer, middle and inner wards, with a barbican at the outer entrance. The inner ward is on the site of the original Norman castle; the foundations are 13th-century, as are the curtain walls and keep. The restored interior includes the striking great hall, which dates largely from the 1840s, though two of the walls are original and the windows are 15th-century.

Cahir Castle

♿ ⏰ 🏠 Castle St ⏰ Hours vary, check website 🚫 24–31 Dec 🌐 heritageireland.ie

---

22

Clonmel

🅰 C5 🏠 Co Tipperary 🚆
🚌 ℹ️ The Main Guard;
www.clonmel.ie

Set on the River Suir, Clonmel is Tipperary's main town. This Anglo-Norman stronghold

---

EAT

Hickey's Bakery and Café

A local institution, Hickey's has been baking bread and cakes for over four generations. Centrally located, it's the perfect place to stop for lunch.

🅰 C5 🏠 West Gate, Clomel 🌐 hickeysbakery.com

€ € €

→

The ruins of Athassel Priory, on the banks of the River Suir

The mighty Cahir Castle, a popular location for film sets

was a fief of the Desmonds and eventually of the Butlers. Its prosperity was founded on milling and brewing. Today, Clonmel is a bustling town with quirky architecture and lively nightlife.

The Franciscan friary by the quays was remodelled in Early English style in Victorian times but retains a 15th-century tower and houses 16th-century Butler tomb effigies. Nearby is O'Connell Street, Clonmel's main shopping street, which is straddled by the West Gate, built in 1831. Visitors to Hearn's Hotel on Parnell Street can see memorabilia of Charles Bianconi (1786–1875), including pictures of the horse-drawn coach service he established between Clonmel and Cahir, which developed into a nationwide passenger service.

23
Athassel Priory

 C5 8 km (5 miles) SW of Cashel, Co Tipperary To Tipperary Daily cashel.ie

This ruined Augustinian priory is situated on the west bank of the River Suir. The tomb of William de Burgh, the Norman founder of the priory, lies in the church. Established in

1192, Athassel is believed to have been the largest medieval priory in Ireland until it burned down in 1447. The scattered monastic site conveys a tranquil atmosphere, from the gatehouse and church to the remains of the cloisters and chapter house. The church has a fine west doorway, nave and chancel walls, as well as a 15th-century central tower.

24
Carrick-on-Suir

 C5 Co Tipperary Heritage centre, Main St; 051 640200

This small market town has a distinctly old-fashioned air. In the 15th century, it was a strategic site commanding access west to Clonmel and southeast to Waterford, but after Tudor times the town sank into oblivion. Apart from **Ormond Castle**, there are few specific sights. However, you can stroll by the old waterside warehouses or shop in the Blarney Woollen Mills.

Although once a fortress, Ormond Castle is the finest surviving Tudor manor house in Ireland. It was built by the powerful Butler family, the Earls of Ormonde, who were given their title by the English Crown in 1328. The castle has a gracious Elizabethan façade overlaying the medieval original; the battlemented towers on the south side

HIDDEN GEM
Fethard Horse Country Experience

Just north of Clonmel is this state-of-the-art exhibition, which explores the relationship between the region's people, land and horses (*www.fhcexperience.ie*).

sit oddly with the gabled façade and its mullioned and oriel windows.

The state rooms contain some of the finest decorative plasterwork in Ireland, and the Long Gallery extends to 30 m (100 ft). The Elizabethan part of the castle was added by Black Tom Butler, the 10th Earl of Ormonde. Following his death, the Ormondes decided to abandon Carrick for Kilkenny (*p136*).

At Kilkieran, 5 km (3 miles) north of Carrick, are three interesting High Crosses, dating from the 9th century. The Plain Cross is unadorned but capped; the West Cross is profusely ornamented though weathered; the Long Shaft Cross has an odd design of stumpy arms on a long shaft.

Ormond Castle

   Castle Park Apr–Oct: for guided tours daily; check website for details heritage ireland.ie

THE WEST OF IRELAND

The rugged Atlantic coastline of the West has been occupied for over 5,000 years. It is rich in prehistoric sites such as the Aran Islands' ring forts, while evidence of the monastic period can be seen in the mysterious remains at Kilmacduagh and Clonfert.

Landlords made their mark in the region throughout the 17th and 18th centuries, building impressive country houses at Clonalis, Strokestown Park and Westport. During the Great Famine, the West – especially Mayo – suffered very badly from emigration. Despite this, strong Gaelic traditions have survived in Galway, which is home to the country's largest Gaeltacht (p234), where almost half the population speaks Irish as a first language.

THE WEST OF IRELAND

THE WEST OF IRELAND

Must Sees

0 kilometres   15

0 miles   15

N

↑ Galway's lively city centre, bustling with locals and street performers

GALWAY

🚩B4 🏠Co Galway 🚉Ceannt Station (091 537581)
🚌Ceannt Station (091 562000) ℹ️The Fairgreen,
Foster St; galwaytourism.ie

On the banks of the River Corrib, Galway is both the centre for surrounding Irish-speaking regions and a lively university city. It was once a prosperous trading post but declined after the Battle of the Boyne *(p251)*, unable to compete with east-coast trade. The city's profile has since been revived as a hub for high-tech industry.

① Eyre Square

This redeveloped square encloses a pleasant plaza and park lined with imposing 19th-century buildings. On the northwest of the square is the Browne Doorway, a 17th-century entrance from a mansion in Abbeygate Street Lower. Beside it is a fountain adorned with a sculpture of a Galway hooker boat. The Eyre Square Centre, overlooking the park, is a modern shopping mall built to incorporate sections of the historic city walls. Walkways link Shoemakers and Penrice towers, two of the 14 wall towers that used to ring the city in the 17th century.

② The Latin Quarter

The bustling "Latin Quarter" is home to Lynch's Castle, now a bank but still the grandest 16th-century townhouse in Galway. It was owned by one of the 14 merchant families, or

"tribes", who controlled the city during the 14th–16th centuries.

A side street leads to the Collegiate Church of St Nicholas, Galway's finest medieval building. The church, founded in 1320, was damaged by the Cromwellians, who used it to stable horses. The west porch is from the 15th century and features some finely carved gargoyles.

③ The Old Quays

The Spanish Arch was built in 1584 to protect the harbour, then outside the city walls. Here, Spanish traders unloaded their ships. Behind the arch is the Galway City Museum, which relates the city's history.

④ The Claddagh

Beyond the Spanish Arch lies the Claddagh, a fiercely independent fishing community, dating from the 5th century and governed by their own "king". The last true King of Claddagh died in 1972, but the title is still used ceremonially. The enduring symbols of this Gaelic-speaking community are Claddagh rings, betrothal rings traditionally handed down from mother to daughter. The design features two clasped hands and a crowned heart.

GALWAY HOOKERS

Galway's traditional wooden sailing boats, featured on the city's coat of arms, were known as *pucans* and *gleotogs* – "hookers" in English. They have broad black hulls, thick masts and white or rust-coloured sails. Once common in the Claddagh district, they were also used along the Atlantic coast to ferry peat, cattle and beer. Hookers can be seen in action at the Cruinniú na mBád festival in Kinvara *(p221)*.

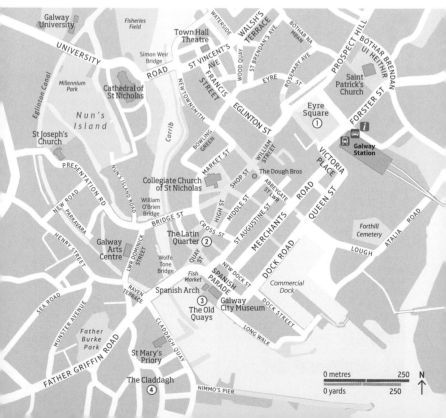

Did You Know?

Aran Islanders who have dressed up for Halloween don't speak all day, to keep their identities secret!

2

ARAN ISLANDS

A4 Co Galway Connemara Airport From Rossaveal: Island Ferries (www.aranislandferries.com); from Doolin: Doolin Ferry Company (www.doolinferries.com); cars cannot be taken to the islands Kilronan, Inishmore; 099 61263 aranislands.ie

Famed for their bleak beauty and woolly jumpers, the Aran Islands are a cluster of three islands located at the mouth of Galway Bay. They are composed of the same limestone that forms the Burren in Co Clare, and their tiny population largely speaks Irish.

The three Aran Islands are known as Inishmore (Inis Mór), Inishmaan (Inis Meáin) and Inisheer (Inis Oírr), and they are formed from a limestone ridge. The largest, Inishmore, is 13 km (8 miles) long and 3 km (2 miles) wide.

Offering stunning coastal views, their austere landscapes are crisscrossed with dry-stone walls and several large prehistoric stone forts. St Enda brought Christianity to the islands in the 5th century, starting a long monastic tradition. Protected for centuries by their isolated position, the islands today are a bastion of traditional Irish culture. Farming, fishing and tourism are the main trades of the islanders.

←

Fishing boats in Kilronan harbour, the main port on Inishmore

↑ The craggy cliffs of
Inishmore, biggest
of the Aran Islands

↑ Dún Aonghasa, Inishmore's Iron
or Bronze Age promontory fort,
with four concentric stone walls

ARAN TRADITIONS

The islands are famous for their
knitwear and for the traditional Aran
costume that was still worn by some
of the older generation not long ago:
for women, a red flannel skirt and
crocheted shawl; for men, a sleeveless
tweed jacket and a colourful knitted
belt. From time to time you may still
see a *currach*, or low rowing boat,
the principal form of transport for
centuries. Land-making, the ancient
and arduous process of creating soil
by covering bare rock with sand and
seaweed, continues to this day.

↑ The ruins of Na Seacht Teampaill,
or the Seven Churches, a monastic
settlement on Inishmore

EXPERIENCE MORE

3

Achill Island

A3 **Co Mayo** **From Westport** **www.achilltourism.com**

Achill is Ireland's largest island, an irregular chunk of mountainous land some 22 km (14 miles) long and 19 km (12 miles) wide. It is reached by a road bridge that can be raised for boats to pass. Achill offers moorland, mountains, rugged cliffs and long beaches, and is a popular spot for angling and watersports. There is evidence that the island was inhabited as many as 5,000 years ago.

For motorists, the best introduction is the Atlantic Coast Drive, a circular, signposted route from Achill Sound, by the Michael Davitt Bridge. The road goes to the island's southern tip, then north around the rest. Between Doeega and Keel in the southwest run the dramatic Minaun Cliffs and Cathedral Rocks. In the north a mountain overlooks Slievemore, a village that was abandoned during the Great Famine (p222).

4

National Museum of Ireland - Country Life

B3 **Turlough Park, Turlough, off the N5, 8 km (5 miles) E of Castlebar, Co Mayo** **10am–5pm Tue–Sat, 1–5pm Mon & Sun** **Good Fri, 25 Dec** **museum.ie**

Explore rural life in Ireland in this award-winning museum set in the grounds of Turlough Park. The collection focuses on the period from 1850 to 1950, when tenant farmers were struggling to become owners of the land they worked. The exhibits illustrate the traditional way of country life while providing historical context of this difficult time. Fascinating artifacts, displayed over four floors, include handcrafted harvest knots and wickerwork; spinning wheels and boats; and hand-operated machinery.

5

Westport

B3 **Co Mayo** **Bridge St; www.westporttourism.com**

Westport is a neat town and has a prosperous air. In the 1770s, architect James Wyatt laid out the wide, tree-lined streets, including the North and South Mall on either side of Carrowbeg River. The town originally traded in yarn, cloth, beer and slate, but industrialization and the Great Famine brought a decline until the 1950s when new industry and visitors were attracted to the area. Beyond the South Mall is shop-lined Bridge Street.

Just west of the town is Clew Bay. At the head of the bay stands **Westport House**, the seat of the Earls of Altamont, descendants of the Browne family, who were Tudor settlers. Designed in

→

The National Museum of Ireland - Country Life, in Turlough Park, inside and out

1732 by Richard Cassels, and completed by James Wyatt in 1778, the limestone mansion is privately owned by the Browne family, who are direct descendants of pirate Grace O'Malley. There is also a miniature railway, birds of prey centre and adventure activity centre.

Westport House

 🏛 Westport
🕐 Mar–Sep: daily; Feb & Nov–Dec: weekends
🌐 westporthouse.ie

---

⑥
Foxford

🅰 B3 🏛 Co Mayo 🚌 From Galway ℹ Westport; 094 9256104

This tranquil market town is mostly known for the **Foxford Woollen Mills**, founded in 1892 by an Irish nun, Mother Arsenius (originally named Agnes). The thriving mill now supplies top fashion houses. A guided tour traces the mill's history, and visitors can see craftspeople at work.

Foxford Woollen Mills

 🏛 Providence Rd
🕐 Daily 🚫 Public hols
🌐 foxfordwoollenmills.com

 →
Bogwood centrepiece in Céide Fields' visitor centre

⑦
Céide Fields

🅰 B2 🏛 8 km (5 miles) W of Ballycastle, Co Mayo
🕐 Apr–Oct: 10am–5pm daily (to 6pm Jun–Sep)
🌐 ceidefields.com

Surrounded by heather-clad moorlands and mountains along a bleak, dramatic stretch of north Mayo coastline is Europe's largest Stone Age monument. Over 10 sq km (4 sq miles) were enclosed by walls to make fields suitable for growing wheat and barley, and grazing cattle. Remains of farm buildings indicate that it was an extensive community. The fields were slowly buried below the creeping bog formation, where they have been preserved for over 5,000 years.

Part of the bog has been cut away to reveal the collapsed stone walls of the ancient fields. The remains are simple but guides help visitors to find and recognize key features. The pyramid-shaped visitor centre has a viewing platform overlooking the site, audiovisual presentations, and displays on local geology and botany.

---

⑧
Knock

🅰 B3 🏛 Co Mayo ✈ 15 km (9 miles) N of Knock 🚌
ℹ Knock; May–Sep; www.discoverireland.ie

In 1879, two local women saw an apparition of the Virgin, St Joseph and St John the Evangelist by the gable of the Church of St John the Baptist. It was witnessed by 13 more onlookers and validated by the Catholic Church amid claims of miracle cures. Every year, over 1.5 million believers make the pilgrimage to the shrine,

including Pope John Paul II in 1979. Its focal point is the gable where the apparition was seen, which is now covered over to form a chapel. **Knock Shrine and Museum**, beside the basilica, has an Apparition section explaining the background to the miracle.

Knock Shrine and Museum

 🕐 Daily 🚫 25 & 26 Dec 🌐 knockshrine.ie

---

⑨
Croagh Patrick

🅰 B3 🏛 Murrisk, Co Mayo
🚌 From Westport
ℹ Westport; www.croagh-patrick.com

Ireland's holy mountain, named after the national saint *(p296)*, is one of Mayo's best-known landmarks. From the bottom it seems cone-shaped, an impression dispelled by climbing to its flat peak. This quartzite, scree-clad mountain has a history of pagan worship from 3000 BC. In AD 441, St Patrick is said to have spent 40 days on the mountain fasting and praying for the Irish.

Since then, penitents, often barefoot, have made the pilgrimage to the summit in his honour, especially on Garland Friday and Reek Sunday in July.

↑ Clare Island lighthouse standing guard at the entrance to Clew Bay

Clare Island

🄰 A3 🄰 Co Mayo 🚢 From Roonagh Quay, 6.5 km (4 miles) W of Louisburgh; www.clareislandferry. com 🛈 Westport; www. clareisland.ie

Clare Island is dominated by two hills, and a square 15th-century castle commands the headland and harbour. In the 16th century the island was the stronghold of Grace O'Malley, pirate queen and patriot, who held sway over the western coast. Although, according to Tudor state papers, she was received at Queen Elizabeth I's court, she stood out against English rule until her death in her seventies in 1603. She is buried here in a tiny Cistercian abbey decorated with medieval murals and inscribed with her motto: "Invincible on land and on sea."

The island is dotted with Iron Age huts and field systems as well as promontory forts and Bronze Age cooking sites. Clare Island is rich in bog flora and fauna, making it popular with walkers. Animal lovers come to see the seals, dolphins, falcons and otters.

The mainland coastal town of Louisburgh offers rugged landscape, sheltered coves and sea angling. The **Granuaile Visitor Centre** tells the story of Grace O'Malley (*Granuaile* in Gaelic) and has displays on Mayo folklore and archaeology.

Granuaile Visitor Centre
⊗ 🄰 St Catherine's Church, Louisburgh 📞 098 66341
🄲 10am–5pm Mon–Fri

Clifden

🄰 A3 🄰 Co Galway 🚌
🛈 Galway Road; Mar–Oct; www.visitclifden.com

Framed by the grandeur of the Twelve Bens mountain range and with a striking skyline dominated by two church spires, this early 19th-century market town passes for the capital of the Connemara region and is a good base for exploring. Clifden was founded in 1812 by John d'Arcy, a local landowner and High Sheriff of Galway, to create a pocket of respectability within the lawlessness of Connemara. The family eventually went bankrupt trying to bring prosperity and order to the town. The Protestant church contains a copy of the Cross of Cong.

Today craft shops have taken over much of the town. In the centre is the square, a place for lively pubs where traditional music is common.

Jutting out into Clifden Bay is a sand spit and beach, signposted from Clifden Square. South of Clifden, at the start of the Roundstone Road, is Owenglen Cascade where, in May, salmon leap on their way to spawn upstream.

The Sky Road is an 11-km (7-mile) circular route with stunning ocean views, which goes northwest from Clifden. It passes desolate scenery and the narrow inlet of Clifden Bay.

The coastal road north from Clifden to the pretty fishing village of Cleggan is spectacular. The village nestles into the head of Cleggan Bay from where boats go to Inishbofin and Inishturk. Cleggan Hill has a ruined Napoleonic Martello tower and a megalithic tomb.

To the south of Clifden, the coastal route to Roundstone skirts a mass of bogland pitted with tiny lakes. The Alcock and Brown Memorial, a tall splinter of dark stone silhouetted on the hillside, overlooks the bog landing site of the first transatlantic flight, made by

↑ Walker taking in the expansive views near the Alcock and Brown landing site in Clifden

John Alcock and Arthur Brown in 1919. Nearby is Marconi's wireless station, which exchanged the first transatlantic radio messages with Nova Scotia in 1907. The Ballyconneely area has craggy islands and the beautiful Coral Strand Beach. The village of Roundstone has a diminutive harbour and a scatter of pubs.

A short drive to the east of Clifden is **Dan O'Hara's Homestead**, an organic farm recreating the tough conditions of life in Connemara before the 1840s. The heritage centre presents an audiovisual display on the history of Connemara.

Dan O'Hara's Homestead

 🅐Connemara Heritage & History Centre, Lettershea, off N59 🕐Apr-Oct: 10am-6pm daily 🌐connemaraheritage.com

---

⑫

Inishbofin

🅐A3 📍Co Galway 🚢From Cleggan; 095 45819 (ferry) ℹClifden; www.inishbofin.com

This mysterious island – whose name means "island of the white cow" – was chosen for its remoteness by the exiled 7th-century St Colman, English Abbot of Lindisfarne. On the site of his original monastery is a late medieval church, graveyard and holy well. At the sheltered harbour entrance lies a ruined castle, occupied in the 16th century by Spanish pirate Don Bosco in alliance with Grace O'Malley. In 1653 it was captured by Cromwellian forces and used as a prison for Catholic priests. Inishbofin was later owned by a succession of absentee landlords and now survives on farming and lobster fishing.

Surrounded by reefs and islets, the island is dotted with stone walls, reed-fringed lakes and hay meadows. Inishbofin's beaches offer bracing walks.

↑ The golden curve of Tra Ghael beach, on Inishbofin Island

EAT

The Owenmore Restaurant

Located in one of Ireland's finest castles, the Owenmore pairs a sophisticated local menu with stunning views. Book ahead.

🅐A3 🏠Ballynahinch Castle Hotel, Connemara 🌐ballynahinch-castle.com

€€€

⑬ Lough Corrib

🅐B3 🚌Co Galway 🚌From Galway and Cong 🚌From Oughterard, Cong and Wood Quay, Galway

An angler's paradise, Lough Corrib offers the chance to fish for brown trout, salmon, pike, perch and eels. The lake is tranquil and, dotted with uninhabited islands and framed by meadows, reedbeds and wooded shores. The waterside is home to swans and coots. On Inchagoill, one of the largest islands, are the ruins of an early Christian monastic settlement and a Romanesque church.

The lake is best appreciated on a cruise. From Galway, the standard short cruise winds through the marshes to the site of an Iron Age fort, limestone quarries and the battlemented Menlo Castle. Longer cruises continue to Cong or include picnics on the islands.

On the banks of Lough Corrib, Oughterard is known as "the gateway to Connemara". The village has craft shops and thatched cottages. It is also popular for golf, angling, hiking and pony trekking. Southeast of Oughterard (off the N59) is **Aughnanure Castle**. This well-restored six-storey tower

house clings to a rocky island on the River Drimneen. The present castle, built by the O'Flaherty clan, is on the site of one dating from 1256. The clan controlled West Connaught from Lough Corrib to Galway and the coast in the 13th to 16th centuries. From this castle the feuding O'Flaherty chieftains held out against the British in the 16th century. In 1545 Donal O'Flaherty married the pirate Grace O'Malley (p216). The tower house has an unusual double bawn (a fortified enclosure) and a murder hole from which missiles could be dropped on invaders.

Aughnanure Castle

♿♿ 🏠Oughterard ⏰Hours vary, check website 🌐heritageireland.ie

⑭ Kylemore Abbey

🅐A3 🏠Connemara, Co Galway 🚌From Galway ⏰Hours vary, check website 🔒24-26 Dec 🌐kylemore abbey.com

Sheltered by the slopes of the Twelve Bens mountain range, this lakeside castle is a romantic Gothic Revival fantasy. It was built for his wife by Mitchell Henry (1826–1911), a Manchester tycoon and later Galway MP. The Henrys also purchased a huge area of moorland, drained the boggy hillside and planted thousands of trees as a windbreak for their new orchards and walled gardens. After the sudden deaths of his wife and youngest daughter, Henry left Kylemore

The imposing Kylemore Abbey on the shores of Kylemore Lough ↑

↑ Gold-tinged route through the main valley of Connemara National Park

and the castle was sold. It later became an abbey when Benedictine nuns, fleeing from Ypres in Belgium during World War I, sought refuge here. For many years the nuns ran it as a girl's school. Today, visitors can explore the abbey's restored rooms and its Victorian walled garden, and stroll in the surrounding woodland and along the lakeshore.

Connemara National Park

⚑ A3 ⬤ Letterfrack, Connemara, Co Galway ⬤ Park: daily; visitor centre: Mar-Oct: 9am–5:30pm daily ⬤ connemara nationalpark.ie

A combination of bogland, lakes and mountains makes up this National Park, established in 1980. Within its more

Did You Know?

Connemara ponies are the world's largest, dwarfing several horse breeds.

HIDDEN GEM
Ashford Castle

Just south of Cong is Ashford Castle, rebuilt in Gothic Revival style in 1870 by Lord Ardilaun of the Guinness family. Now one of Ireland's best hotels, its grounds can be visited by boat from Galway and Oughterard.

than 20 sq km (8 sq miles) are four of the Twelve Bens, including Benbaun, the highest mountain in the range, and the peak of Diamond Hill. Visitors come for the spectacular landscape and the famous Connemara ponies. There are traces of the land's previous uses all over the park: megalithic tombs, up to 4,000 years old, can be seen, plus old ridges marking former grazing areas and arable fields.

The visitor centre near the entrance has displays on local flora and fauna and on how the landscape developed. From the visitor centre there are four walking trails around Diamond Hill, and guided walks are arranged throughout the year Climbing the Twelve Bens should be attempted only by experienced walkers equipped for all weather conditions.

Cong

⚑ B3 ⬤ Co Mayo ⬛ ⓘ Old Courthouse; Mar-Oct: daily; www.discoverireland.ie

This picturesque village lies on the shores of Lough Corrib, just within County Mayo. Cong means isthmus – the village lies on the strip of land between Lough Corrib and Lough Mask. During the 1840s a canal was built linking the two lakes, but the water drained through the porous limestone bed. Stone bridges and stone-clad locks are still in place along the dry canal.

Cong Abbey lies close to the main street. It was founded in the early 12th century by Turlough O'Connor, King of Connaught and High King of Ireland. The Cross of Cong, an ornate processional cross intended for the abbey, is in the National Museum of Ireland in Dublin (p68). The most fascinating remains of the abbey are the Gothic chapter house, stone bridges and the monks' fishinghouse that overhangs the river – the monks had a system where a bell rang in the kitchen when a fish took the bait. A short walk from the abbey is the Quiet Man Museum, devoted to the 1952 movie that was filmed in Cong.

17

Kilmacduagh

🅰B4 🚩Outside Gort on Corofin Rd, Co Galway 🚌To Gort 🕐Daily

This monastic settlement is in a remote spot on the borders of counties Clare and Galway. The sense of isolation is accentuated by the stony moonscape of the Burren to the west (p188). Reputedly founded by St Colman MacDuagh in the early 7th century, Kilmacduagh owes more to the monastic revival which led to rebuilding from the 11th century onwards.

The centrepiece of the extensive site is a large leaning 11th- or 12th-century round tower and a roofless church, known as the cathedral or Teampall. The cathedral is a pre-Norman structure, which was later remodelled in Gothic style, with flamboyant tracery and fine tomb carvings.

Round tower and cathedral ruins standing in an isolated spot at Kilmacduagh ↑

18

Thoor Ballylee

🅰B4 🚩Gort, Co Galway 🚌To Gort 🕐Hours vary, check website 🌐yeats thoorballylee.org

For much of the 1920s, this beguiling tower house was a summer home to the poet W B Yeats. Yeats was a regular visitor to nearby Coole Park, the home of his friend Lady Gregory (1852–1932), who was a cofounder of the Abbey Theatre (p102).

On one visit to Coole Park, Yeats came upon Ballylee Castle, a 14th-century de Burgo tower adjoining a cosy cottage with a walled garden and stream. In 1902, both the tower and the cottage became part of the Gregory estate and Yeats bought them in 1916. From 1919 onwards, his family divided their time between Dublin and their Galway tower. Yeats took the name Thoor Ballylee as the address, using the Irish word for tower to "keep people from suspecting us of modern gothic and a deer park". His collection, *The Tower* (1928), includes several poems inspired by the house.

An audiovisual tour includes readings from Yeats's poetry, but the charm of a visit lies in the tower itself, with its spiral stone steps and views from the battlements over forest and farmland.

To the north of nearby Gort town is **Coole Park**, once the home of Lady Gregory. Although the house was demolished in 1941, the estate farm has been restored and the fine gardens survive. Within Coole Park's gardens is the "autograph tree", a spreading copper beech carved with the initials of George Bernard Shaw, W B Yeats, J M Synge and Jack Yeats. In the farm buildings is an audiovisual display, and the emphasis of the visitor centre is on the life of Lady Gregory. It is the start of two signposted walks, one around the gardens and the other through beech, hazel, birch and ash woodland to Coole Lake.

Coole Park

☺ 🚩3 km (2 miles) NE of Gort 🕐Visitor centre: Easter–Sep: daily; park: open all year 🌐coolepark.ie

19

Portumna

🅰C4 🚩Co Galway 🚌 ℹGalway; 091 537700

Portumna is a historic market town with scattered sights, many of which have been restored. Situated on Lough Derg, it is a convenient base for cruising the River Shannon (p196) and has a modern marina. The imposing bulk of **Portumna Castle**, built in the early 17th century in medieval and Renaissance style, was the main seat of the de Burgo

> Within Coole Park's gardens is the "autograph tree", a spreading copper beech carved with the initials of George Bernard Shaw, W B Yeats, J M Synge and Jack Yeats.

→

Dunguaire Castle set on a grass promontory, north of Kinvara

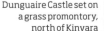

EAT

Moran's Oyster Cottage

This thatched cottage has been in the Moran family for seven generations. Oysters are of course the focus, but there are also plenty of delicious seafood dishes on offer.

🅰 B4 🏠 The Weir, Kilcolgan
🌐 moransoyster cottage.com

€€€

---

❷⓪

Kinvara

🅰 B4 🏠 Co Galway 🚌
ℹ Galway; 091 537700

The appeal of Kinvara, one of the most charming fishing villages on Galway Bay, lies in its sheltered harbour and traditional seafaring atmosphere. The pier is bordered by a row of fishermen's cottages. Kinvara is well known for the Cruinniú na mBád (gathering of the boats) festival held in August. Rambles around the village include historical and nature trails. Bird-watchers may spot teal, curlews and oystercatchers by the shore.

North of Kinvara, on a promontory on the shore of Galway Bay, lies **Dunguaire Castle**. It is named after the 7th-century King Guaire of Connaught, whose court here was renowned as the haunt of bards and balladeers. Medieval earthworks survive, but the present castle was built in the 16th century, a quintessential tower house with sophisticated machicolations. The banqueting hall is still used for "medieval banquets" with Celtic harp music and the recital of Irish poetry.

Dunguaire Castle

⊗ ⊙ 🕐 Apr–Sep: daily
🌐 dunguairecastle.com

---

❷①

Clonfert Cathedral

🅰 C4 🏠 Clonfert, Co Galway
🕐 Daily

Situated near a bleak stretch of the Shannon bordering the boglands of the Midlands, Clonfert is one of the jewels of Irish-Romanesque architecture. The tiny cathedral occupies the site of a monastery, which was founded by St Brendan in AD 563, and is believed to be the burial place of the saint.

Although a great scholar and enthusiastic founder of monasteries, St Brendan is best known as the "great navigator". His journeys are recounted in *Navigatio Sancti Brendani*, written in about 1050, which survives in medieval manuscripts in several languages.

The highlight of Clonfert is its intricately sculpted sandstone doorway. The round arch above the door is decorated with carvings of animal and human heads, foliage and symbolic motifs. The carvings on the triangular tympanum above the arch are of strange human heads. In the chancel, the 13th-century east windows are fine examples of late Irish-Romanesque art. The 15th-century chancel arch is adorned with sculptures of a mermaid and angels. Although Clonfert was built over several centuries, the church has a profound sense of unity.

---

family. It is adorned with some elaborate interior stonework and has beautiful formal gardens. Nearby is Portumna Priory. Most of the remains date from 1414 when it was founded by the Dominicans, but traces can also be found of the Cistercian abbey that was previously located on the site. The de Burgo estate to the west of the town now forms Portumna Forest Park, with picnic sites and signposted woodland trails leading to Lough Derg.

Portumna Castle

⊗ ⊗ 🕐 Apr–Oct
🌐 heritageireland.ie

Turoe Stone

B4 **Turoe, Bullaun, Loughrea, Co Galway** **Hours vary, check website** **turoepetfarm.com**

The Turoe Stone stands at the centre of the Turoe Pet Farm and Leisure Park. The white granite boulder dates back to the 3rd or 2nd century BC. Its top half is carved in a graceful Celtic style known as La Tène. The lower half has a smooth section and a band of step-pattern carving. The stone was originally found at an Iron Age ring fort nearby, and is thought to have been used there in fertility rituals. Efforts at preservation sometimes hamper viewing, so check the website before you visit.

Roscommon

C3 **Co Roscommon** **Market Sq; www.visitroscommon.com**

The county capital is a busy market town. In Main Street is the former gaol, which had a woman as its last executioner. "Lady Betty", as she was known, was sentenced to death for the murder of her

THE GREAT FAMINE

The failure of the Irish potato crop in 1845, 1846 and 1848, due to potato blight, had disastrous consequences for the people of Ireland. More than a million died of starvation and disease, and by 1856 over two and a half million had been forced to emigrate. The crisis was worsened by landlords who often continued collecting rents. The Famine had far-reaching effects: mass emigration became a way of life (p176) and rural communities, particularly in the far west, were decimated.

son in 1780, but negotiated a pardon by agreeing to become a hangwoman.

Roscommon Castle, north of the town, was built in 1269 by Robert d'Ufford, Lord Justice of Ireland, on land seized from the Dominican friary, and rebuilt 11 years later after being destroyed by the Irish, led by Hugh O'Conor, King of Connaught.

Strokestown Park

C3 **Strokestown, Co Roscommon** **Mid-Mar-Oct: 10:30am–5:30pm daily (to 4:30pm Nov–mid-Mar)** **A week at Christmas** **strokestownpark.ie**

This truly impressive Palladian mansion was built in the 1730s for Thomas Mahon, an MP whose family was granted the lands by Charles II after the

Restoration. It incorporates an earlier 17th-century tower house. The design of the new house owes much to Richard Cassels, architect of Russborough (p144). The galleried kitchen, panelled stairwell and groin-vaulted stables are undoubtedly his work, tailoring Palladian principles to the requirements of the Anglo-Irish gentry.

The house stayed in the family's hands until 1979, when major restoration began. In its heyday, the estate included ornamental parkland, a mausoleum, deer park, folly and the village of Strokestown itself. By 1979, the estate's original 12,000 ha (30,000 acres) had dwindled to 120 ha (300 acres), but the re-creation of the Pleasure Gardens and the Fruit and Vegetable Garden have greatly increased the area.

Set in the stable yards, the Famine Museum uses the

Strokestown archives to tell the story of tenants and landlords during the 1840s Famine. A section of the exhibition deals with continuing famine and malnutrition worldwide.

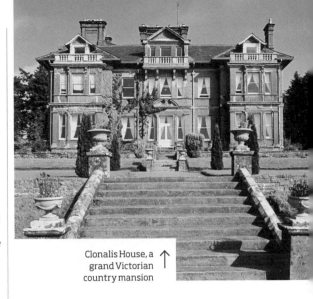

Clonalis House, a grand Victorian country mansion ↑

Clonalis House

🅰B3 🏠**Castlerea, Co Roscommon** ⏰**Jun–Aug: 11am–5pm Mon–Sat** 🌐**clonalis.com**

Dating from 1878, this splendid Victorian manor just outside Castlerea is the ancestral home of the O'Conors, the last High Kings of Ireland and Kings of Connaught. This old Gaelic family can trace its heritage back 1,500 years. The ruins of their gabled 17th-century home are still visible in the grounds. On the lawn lies the O'Conor coronation stone, which dates from 90 BC.

The interiors, which are open both for day visits and overnight stays, include a library of many books and documents recording Irish history, a tiny private chapel and a gallery of family portraits spanning 500 years. In the billiard room is the harp once played by Turlough O'Carolan (1670–1738), a blind harpist and last of the Gaelic bards.

26 Boyle

🅰C3 🏠**Co Roscommon** 🚌 ℹ️**King House; Jun–Sep; www.unabhan.ie**

Boyle, County Roscommon's most charming town, is blessed with fine Georgian and medieval architecture. **Boyle Abbey** is a well-preserved Cistercian monastery founded in 1161 as a sister house to Mellifont in

East wall and gatehouse at Roscommon Castle, an Anglo-Norman fortress

County Louth (*p256*). The monastery survived raids by Anglo-Norman barons and Irish chieftains, as well as the 1539 suppression of the monasteries. In 1659 it was turned into a castle. The abbey is still remarkably intact, with a church, cloisters, cellars, sacristy and kitchens. The nave of the church has both Romanesque and Gothic arches and there are well-preserved 12th-century capitals.

King House, a Georgian mansion, is the ancestral home of the Anglo-Irish King family, later Earls of Kingston. Inside is a contemporary art gallery, and displays on Georgian architecture, the history of the surrounding area and the Connaught chieftains. The house also holds musical, dramatic and cultural events.

A short drive from Boyle, Lough Key is an island-studded lake surrounded by woodland – a glorious setting for the **Lough Key Forest Park**. The 320-ha (790-acre) park formed part of the Rockingham estate until 1957, when Rockingham House, a John Nash design, burned down. The woods were added by 18th-century landlords. The Lough Key Experience takes visitors on an audio journey through the

19th-century underground tunnels, up to the Moylurg viewing tower and along Ireland's first Tree Canopy Trail.

Boyle Abbey

⏰**Easter–Sep: 10am–6pm daily** 🌐**heritageireland.ie**

King House

🏠**Main St** ⏰**Apr–Sep: 11am–5pm Tue–Sun & public hols** 🌐**visitkinghouse.ie**

Lough Key Forest Park

🏠**N4 8 km (5 miles) E of Boyle** ⏰**Hours vary, check website** 🌐**loughkey.ie**

STAY

Clonalis House
Live like the High Kings of Ireland for a night at this historic house, overlooking stunning parkland. The period rooms are lavishly decorated, particularly the book-lined library.

🅰B3 🏠**Castlerea** 🌐**clonalis.com**

€€€

The Anvil cliff edge, jutting off the coast of Tory Island

NORTHWEST IRELAND

In Celtic mythology, Sligo, in the south of the region, was the power base of warrior-queen Maeve of Connaught, and the county's numerous prehistoric sites demonstrate that the area was heavily populated during Celtic times. Later, both Sligo and Leitrim (further inland) seem to have been little affected by events taking place in the rest of Ireland – the Normans, for example, barely disturbed the rule of local Gaelic clans.

Comprising the majority of the region, Donegal, by contrast, is part of Ulster and has played an active role in the history of the north. The O'Donnell family held sway over most of the county during the Middle Ages, but they fled to Europe in 1607 following their ill-fated stand against the English alongside the O'Neills *(p263)*. Protestant settlers moved onto land confiscated from the two clans, but left much of Donegal and its poor soil to the native Irish, who lived there in isolation from the rest of Ulster. Donegal remains one of the most remote parts of Ireland, and it is no coincidence that it is home to the country's largest number of Gaelic speakers.

NORTHWEST IRELAND

Must See

1 Slieve League

Experience More

2 Tory Island
3 Bloody Foreland
4 Derryveagh Mountains
5 Horn Head
6 Grianán Ailigh
7 The Rosses
8 Rosguill Peninsula
9 Fanad Peninsula
10 Letterkenny
11 Ardara
12 Glencolmcille
13 Donegal
14 Killybegs
15 Lough Derg
16 Rossnowlagh
17 Ballyshannon
18 Lissadell House
19 Sligo
20 The Organic Centre
21 Lough Arrow
22 Carrick-on-Shannon
23 Parke's Castle

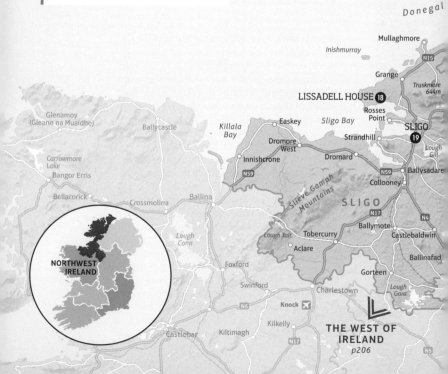

Owey Island (Uaigh)

Arranmore
(Árainn Mhór)

Burtonport (Ailt an Chorráin)

Crohy Head

Gweebarra Bay

Dawros Head   Naran

Loughros Point

ARDARA
11

GLENCOLMCILLE

12

Malin More
(Málainn Mhóir)   Carrick
(An Charraig)

1

SLIEVE LEAGUE

14

KILLYBEGS

St John's Point

Donegal

Mullaghmore

Inishmurray

N15

Grange

Truskmore
644m

LISSADELL HOUSE 18

Rosses
Point

SLIGO
19

Glenamoy
(Gleann na Muaidhe)

Ballycastle

Killala
Bay

Easkey   Sligo Bay

Lough
Gill

Carrowmore
Lake

Bangor Erris

Dromore
West

Innishcrone

Strandhill

Dromard

N59

Ballysadare

Bellacorick   Crossmolina   Ballina

N59

Slieve Gamph
Mountains

Collooney

SLIGO

N17   N4

NORTHWEST
IRELAND

Lough
Conn

Lough Talt   Tobercurry

Aclare

Ballymote

Castlebaldwin

Ballinafad

Foxford

Gorteen   Lough
Gara

Swinford   Charlestown

N5

Knock ✈

Kilkelly

THE WEST OF
IRELAND
p206

Castlebar   Kiltimagh

N17   N5

Did You Know?

Huge rocks near Bunglass Point once spelled "ÉIRE" – a message for pilots during World War II.

SLIEVE LEAGUE

B2 **Co Donegal** **sliabhliag.com**

One of Ireland's best-kept secrets, this craggy coastline is a sight to rival the Cliffs of Moher *(p190)*. Soaring nearly three times their height, and without Moher's crowds or admission charge, the sea cliffs of Slieve League (*Sliabh Liag* in Irish) are a key attraction along the Wild Atlantic Way.

Slieve League is spectacular not only for its sheer elevation – these massive precipices are among the highest in Europe – but also for its colour: at sunset the rock is streaked with changing shades of red, amber and ochre. Start your day at the Slieve League Cultural Centre in Teelin, which focuses on the natural and cultural history of the area, and offers archaeological tours of nearby Neolithic and monastic sites. From Teelin you can follow the

↑ Hikers taking in sublime views across the cliffs

> **INSIDER TIP**
> ### Sea Views
>
> During the summer months, those hoping for spectacular views without the strenuous climb can pay a Teelin boat-owner to take them to see the cliffs from the sea.

↑ Sheer cliff faces rising above the crashing sea below

meandering Pilgrim's Path up the cliffs, or it's a 10-minute drive to Bunglass Point, where the best views can be found. The main viewing platform is located here, and allows visitors to take in the whole of Slieve League, its cliff faces rising abruptly from the ocean. There's a magnificent view behind, too – on clear days you'll be able to look right across Donegal Bay to the counties of Leitrim, Sligo and Mayo.

↑ Slieve League's immense sea cliffs stretching out into the Atlantic

ONE MAN'S PASS

Only experienced hikers should attempt the treacherous ledges of One Man's Pass. This is part of a trail that climbs sharply westwards out of Teelin and up to the highest point of Slieve League - from where you can admire the Atlantic Ocean shimmering nearly 600 m (1,970 ft) below. The path then continues 16 km (10 miles) west to Malinbeg, a secluded crescent-shaped bay surrounded by cliffs.

EXPERIENCE MORE

Tory Island

🅰 C1 🏠 Co Donegal ⛴ From Mahgeroarty Pier near Gortahork (2–3 ferries daily; weather permitting: 087 199 3710); toryferry.com

The turbulent Tory Sound separates this island from the northwestern corner of mainland Donegal. Given that rough weather can cut off the tiny island for days, it is not surprising that Tory's inhabitants have developed a strong sense of independence. Most of the islanders speak Gaelic and they even have their own monarch: the powers of this non-hereditary position are minimal, but can encompass promoting the interests of their "subjects" and attracting visitors to the island.

During the 1970s, the Irish government tried to resettle most of the islanders on the mainland, but they refused to move. Their campaign of resistance was led by Tory's school of Primitive artists. This emerged after 1968, inspired by a local man called James Dixon who claimed he could do better than a visiting English painter, Derek Hill. Since then the school has drawn a growing number of tourists; the **Dixon Gallery** opened in 1992 in the main village of West Town. There are ruins of a monastery founded by St Columba nearby, or else you can explore the island's dramatic cliffs and sea bird rookeries.

Dixon Gallery

🏠 West Town 📞 086 262 0154 🕐 Easter–Sep: daily

Bloody Foreland

🅰 C1 🏠 Co Donegal 🚌 To Letterkenny

Bloody Foreland, which gets its name from the rubescent glow of the rocks at sunset, boasts magnificent scenery. The R257 road skirts the coast around the headland, providing lovely views. The most scenic viewpoint is on the north coast and looks across to the cliffs of nearby offshore

Did You Know?

Glenveagh National Park was given to the nation by Henry McIlhenny, whose family invented Tabasco sauce.

islands, including Tory. A short distance further south, the tiny village of Bunbeg has a pretty harbour, but elsewhere the landscape is somewhat spoiled by holiday bungalows.

Derryveagh Mountains

🅰 C1 🏠 Co Donegal

The wild beauty of these mountains provides one of the high spots of a visit to Donegal. Errigal Mountain, the range's tallest peak at 751 m (2,464 ft), attracts keen hikers, but the cream of the scenery lies within **Glenveagh National Park**. Covering nearly 16,000 ha (40,000 acres), this takes in the beautiful valley occupied by

↑ Glenveagh Castle, a splendid fortress within the Derryveagh Mountains

Lough Veagh, and Poisoned Glen, a marshy valley enclosed by dramatic cliffs. The park also protects the largest herd of red deer in the country.

Standing on the southern shores of Lough Veagh, **Glenveagh Castle** is a splendid granite building constructed in 1870 by John Adair, notorious for his eviction of many local families during the Famine (*p222*). The castle was given to the nation in the 1970s by its last owner, a wealthy art dealer from Pennsylvania. Shuttle buses whisk you up the private road to the castle from the visitor centre. You can go on a guided tour of the sumptuous interior or just stroll through the formal gardens and rhododendron woods. Trails weave all around the castle grounds; one path climbs steeply to reward you with a lovely view over Lough Veagh.

Overlooking Lough Gartan, 6 km (4 miles) south of the visitor centre, **Glebe House and Gallery** was once the home of landscape painter and collector Derek Hill. This modest Regency mansion, which can be explored by a guided tour only, reveals his varied tastes, with William Morris wallpapers, Islamic ceramics and paintings by Tory Island artists. The gallery contains works by artists such as Picasso, Guttuso and Hokusai among others.

The **Colmcille Heritage Centre**, less than 3 km (2 miles) south, traces the life of St Columba (Colmcille in Gaelic), who was born in nearby Church Hill in AD 521. A flagstone in Lacknacoo is said to mark the site of the saint's birthplace.

Glenveagh National Park and Castle

♿♿🅿️☕🖼️ ◻ Off R251, 16 km (10 miles) N of Churchill ◻ Daily 🌐 glenveagh nationalpark.ie

Glebe House and Gallery

♿♿☕ ◻ May–Jun & Sep–Oct: Sat–Thu; Jul & Aug: daily 🌐 glebegallery.ie

Colmcille Heritage Centre

♿ ◻ Easter & May–Sep: daily 🌐 colmcilleheritagecentre.ie

---

⑤

Horn Head

🅰️ C1 ◻ Co Donegal 🚌 To Dunfanaghy from Letterkenny 🌐 dunfanaghy.info

Carpeted in heather and rich in birdlife, this is the most scenic of the northern Donegal headlands, with lovely views of the sea and mountains. Its appeal is enhanced by Dunfanaghy, a delightful town with an air of affluence and Presbyterianism unusual in this area. The town is the perfect place to enjoy outdoor activities such as surfing, hill walking, rock climbing and horse-riding. Dunfanaghy's local beach, Killahoey Strand, offers excellent swimming and is often deserted.

> **Bloody Foreland, which gets its name from the rubescent glow of the rocks at sunset, boasts magnificent scenery.**

←

Sun setting over the rocky landscape of Bloody Foreland

6

Grianán Ailigh

C1 Co Donegal From Letterkenny or Derry 10am–4pm daily Letterkenny; 074 912 1160

Donegal's most impressive and intriguing ancient monument stands just 10 km (6 miles) west of the city of Derry (p280) at the entrance to the lovely Inishowen Peninsula. Its name is roughly translated as "sun palace".

Overlooking Lough Swilly and Lough Foyle, the circular stone structure, measuring 23 m (77 ft) in diameter, is believed to have been built as a pagan temple around the 5th century BC, although the site was probably a place of worship before this date. Later, Christians adopted the fort: St Patrick is said to have baptized Eoghan, founder of the O'Neill dynasty, here in AD 450. It became the royal residence of the O'Neills, but was damaged in the 12th century by the army of Murtagh O'Brien, King of Munster.

The fort was restored in the 1870s. Two doorways lead from the outside into a grassy arena ringed by three terraces. The most memorable feature of the fort, however, is its magnificent vantage point, which affords stunning views in every direction.

At the foot of the hill stands an attractive church, dedicated to St Aengus and built in 1967. Its circular design echoes that of the Grianán.

INSIDER TIP
Sun Circle

Grianán Ailigh is originally thought to have been built as a place of sun worship. Visit at sunrise during one of the equinoxes to see beams align precisely with the entrance.

 Jagged red rocks that line the Rosses' dramatic coastline

7

The Rosses

C1 Co Donegal To Dungloe or Burtonport from Letterkenny To Arranmore from Burtonport (074 954 2233; arranmore ferry.com) Dungloe; 074 952 2198; seasonal

A rocky headland dotted with more than 100 lakes, the Rosses is one of the most picturesque and unspoilt corners of Donegal. It is also a strong Gaeltacht area (p234), with many people speaking Gaelic.

The hub of the Rosses, at the southern end of the headland, is Dungloe, a bustling market town and major angling centre.

There is a glorious sheltered beach 8 km (5 miles) west of Dungloe at Maghery Bay, from where you can also walk to nearby Crohy Head, an area known for its caves, arches and unusual cliff formations. From the small fishing village of Burtonport, 8 km (5 miles) north of Dungloe, car ferries sail daily to Donegal's largest island, Arranmore. The rugged northwest coast here is ideal for cliff-top walks, and from the south coast you can enjoy fine views across to the Rosses. Most of Arranmore's population of 500 lives in Leabgarrow, where the harbour is located.

8

Rosguill Peninsula

C1 Co Donegal

Rosguill Peninsula juts out into the Atlantic Ocean between Sheephaven and Mulroy bays. The simplest way to see it is to follow the 11-km (7-mile) Atlantic Drive,

Old warehouses standing waterside at Rathmelton, on the Fanad Peninsula

a circular route that skirts the clifftops at the tip of the headland. Doe Castle, 5 km (3 miles) north of Creeslough village, is worth a visit as much for its setting on a promontory overlooking Sheephaven Bay as for its architectural or historical interest. It has been restored from the remains of a castle erected in the 16th century by the MacSweeneys, a family of Scottish mercenaries.

Fanad Peninsula

🅰️C1 🏠Co Donegal 🚌To Rathmelton & Portsalon from Letterkenny

A panoramic route winds between the hilly spine and rugged coast of this tranquil peninsula. The eastern side is by far the most enjoyable and begins at Rathmelton, a charming Plantation town founded in the 17th century. Elegant Georgian homes and handsome old warehouses flank its tree-lined Main Street.

Further north, Portsalon offers safe bathing and great views from nearby Saldanha Head. Near Doagh Beg, on the way to Fanad Head in the far north, the cliffs have been eroded into arches and other dramatic shapes.

Letterkenny

🅰️C1 🏠Co Donegal
🚉 ℹ️Neil T Blaney Rd; 074 912 1160

Straddling the River Swilly, with the Sperrin Mountains to the east and the Derryveagh Mountains (p230) to the west, Letterkenny is Donegal's largest town. It is also the region's leading business centre, a role it took over from Londonderry after partition in 1921. The likeable town makes a good base from which to explore the northern coast of Donegal and, for anglers, is well placed for access to the waters of Lough Swilly.

Letterkenny has one of the longest main streets in Ireland, which is dominated by the 65-m (215-ft) steeple of St Eunan's Cathedral. A Neo-Gothic creation built in the late 19th century, it contains Celtic-style stonework, a rich marble altar and striking stained-glass windows, and looks particularly impressive when floodlit at night.

Located in a former workhouse, **Donegal County Museum** offers informative displays on local history from the Stone Age to the 20th century, as well as a collection of archaeological

artifacts found in Donegal, some of them dating from the Iron Age.

Donegal County Museum
🏠High Rd 📞074 912 4613
🕐Mon–Sat (pm only Sat)
🚫Christmas and public hols

A hand-loom worker
weaving his wares at an
Ardara store

⑪
Ardara

 C2 ⬛ Co Donegal
🚌 From Killybegs or
Donegal 🅸 Heritage
centre; www.ardara.ie

Ardara, the weaving capital of Donegal, is lined with shops selling locally made tweeds and hand-knitted sweaters; some larger stores put on displays of hand-loom weaving. Ardara is also worth a stop for its pubs, much loved for their fiddle sessions.

A drive along the narrow peninsula to Loughros Point, 10 km (6 miles) west of town, provides dramatic coastal views. Another picturesque route runs southwest from Ardara to Glencolmcille, going over Glengesh Pass, a series of bends through a wild, deserted landscape.

⑫
Glencolmcille

⬛ B2 ⬛ Co Donegal 🚌 From Killybegs 🅸 Donegal; www.glencolmcille.ie

Glencolmcille, a quiet, grassy valley scattered with brightly coloured cottages, feels very much like a backwater, in spite of the sizeable number of visitors who come here.

The "Glen of St Colmcille" is a popular place of pilgrimage due to its associations with the saint more commonly known as St Columba. Just north of the village of Cashel, on the way to Glen Head, is the church where St Columba worshipped: it is said that between prayers the saint slept on the two stone slabs still visible in one corner.

The main attraction here is the **Folk Village Museum**, a cluster of replica cottages perched on the hillside, which depicts rural Donegal lifestyles through the ages. It was started in the 1950s by a local priest called Father James McDyer, who concerned about the high rate of emigration from this poor region, sought to provide jobs and a sense of regional pride, partly by encouraging people to set up craft cooperatives. There are regular craft demonstrations – such as spinning – at the museum and the folk village shop sells local wares.

There is plenty to explore in the valley, which is littered with cairns, dolmens and other ancient monuments. The nearby coast is lovely too, with the best walks taking you west across the grassy foreland of Malinbeg, a tiny Gaeltacht village. Slightly further, beyond the small resort of Malin More, steps drop down to an idyllic sandy cove that is hemmed in by cliffs.

Folk Village Museum
⊛⊛⊜⊕ ⬛ Dooey
⬛ Easter-Oct: daily
🅦 glenfolkvillage.com

THE IRISH GAELTACHTS

The term "Gaeltacht" refers to Gaelic-speaking areas of Ireland. Up to the 16th century, virtually the entire population spoke the native tongue. British rule, however, undermined Irish culture, and the Famine (p222) drained the country of many of its Gaelic speakers. The use of the local language has fallen steadily since. Even so, in the Gaeltachts 75 per cent of the people still speak it, and road signs are exclusively in Irish - unlike in most other parts of Ireland.

The Donegal Gaeltacht stretches almost unbroken along the coast from Fanad Head to Slieve League and boasts the largest number of Irish speakers in the country. Ireland's other principal Gaeltachts are located in Galway and Kerry.

Donegal

C2 **Co Donegal**
The Quay;
www.donegaltown.ie

Donegal means "Fort of the Foreigners", and is named for the Vikings who built a garrison here. However, it was under the O'Donnells in the 15th century that the town began to take shape. The restored **Donegal Castle** incorporates the gabled tower of a fortified house built by the family. The adjoining house and other features are Jacobean – added by Sir Basil Brooke, who moved in after the O'Donnells were ousted by the English in 1607.

Brooke was also responsible for laying out the market square, known as the Diamond. An obelisk in the centre commemorates four Franciscan monks who wrote the *Annals of the Four Masters* in the 1630s, tracing the history of the Gaelic people from 40 days before the Great Flood up until the end of the 16th century. Part

of it was written at Donegal Abbey, south of the Diamond. Built in 1474, little remains of the abbey except a few Gothic windows and cloister arches. About 1.5 km (1 mile) further on is **Donegal Craft Village**, which showcases local and contemporary arts and crafts.

Donegal Castle

Tirchonaill St
Easter-mid-Sep: daily;
mid-Sep-Easter: Thu-Mon
heritageireland.ie

Donegal Craft Village

Ballyshannon Rd
Apr-Sep: Mon-Fri; Oct-Mar: Tue-Fri **donegal craftvillage.com**

Killybegs

C2 **Co Donegal**
From Donegal **Shore Rd; www.killybegs.ie**

Narrow winding streets lined with traditional cottages give Killybegs a timeless feel. This small town is known in particular for the manufacture of Donegal carpets. Killybegs is also one of Ireland's busiest fishing ports and the quays are well worth seeing when

the trawlers arrive to offload their catch: gulls squawk overhead and the smell of fish fills the air. Trawlermen come from far and wide – so do not be surprised to hear Eastern European voices as you wander the town.

TOP 5 BEACHES IN DONEGAL

Culdaff Beach
D1
A stunning village bay.

Five Fingers Strand
C1
Best for solitude-seekers.

Murder Hole Beach
C1
A hidden gem.

Ballymastocker Bay
C1
Best for golden sands.

Tullan Strand
C2
A surfer's paradise.

↑ Colourful fishing trawlers moored in Killybegs port

↑ A statue of St Patrick on the shores of Lough Derg

 Lough Derg

🗺C2 🏠Co Donegal 📅May-Sep (pilgrims only) 🚌To Pettigo from Donegal 🌐loughderg.org

Pilgrims have made their way to Lough Derg ever since St Patrick spent 40 days praying on one of the lake's islands in an attempt to rid Ireland of all evil spirits. The Pilgrimage of St Patrick's Purgatory began in around 1150 and still attracts thousands of Catholics every summer. Their destination is the tiny Station Island, close to Lough Derg's southern shore and reached by boat from a jetty located 8 km (5 miles) north of the border village of Pettigo. The island is totally occupied by a religious complex, which includes a basilica, built in 1921, and hostels for the pilgrims.

The pilgrimage season runs from May to August. There are one-day retreats and three-day pilgrimages; the latter entails fasting, praying and walking. Although only pilgrims can visit Station Island, it is interesting to go to the jetty to savour the atmosphere and get a good view of the basilica near the shore.

⑯ **Rossnowlagh**

🗺C2 🏠Co Donegal 🚌From Bundoran & Donegal ℹThe Bridge, Bundoran; www.discoverbundoran.com

At Rossnowlagh, Atlantic waves break on to one of Ireland's finest beaches, drawing crowds of both bathers and surfers to this tiny place. Even so, the village remains far more peaceful than the resort of Bundoran, 14 km (9 miles) south. In addition, the cliffs at Rossnowlagh provide scope for exhilarating coastal walks. Away from the sea, you can visit the **Donegal Historical Society Museum**, housed in a striking Franciscan friary built in the 1950s. The tiny but fascinating collection includes displays of Stone Age flints, Irish musical instruments and other local artifacts.

Rossnowlagh never fails to make the news in July, when it hosts the only parade to take place in the Republic by the Protestant organization the Orange Order.

Donegal Historical Society Museum

🏠Ardeelan Lower 🕐Daily 🌐donegalhistory.com

⑰ **Ballyshannon**

🗺C2 🏠Co Donegal 🚌From Bundoran & Donegal ℹBus Station, The Bridge; www.discoverballyshannon.ie

In the one-time garrison town of Ballyshannon, well-kept Georgian homes jostle for space along hilly streets on the banks of the River Erne, near where it flows into Donegal Bay. This is a bustling town, full of character and off the main tourist track –

DRINK

Stanford Village Inn

Decorated with flagstones from a ruined castle, this traditional pub has been in the same family for generations. Come for delicious food and convivial company.

🗺C2 🏠Main St, Dromahair
📞071 916 4140

though it does get packed during August's festival of traditional music, which is one of the best of its kind in Ireland.

The music festival apart, Ballyshannon is most famous as the birthplace of poet William Allingham (1824–89), who recalled his home town in the lines "Adieu to Ballyshanny and the winding banks of the Erne". He lies buried in the graveyard of St Anne's Church, off Main Street. There is a fine view over the river from here: you can see the small island of Inis Saimer where, according to legend, Greeks founded the first colony in Ireland after the Great Flood. Beyond, you can glimpse a large Irish Army base: Ballyshannon's position on a steeply rising bluff overlooking the River Erne has always made the town a strategic military site.

About 1.5 km (1 mile) northwest of town lie the scant ruins of Assaroe Abbey, founded by Cistercians in 1184. A graveyard with some ancient burial slabs and headstones is all that remains. Nearby, two water wheels installed by the monks have been restored. **The Water Wheels** is in an exceptional setting overlooking the Erne Estuary and Atlantic Ocean, and has a small heritage centre and a café.

The Water Wheels

⊜⊕ 🄰 Assaroe Abbey
📞 071 985 1260 🄲 Easter-Oct: Sun only

→

Lissadell House interior, filled with Gore-Booth treasures

18 (◈)(◈)(▭)

Lissadell House

🄰 B2 🄲 Carney, Co Sligo
🚆🚍 To Sligo 🄲 Mid-Apr-mid-Oct: 10:30am–6pm daily 🅆 lissadellhouse.com

A Greek Revival mansion built in the 1830s, Lissadell is better known for its occupants than its architecture. It was the home of the Gore-Booths who, unlike some of the Anglo-Irish gentry, have contributed much to the region over the four centuries they have been in County Sligo. During the Famine *(p222)*, Sir Robert mortgaged the house to help feed his employees.

The most famous member of the Gore-Booth family is Sir Robert's granddaughter, Constance Markievicz (1868–1927), a leading nationalist who took part in the 1916 Rising. She was the first woman to be elected to the British House of Commons and later became Minister for Labour in the first Dáil.

Built in grey limestone, the exterior of Lissadell House is rather austere. The interior, on the other hand, has an appealing atmosphere of faded grandeur, with copious memorabilia of the building's former occupants. The finest rooms are the gallery and the dining room, decorated with full-length murals of the Gore-Booth family, their famous butler Thomas Kilgallon, the gamekeeper, head woodsman and a dog.

The house is now a private family home but is open to the public for guided tours (check the website for the latest details). There are also delightful alpine and kitchen gardens, from where you can savour gorgeous views of the beach and across the bay.

19

Sligo

C2 ▣ Co Sligo ✈ 071 916 8280 ▣ ▣ ℹ Old Bank Building, O'Connell St; www.sligotourism.ie

The port of Sligo sits at the mouth of the River Garavogue, sandwiched between the Atlantic and Lough Gill. The largest town in the northwest, it rose to prominence under the Normans, being well placed as a gateway between the provinces of Ulster and Connaught. The appearance of Sligo today is mainly the result of growth during the late 18th and 19th centuries.

Sligo is perfectly situated for touring the ravishing countryside nearby, and it is also a good centre for traditional music. However, its real renown comes from its status as the arts capital of northwest Ireland.

Sligo's link with the Yeats family is a big draw to the town. W B Yeats, Ireland's best-known poet, was born into a prominent local family. The Pollexfen warehouse, at the western end of Wine Street, has a rooftop turret from which the poet's grandfather would watch his merchant fleet moored in the docks. The town's sole surviving

1923

The year W B Yeats became the first Irishman to receive a Nobel Prize.

medieval building is **Sligo Abbey**, founded in 1253. Some original features remain, such as the delicate lancet windows in the choir, but this ruined Dominican friary dates mainly from the 15th century. The best features are a beautifully carved altar and the cloisters. A short distance west from the abbey is O'Connell Street, with the town's main shops and Hargadon Bros – an old Sligo institution complete with a dark, wooden interior, snugs and a grocery counter. Near the junction with Wine Street, overlooking Hyde Bridge, is the Yeats Memorial Building. This houses the Yeats Society, dedicated to commemorating the life of the poet. The Yeats International Summer School is held here too: a renowned annual festival of readings and lectures on the poet's life and work. Just the other side of Hyde Bridge is a statue of the poet, engraved with lines from his own verse.

Sligo County Museum has Yeatsian memorabilia and local artifacts but the entire Niland Collection, including paintings by Jack B Yeats and Paul Henry, is in **The Model** in the Mall. This outstanding centre also puts on temporary exhibitions of major Irish and international contemporary art.

Improbably set in the suburbs of Sligo, **Carrowmore Megalithic Cemetery** once held the country's largest collection of Stone Age tombs. Quarrying destroyed much, but about 40 passage tombs and dolmens survive among the abandoned gravel pits, with some in private gardens and cottages.

Just west of Sligo, the huge unexcavated cairn atop Knocknarea mountain dates back 5,000 years and is said to contain the tomb of the legendary Queen Maeve of Connaught. It is an hour's climb, starting 4 km (2 miles) west of Carrowmore.

Tobernalt Holy Well, by Lough Gill, 5 km (3 miles) south of Sligo, means "cliff well", after a nearby spring with alleged curative powers. It was a holy site in Celtic times and later it became a Christian shrine. Priests came to the site to celebrate Mass in secret during the 18th century, when Catholic worship was illegal. The Mass

↑ The tomb of Queen Maeve of Connaught, atop Sligo's Knocknarea mountain

rock, next to an altar erected around 1900, remains a place of pilgrimage.

Sligo Abbey

Abbey St ◻ Apr-Oct: daily ◻ heritageireland.ie

Sligo County Museum

Stephen St ◻ 071 911 1679 ◻ Tue-Sat (Oct-Apr: am only)

The Model

The Mall ◻ Tue-Sun ◻ themodel.ie

Carrowmore Megalithic Cemetery

Easter-Oct: daily ◻ heritageireland.ie

The Organic Centre

◻ C2 ◻ Rossinver, Co Leitrim ◻ 10am-5pm daily ◻ theorganiccentre.ie

Situated about 3 km (2 miles) from Rossinver on the Kinlough Road, The Organic Centre is a not-for-profit company that provides training, information and demonstrations of organic gardening, cultivation and farming. The centre is located on a large 7.7-ha (19-acre) site in the unspoilt countryside of sparsely populated north Leitrim. There are several display gardens for visitors to wander through, including a children's garden, a taste garden and a heritage garden. The Eco Shop sells seeds, cuttings and vegetables, as well as books and kitchen equipment. Some items can also be bought online.

SURFING IN SLIGO

Ireland's west coast is hailed worldwide as a great surfing spot. From gentle conditions suitable for beginners to the elusive big one – the monstrous Aileen's Wave, found off the Cliffs of Moher (p190) – there's great surf for all abilities. Perhaps the most popular destination of all is Sligo – and, with its stunning beaches and wealth of surf schools, it's easy to see why. Beginners should head for Enniscrone beach, which offers the perfect place to learn amid 5 km (3 miles) of golden sand and gentle breaking waves. Experienced surfers will find more of a challenge at Mullaghmore; with strong winds and waves reaching up to 9 m (30 ft) high, it's considered one of the world's prime big-wave destinations and is suitable only for expert-level surfers.

↑ A surfer riding the waves on Ireland's west coast, a world-renowned surfing hot spot

←

The remarkably well-preserved medieval ruins of Sligo Abbey

Lough Arrow seen from a passage tomb in Carrowkeel cemetery ↑

21

Lough Arrow

 C3 ◉ Co Sligo ▦ To Ballinafad ℹ Boyle; Jun–Sep; www.discoverireland.ie

This large, scenic lake lies mostly in County Sligo with a very small section in County Roscommon. People go to Lough Arrow to sail and fish for the local trout, and simply to enjoy the glorious countryside. You can explore the lake by boat, but the views from the shore are the real joy of Lough Arrow. A full circuit of the lake is recommended, but for the most breathtaking views head for the southern end around Ballinafad. This small town lies in a gorgeous spot, enclosed to the north and south by the Bricklieve and Curlew mountains.

The Carrowkeel Passage Tomb Cemetery occupies a remote and eerie spot in the Bricklieve Mountains to the north of Ballinafad. The best approach is up the single track road from Castlebaldwin, 5 km (3 miles) northeast of the site.

The 14 Neolithic passage graves, which are scattered around a hilltop overlooking Lough Arrow, are elaborate corbelled structures. One is comparable with Newgrange (p248), except that the burial chamber inside this cairn is lit by the sun on the day of the summer solstice (21 June) as opposed to the winter solstice. On a nearby ridge are the remains of Stone Age huts, presumably those occupied by the farmers who buried their dead in the Carrowkeel passage graves.

SHANNON-ERNE WATERWAY

This labyrinthine system of rivers and lakes links Leitrim village, on the Shannon, with Upper Lough Erne, in Fermanagh. It follows the course of a canal, which was completed and then abandoned in the 1860s. The channel was reopened in 1994, enabling the public to enjoy both the Victorian stonework (including 34 bridges) and the state-of-the-art technology used to operate the 16 locks.

22

Carrick-on-Shannon

🅰 C3 🏠 Co Leitrim 🚂 🚌
ℹ The Old Barrel Store; May-Sep; www.leitrim tourism.com

The tiny capital of Leitrim, one of the least populated counties in Ireland (although this is changing), stands in a lovely spot on a tight bend of the River Shannon.

The town's river location and its proximity to the Grand Canal were crucial to Carrick's development, and are also the main reasons for its now thriving tourist industry. There is a colourful, modern marina, where private boats can moor in summer and boats are available for hire.

Already a major boating centre, Carrick has benefited from the reopening of the Shannon–Erne Waterway, one end of which begins 6 km (4 miles) north at the village of Leitrim. It was restored in a cross-border joint venture billed as a symbol of peaceful cooperation between Northern Ireland and the Republic.

Away from the bustle of the marina, Carrick is an old-fashioned place, with 19th-century churches and convents, and refined Georgian houses and shopfronts. The town's most curious building is the quaint Costello Chapel on Bridge Street, one of the smallest in the world. It was built in 1877 by local businessman Edward Costello, to house the tombs of himself and his wife.

23

Parke's Castle

🅰 C2 🏠 6 km (4 miles) N of Dromahair, Co Leitrim
🚂 🚌 To Sligo 🕐 Late Mar-Sep: 10am-6pm daily (last adm: 5:15pm)
🌐 heritageireland.ie

Dominating the eastern end of Lough Gill, this fortified manor house was was built in 1609 by Captain Robert Parke, an English settler who later became MP for Leitrim. It has been beautifully restored by the Office of Public Works using 17th-century building methods and native Irish oak.

Parke's Castle was erected on the site of a 16th-century tower house belonging to the O'Rourkes, a powerful local clan, and stones from this earlier structure were used in the new building. The original foundations and part of the moat were incorporated, but otherwise Parke's Castle is the epitome of a Plantation manor house. It is protected by a large enclosure or bawn, whose sturdy wall includes a gatehouse and turrets as well as the house itself.

Among the most distinctive architectural features of Parke's Castle are the diamond-shaped chimneys, mullioned windows and the parapets. There is also a curious stone hut, known as the "sweathouse", which was an early Irish sauna. Inside, an exhibition and audiovisual display cover Parke's Castle and various historic and prehistoric sites in the area. There is also a working forge.

From the shore there is a good view of the tiny wooded island of Innisfree, the subject of W B Yeats's popular poem, "The Lake Isle of Innisfree". Boat trips around sights on Lough Gill leave from outside the castle walls.

A DRIVING TOUR
YEATS COUNTRY

Length 88 km (55 miles) **Stopping-off points** Rosses Point; Drumcliff; Dromahair **Terrain** Some narrow country roads

Even for those unfamiliar with the poetry of W B Yeats, Sligo's engaging landscapes are reason enough to make a pilgrimage to the home of the Irish poet. This tour follows a varied route, taking you past sandy bays and dramatic limestone ridges, through forest and alongside rivers and lakes. Lough Gill lies at the heart of Yeats country, enclosed by wooded hills crisscrossed by walking trails. In summer, boats ply the length of the lough, or you can head to one of the northwest's best beaches, at Rosses Point.

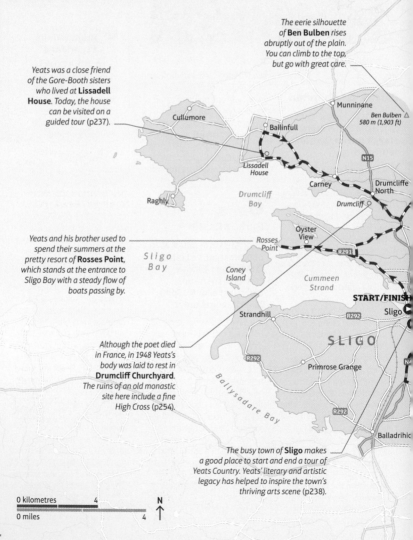

The eerie silhouette of **Ben Bulben** rises abruptly out of the plain. You can climb to the top, but go with great care.

Yeats was a close friend of the Gore-Booth sisters who lived at **Lissadell House**. Today, the house can be visited on a guided tour (p237).

Yeats and his brother used to spend their summers at the pretty resort of **Rosses Point**, which stands at the entrance to Sligo Bay with a steady flow of boats passing by.

Although the poet died in France, in 1948 Yeats's body was laid to rest in **Drumcliff Churchyard**. The ruins of an old monastic site here include a fine High Cross (p254).

The busy town of **Sligo** makes a good place to start and end a tour of Yeats Country. Yeats' literary and artistic legacy has helped to inspire the town's thriving arts scene (p238).

Munninane

Ben Bulben △
580 m (1,903 ft)

N15

Cullamore

Ballinfull

Lissadell House

Carney

Drumcliffe North

Drumcliff

Raghly

Drumcliff Bay

Oyster View

Rosses Point

R291

Sligo Bay

Coney Island

Cummeen Strand

START/FINISH

Strandhill

R292

Sligo

SLIGO

Primrose Grange

Ballysadare Bay

R292

R292

Balladrihid

0 kilometres   4
0 miles   4

N ↑

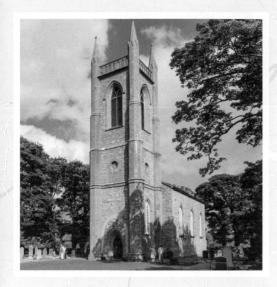

← St Columba's Church in Drumcliff, Sligo

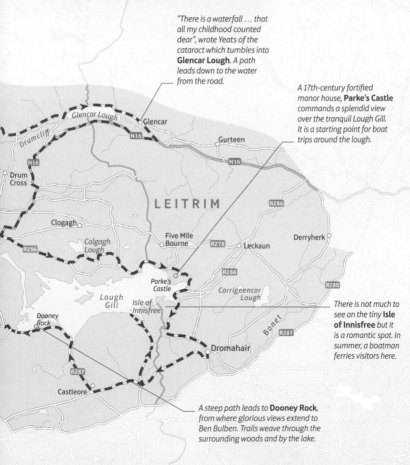

"There is a waterfall … that all my childhood counted dear", wrote Yeats of the cataract which tumbles into **Glencar Lough**. A path leads down to the water from the road.

A 17th-century fortified manor house, **Parke's Castle** *commands a splendid view over the tranquil Lough Gill. It is a starting point for boat trips around the lough.*

There is not much to see on the tiny **Isle of Innisfree** *but it is a romantic spot. In summer, a boatman ferries visitors here.*

A steep path leads to **Dooney Rock***, from where glorious views extend to Ben Bulben. Trails weave through the surrounding woods and by the lake.*

THE MIDLANDS

County Meath's fertile Boyne Valley was settled during the Stone Age and became the most important centre of habitation in the country. The remains of ancient sites from this early civilization include Newgrange, Ireland's finest Neolithic tomb. In Celtic times the focus shifted south to the legendary Hill of Tara. Beyond these, historical highlights of the region include monasteries such as Fore Abbey and Clonmacnoise.

Norman castles, such as the immense fortress at Trim, attest to the shifting frontiers around the area of English influence known as the Pale (p145). By the end of the 16th century, this zone incorporated nearly all the counties in the Midlands.

Although part of the Republic since 1921, Monaghan and Cavan also belong to the ancient province of Ulster, and the former retains strong links with Northern Ireland. The rounded hills called drumlins, found in both counties, are typical of the border region between the Republic and Northern Ireland.

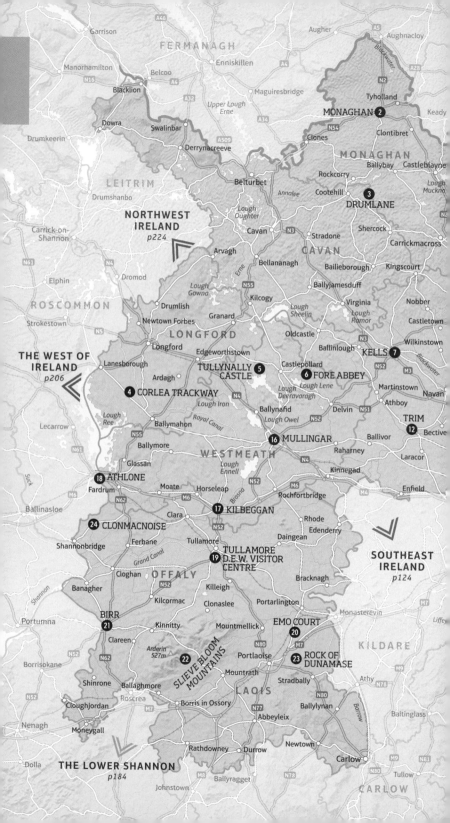

THE MIDLANDS

Must See
1 Newgrange and the Boyne Valley

Experience More
2 Monaghan
3 Drumlane
4 Corlea Trackway
5 Tullynally Castle
6 Fore Abbey
7 Kells
8 Carlingford
9 Monasterboice
10 Dundalk
11 Drogheda
12 Trim
13 Hill of Tara
14 Slane
15 Old Mellifont Abbey
16 Mullingar
17 Kilbeggan
18 Athlone
19 Tullamore D.E.W. Visitor Centre
20 Emo Court
21 Birr
22 Slieve Bloom Mountains
23 Rock of Dunamase
24 Clonmacnoise

THE
MIDLANDS

Visitors queue to enter Newgrange, Ireland's most famous prehistoric site ↑

NEWGRANGE AND THE BOYNE VALLEY

📍 D3 🚗 8 km (5 miles) E of Slane, Co Meath 🚂 To Drogheda 🚌 To Drogheda and Drogheda to Brú na Bóinne Visitor Centre 🕐 Hours vary, check website 📅 24-27 Dec 🌐 newgrange.com

Known as Brú na Bóinne, the "Palace of the Boyne", this Midlands river valley is rich in associations with Ireland's history. It is home to three ancient passage graves that together have been designated a UNESCO World Heritage Site – the most significant of these being the immense Newgrange. The valley is also renowned as a burial ground for the legendary kings of Tara and the location of the Battle of the Boyne.

INSIDER TIP
Solar Spectacle

Enter a lottery to visit Newgrange at dawn during the winter solstice. Applications hugely outnumber the slots available – no surprise given the awe-inspiring experience.

NEOLITHIC NEWGRANGE

The origins of Newgrange, one of the most important passage graves in Europe, are steeped in mystery. Built in around 3200 BC – meaning that it predates Egypt's pyramids by more than 600 years – the grave was left untouched by all invaders until it was rediscovered in 1699. When the site was excavated in the 1960s, archaeologists discovered that on and around the winter solstice (21 December), rays of sun enter the tomb and light up the burial chamber – making it the world's oldest solar observatory.

The massive structure is located on a low ridge north of the River Boyne, reaching

CONSTRUCTION OF NEWGRANGE

The tomb at Newgrange was designed by people with clearly exceptional artistic and engineering skills, who had use of neither the wheel nor metal tools. About 200,000 tonnes of loose stones were transported to build the mound, or cairn, which protects the passage grave. Larger slabs were used to make the circle around the cairn (12 out of a probable 35 stones have survived), the kerb and the tomb itself. Many of the kerbstones and the slabs lining the passage, the chamber and its recesses are decorated with zigzags, spirals and other geometric motifs. The grave's corbelled ceiling consists of smaller, unadorned slabs and has proved completely waterproof for the last 5,000 years.

↑ Newgrange's elaborately carved entrance stone, forming part of the ring of huge slabs around the cairn

80 m (262 ft) in diameter and 13 m (43 ft) high. Newgrange is ringed by 97 large stones called kerbstones, which are intricately carved with megalithic art. The most striking of these guards the entrance. Inside, chiselled basin stones in each recess would have contained funerary offerings and cremated human remains.

All visitors to Newgrange and Knowth *(p250)*, which are viewed as part of the same tour, are admitted through the Brú na Bóinne Visitor Centre, which itself has an illuminating exhibition on the site.

↑ An engraved kerbstone on the northwest side of Newgrange

KNOWTH

The two sister graves included in the World Heritage Site are called Knowth and Dowth. Similar in size to Newgrange, Knowth outshines its more famous neighbour in several respects; above all in the quantity of its treasures, which form the greatest concentration of megalithic art in Europe. The site was also occupied for a much longer period – from Neolithic times until about 1400. Unusually, Knowth has two passage tombs rather than one, with entrances on opposite sides. The grave is surrounded by 18 smaller satellite mounds. As with Newgrange, excavations began here in 1962, and the restored site is now open, although the tombs can only be viewed externally to prevent further decay.

> **Similar in size to Newgrange, Knowth outshines its more famous neighbour in many respects; above all in the quantity of its treasures.**

years as a swan. When Caer became a bird that winter, Oengus went to her and was transformed as well. Together they flew back to Newgrange, and the site still serves as a wintering ground for a flock of whooper swans today.

Although Newgrange predates them, Celtic lore maintains that the legendary high kings of Tara *(p256)* were buried here, and the site has furnished Irish museums with many precious artifacts. Most of these – which include jewellery and Roman coins – are assumed to be votive offerings.

As with most of Ireland's ancient sites, Newgrange is saturated with myths and legends. One tale tells the story of Oengus (also spelled Aonghus), a chieftain god who fell in love with a girl named Caer after seeing her image in a dream. Oengus searched the length and breadth of Ireland for a year, before finally finding Caer and learning that she was doomed to spend alternate

DRINK

Listoke Distillery and Gin School
Ireland's only gin school is located in the heart of the Boyne Valley. Visitors are greeted with a Listoke 1777 G&T before a tour of the distillery. After a lesson in the brand's history and a quick introduction to botanicals, they can then begin to design and distil their own 700ml bottle of gin.

🅐D3 🄰Tenure Business Park, Monasterboice
🅦listokedistillery.ie

Dowth, the third of the principal tombs, was subjected to an unprofessional excavation in the mid-1800s, and was badly damaged as a result. Its passage tombs are less spectacular than within the other two burial mounds, and, unlike at Newgrange or Knowth, many of its surrounding kerbstones are partially or completely buried. Dowth is closed to the public (though it can be viewed from the road), and is therefore not included on the official visitor centre tour that takes in its two sister sites.

↓ Knowth passage tomb and some of its surrounding satellite graves

BATTLE OF THE BOYNE

A more recent, but equally significant, event in the region's history occurred in the 17th century. In 1688 the Catholic King James II of England was deposed from his throne, to be replaced by his Protestant daughter, Mary, and her husband, William of Orange. Determined to win back the crown, James sought the support of Irish Catholics, and challenged William by the River Boyne. The Battle of the Boyne took place on 1 July 1690, with James's poorly trained force of 25,000 French and Irish Catholics facing William's 36,000-strong hardened army. The Protestants triumphed and James fled to France, signalling the beginning of total Protestant power over Ireland and sealing the country's fate for the next 300 years.

Did You Know?

The Battle of the Boyne was the largest ever gathering of troops on Irish soil.

EXPERIENCE MORE

Monaghan

 D2 Co Monaghan
Market House, Market St; Jun-Sep; www. monaghantourism.com

The spruce and thriving town of Monaghan is the urban highlight of the northern Midlands. Planted by James I in 1613, it developed into a prosperous industrial centre, thanks mainly to the local manufacture of linen. A crannog off Glen Road is the sole trace of the town's Celtic beginnings.

Monaghan centres on three almost contiguous squares. The main attraction in Market Square is the 18th-century Market House (now an arts centre), a squat but charming building with the original oak beams still visible. To the east lies Church Square, the heart of modern Monaghan and lined with dignified 19th-century buildings, such as the Classical-style courthouse. The third square, which is known as the Diamond, was the original marketplace. It contains the Rossmore Memorial, a large Victorian drinking fountain with an ornate stone canopy supported by marble columns.

The award-winning **County Museum** tells the story of Monaghan's linen and lace-making industries. The pride of the historical collection is the Cross of Clogher, an ornate bronze altar cross that dates from around 1400.

County Museum
Hill St 047 82928
11am-5pm Mon-Fri, noon-5pm Sat Public hols

Drumlane

C3 1 km (0.5 miles) S of Milltown, Co Cavan To Belturbet

Standing alone by the River Erne, Drumlane's medieval church and round tower merit a visit for their

delightful setting as much as for the ruins themselves. The abbey church, founded in the early 13th century but altered about 200 years later, features fine Romanesque carvings. The nearby round tower has lost its cap but is unusual for the well-finished stonework, with carvings of birds on the north side.

Corlea Trackway

C3 Kenagh, Co Longford To Longford Apr-Sep: 10am-6pm daily (last adm: 1hr before closing) heritage ireland.ie

The Corlea Trackway Visitor Centre interprets an Iron Age bog road built in the year 148 BC. The oak road is the longest of its kind in Europe; an 18-m (60-ft) length of preserved road is on permanent display in a hall specially designed to prevent the ancient wood from cracking in the heat.

Just 10 km (6 miles) north of Corlea Trackway, Ardagh is one of the prettiest villages in Longford, with charming stone cottages around a green.

Rossmore Memorial at the centre of the Diamond in Monaghan

↑ The ruins of Fore Abbey, a medieval Benedictine priory that stands in a lovely wooded setting

Tullynally Castle

C3 **Castlepollard, Co Westmeath** **To Mullingar** **Castle: to pre-booked groups only; gardens: Apr-Sep: 11am-5pm Thu-Sun** **tullynallycastle.ie**

This huge structure, festooned with turrets and battlements, is one of Ireland's largest castles. The original 17th-century tower house was given a Georgian gloss, but this was all but submerged under later Gothic Revival changes. The Pakenham family (headed by the Earls of Longford) have lived at Tullynally since 1655; Thomas Pakenham now manages the estate.

The imposing great hall leads to a fine panelled dining room hung with family portraits, though of equal interest are the Victorian kitchen, laundry room and the adjacent drying room. The 8,000-volume library looks out on to rolling wooded parkland, much of which was landscaped in the 1760s. The grounds include Victorian terraces, a walled kitchen and flower gardens, two small lakes and a Chinese and Tibetan garden.

Fore Abbey

C3 **Fore, Castlepollard, Co Westmeath** **To Castlepollard** **Daily** **heritageireland.ie**

The ruins of Fore Abbey lie in glorious rolling countryside. St Fechin set up a monastery here in AD 630, but what you see now are the only remains of a Benedictine abbey in Ireland, founded around 1200. On the northern border of the Pale (*p145*), Fore Abbey was fortified in the 15th century as protection against the native Irish. The ruined church was part of the original Norman priory, but the cloister and refectory date from the 1400s.

Kells

D3 **Co Meath** **Headfort Place; 9am-5pm Tue-Sat; www.visitingkells.ie**

Signposted by its Irish name, Ceannannus Mór, this modest town provides an unlikely backdrop to the monastery for which it is so famous.

Kells Monastery was set up by St Columba in the 6th century, but its heyday came after 806, when monks fled here from Iona. They may have been the scribes who illuminated the superb *Book of Kells*, now kept at Trinity College, Dublin (*p66*).

The monastery, centred on an 18th-century church, beside a decapitated round tower, has several intricately carved 9th-century High Crosses.

Just north of the enclosure is St Columba's House, a tiny steep-roofed stone oratory.

The Market Cross, a High Cross that once served to mark the entrance to the monastery, now stands outside the Old Courthouse. It was used as a gallows during the uprising in 1798. The battle scene on the base is a subject rarely used in High Cross art.

Dramatic scenery in
Slieve Foye Forest Park,
near Carlingford ↑

⑧ Carlingford

D3 ⌂ Co Louth 🚌
ℹ Old Railway Station;
www.carlingford.ie

This picturesque fishing village,
located between the moun-
tains of the Cooley Peninsula
and Carlingford Lough, is a
delightful place to explore,
featuring pretty whitewashed
cottages and ancient buildings
that cluster along medieval
alleyways. The newly restored
ruins of King John's Castle,
built by the Normans to protect
the entrance to the lough, still
dominate the village; there
are guided tours daily at 11am
and 3pm. The **Carlingford
Heritage Centre**, housed in
a medieval church, traces
the history of the port from
Anglo-Norman times.

In summer, there are cruises
around the lough, which is
also popular with watersports
enthusiasts, while in August
Carlingford hosts a popular
Oyster Festival.

From the coast 3 km
(2 miles) northwest of
Carlingford, a dramatic cork-
screw road climbs through
Slieve Foye Forest Park to give
amazing panoramic views.

Carlingford Heritage Centre

⊛ ⌂ Old Holy Trinity,
Church Rd 🕙 10am-
12:30pm & 2-4:30pm
Mon-Fri 🅦 carlingford
heritagecentre.com

IRELAND'S HIGH CROSSES

High Crosses exist in Celtic parts of both Britain and
Ireland. Yet in their profusion and craftsmanship, Irish
High Crosses are exceptional. The distinctive ringed
cross has become a symbol of Irish Christianity and is
still imitated today. The beautiful High Crosses
associated with medieval monasteries were carved
between the 8th and 12th centuries. The early crosses
bore only geometric motifs, but in the 9th to 10th
centuries a new style emerged when sculpted scenes
from the Bible were introduced. Referred to as "sermons
in stone", these later versions may have been used to
educate the masses. In essence, though, the High Cross
was a status symbol for the monastery or a local patron.

---

⑨ Monasterboice

D3 ⌂ Co Louth 🚌 To
Drogheda ℹ Daily; 041 983
7070

Founded in the 5th century
by an obscure disciple of
St Patrick called St Buite, this
monastic settlement is one
of the most famous religious
sites in the country. The ruins
of the medieval monastery
are enclosed within a graveyard
in a secluded spot north of
Drogheda. The site includes a
roofless round tower and two
churches, but Monasterboice's
greatest treasures are its
10th-century High Crosses.

Muiredach's High Cross is
the finest of its kind in Ireland,
and its sculpted biblical
scenes are still remarkably
fresh. They depict the life of
Christ on the west face, while
the east face features mainly
Old Testament scenes. The
cross is named after an
inscription on the base that
reads "A prayer for Muiredach
by whom this cross was made",
which is perhaps a reference to
the abbot of Monasterboice.
The 6.5-m (21-ft) West Cross,
also known as the Tall Cross, is
one of the largest in Ireland.
The carving has not lasted as
well as on Muiredach's Cross,
but you can still make out

scenes from the Death of Christ. The North Cross features a crucifixion and a carved spiral pattern.

Dundalk

🅐D3 🅐Co Louth 🚂
🚌 *i* Market Square;
www.visitlouth.ie

Dundalk once marked the most northerly point of the Pale, the area controlled by the English during the Middle Ages *(p145)*. Now it is the last major town before the Northern Ireland border.

Dundalk is also a gateway to the magnificent countryside of the Cooley Peninsula. Housed in a superbly restored 18th-century distillery, the **County Museum** has three exhibition galleries displaying an imaginative history of the county, from the Stone Age to the present day.

County Museum
⊗ 🅐Jocelyn St
🕒10am–5pm Tue–Sat
🅧Public hols 📞42 939 2999

→

St Peter's Cathedral on West Street, one of two churches thus named in Drogheda

Drogheda

🅐D3 🅐Co Louth 🚂 🚌
i The Thosel, West St;
www.drogheda.ie

In the 12th century, this busy Norman port spanning both banks of the River Boyne was one of Ireland's most important towns. However, Drogheda never managed to regain this status following the trauma of a vicious attack by Oliver Cromwell in 1649, in which 2,000 citizens were killed. Even so, the town still has its original street plan and has a rich medieval heritage.

Little remains of Drogheda's medieval defences but St Lawrence Gate, a fine 13th-century four-floor barbican, has survived. Nearby, there are two churches called St Peter's. The one belonging to the Church of Ireland, built in 1753, is the more striking and has some splendid grave slabs. The Catholic church is home to the embalmed head of Oliver Plunkett, an archbishop martyred in 1681.

South of the river you can climb the steep steps to Millmount, a Norman motte topped by a Martello tower. It provides a good view and is the site of the **Drogheda Museum**, which contains interesting historical artifacts and documented stories, including guns used in the War of Independence and a recreated dairy room that demonstrates butter-making.

Drogheda Museum
⊗ ⊗ 🅐Millmount Square
🕒10am–5:30pm Mon–Sat,
2–5pm Sun & bank hols
🅧Week at Christmas
🆆droghedamuseum.ie

↑ Brightly painted cottages lining the streets of Trim village

12 Trim

🅰D3 🅰Co Meath 🚌
ℹ️Castle St; www.
discoverboynevalley.ie

Trim is one of the most pleasing Midlands market towns. A Norman stronghold on the River Boyne, it marked a boundary of the Pale *(p145)*, a history examined in a multimedia exhibition at the Trim Visitor Centre. It is also the starting point for a heritage trail, which takes in eight sites, including the town's two castles and two cathedrals.

The dramatic **Trim Castle** was founded in the 12th century by Hugh de Lacy, a Norman knight, and is one of the largest medieval castles in Europe. It makes a spectacular backdrop for films and was used in Mel Gibson's *Braveheart* in 1995.

Over the river is Talbot Castle, an Augustinian abbey converted to a manor house in the 15th century. Just north of here, St Patrick's Cathedral incorporates part of a medieval church with a 15th-century tower and sections of the original chancel. The trail leads to the Saints Peter and Paul Cathedral further east.

A lovely walk leads from the castle along the River Boyne to Newtown Abbey.

Trim Castle

⊛⊛ 🕐Mid-Mar-Sep: 10am-5pm daily; Feb-mid-Mar & Oct: 9:30am-4:30pm daily; Nov-Jan: 9am-4pm Sat & Sun
🔳heritageireland.ie

13 Hill of Tara

🅰D3 🅰Nr Killmessan Village, Co Meath 🚌To Navan 🕐Mid-May-mid-Sep: 10am-6pm daily (last adm: 1hr before closing)
🔳heritageireland.ie

A site of mythical importance, Tara has more than 30 visible monuments. It was once the political and spiritual centre of Celtic Ireland and the seat of the High Kings until the 11th century. The spread of Christianity, which eroded the importance of Tara, is marked by a statue of St Patrick. The symbolism of the site was not lost on Daniel O'Connell, who chose Tara for a rally in 1843, attended by over one million people.

Tours from the interpretative centre take in a Stone Age passage grave and Iron Age hill forts, which, to the untutored eye, look like mere hollows and grassy mounds. Clearest is the Royal Enclosure, an oval fort, in the centre of which is Cormac's House, containing the "stone of destiny" *(Liath Fáil)*, fertility symbol and inauguration stone of the High Kings. Most moving, however, is the poignant atmosphere and views over the Boyne Valley.

14 Slane

🅰D3 🅰Co Meath 🚌

An estate village just 30 minutes north of Dublin, Slane is centred on a crossroads containing a quartet of identical, limestone Georgian houses that face each other across the square. The Boyne flows through the town and skirts **Slane Castle**, which is set in glorious grounds laid out in the 18th century. Guided tours of the castle and on-site whiskey distillery are available.

Just to the north rises the Hill of Slane where, in AD 433, St Patrick is said to have lit a Paschal (Easter) fire as a challenge to the pagan High King of Tara. The event symbolized the triumph of Christianity over paganism.

Slane Castle

⊛⊛⊛⊛⊛ 🕐Jul-Sep: noon-5pm Mon-Fri, noon-6pm Sat & Sun 🔳slanecastle.ie

15   Old Mellifont Abbey

🅰D3 🅰Tullyallen, Cullen, Co Louth 🚇To Drogheda 🚌To Drogheda or Slane 🕐May-Sep: 10am-6pm daily (last adm: 45 mins before closing)
🔳mellifontabbey.ie

On the banks of the River Mattock, 10 km (6 miles) west of Drogheda, lies the first Cistercian monastery to have been built in Ireland. Mellifont was founded in 1142 on the orders of St Malachy, the

→

Ruins of Old Mellifont Abbey, on the banks of the River Mattock

Archbishop of Armagh. He was greatly influenced by St Bernard who, based at his monastery at Clairvaux in France, was behind the success of the Cistercian Order in Europe. The archbishop introduced not only Cistercian rigour to Mellifont, but also the formal style of monastic architecture that was used on the Continent. His new monastery became a model for other Cistercian centres built in Ireland, retaining its supremacy over them until 1539, when the abbey was eventually closed and turned into a fortified house.

William of Orange used Mellifont as his headquarters during the Battle of the Boyne in 1690. The abbey is now a ruin, but it is still possible to appreciate the scale and ground plan of the original complex. Little survives of the abbey church, but to the south of it, enclosed by what remains of the Romanesque cloister, is the most interesting building at Mellifont: a unique 13th-century octagonal lavabo where monks washed their hands in a fountain before eating. Four of the building's eight sides survive, each with a Romanesque arch. Standing to the east of the cloister is the 14th-century chapter house, with its impressive vaulted ceiling and medieval tiled floor.

 16

Mullingar

AC3 **A**Co Westmeath **A** **A**
iMarket Square; www. mullingar.ie

Westmeath's county town, Mullingar is a prosperous market town encircled by the Royal Canal, which links Dublin with the River Shannon.

Mullingar's main appeal is as a base to explore the surrounding area, but pubs such as Canton Casey's and Con's are a pleasant interlude.

The Dublin to Mullingar stretch of the Royal Canal features attractive towpaths for walkers, and fishing.

Just off the Kilbeggan road from Mullingar stands **Belvedere House**, a romantic Palladian villa overlooking Lough Ennel. The house, built in 1740 by Richard Cassels, is decorated with Rococo plasterwork and set in beautiful grounds. There are delightful woodland walks through exotic conifers, yew, lime and beech, and along the lakeshore.

Shortly after the house was built, the first Earl of

 INSIDER TIP
Castle Concerts

The sloping grounds at Slane Castle form a natural amphitheatre, meaning that it is often used as a unique concert venue. Acts who have previously performed here include Queen, David Bowie and U2.

Belvedere accused his wife of having an affair with his brother, and imprisoned her for 31 years in a nearby house. In 1760, the earl built a Gothic folly – the Jealous Wall – to block the view of his second brother's more opulent mansion across the way. The Jealous Wall still stands today, as does an octagonal gazebo and follies.

Charming terraces descend to the lake. Located on the other side of the house is a picturesque walled garden, which is enclosed by a splendid arboretum and lush green parkland.

Belvedere House
⊘ ☺ ⊚ **A**6.5 km (4 miles) S of Mullingar **O**Daily, check website for times
Wbelvedere-house.ie

⑰ Kilbeggan

🅐 C3 🏠 Co Westmeath 🚌

Situated between Mullingar and Tullamore, this pleasant village has a small harbour on the Grand Canal. However the main point of interest is **Kilbeggan Distillery Experience**. Founded in 1757, it claims to be the oldest licensed pot still distillery in the world to be still producing whiskey. Unable to compete with Scotch whisky manufacturers, the company went bankrupt in 1953, but the aroma hung in the warehouses for years and was known as "the angel's share". The distillery reopened as a museum in 1987, production started in 2007, and the results have been on sale since 2014. The building is authentic, a solid structure complete with waterwheel and steam engine. A tour traces the process of Irish whiskey-making, from the mash tuns to the vast fermentation vats and creation of wash (rough beer) to the distillation and maturation stages. At the tasting stage, workers would sample the whiskey in the can pit room. Visitors can still taste whiskeys in the bar.

Kilbeggan Distillery Experience

⊛⊛🍸⌂ 🏠 Lower Main St 🕐 Apr–Oct: 9am–6pm daily; Nov–Mar: 10am–4pm daily 🌐 kilbegganwhiskey.com

Athlone Castle beneath the towers of St Peter and St Paul, by the River Shannon ↑

⑱ Athlone

🅐 C3 🏠 Co Westmeath 🚆 🚌 ℹ Castle Street; 090 649 4630

The town owes its historical importance to its position by a natural ford on the River Shannon. Lying in the shadow of the 19th-century church of St Peter and St Paul, the impressive **Athlone Castle** is a 13th-century fortress. It was badly damaged in the Jacobite Wars. Across the river from the castle, boats depart for Clonmacnoise *(p261)* or Lough Ree.

The Lough Ree Trail starts 8 km (5 miles) northeast of Athlone, at Glassan, and is a popular cycling tour that runs around the shores and into County Longford.

Athlone Castle

⊛⊛ 🏠 Visitor centre, St Peter's Sq 🕐 Daily, check website for times 🔒 Mar–May & Sep–Oct: Mon; Nov–Feb: Mon & Tue 🌐 athlonecastle.ie

←

Oak whiskey barrels on view at the Kilbeggan Distillery Experience

⑲  Tullamore D.E.W Visitor Centre

🅐 C4 🏠 Bury Quay, Tullamore, Co Offaly - access from Dublin–Galway M6 & Dublin–Cork M7 roads 🕐 9:30am–6pm Mon–Sat, 11:30am–5pm Sun 🔒 25–26 Dec & 31 Dec–2 Jan 🌐 tullamoredew.com

The charming town of Tullamore and its most famous export, Tullamore Dew Whiskey, are intrinsically

linked. It makes sense, therefore, that the Tullamore Dew Heritage Centre should attempt to explore not only the history of the Tullamore Dew brand but also that of the town itself.

The refurbished centre is housed in the handsome Victorian Tullamore Dew distillery, which dates back to 1897. The distillery and the whiskey are both named after Daniel E Williams, the founder. Visitors can wander through the fascinating re-created working stations of the distillery, such as the malting, bottling, corking and cooperage areas, as well as the warehouse where the old oak barrels filled with whiskey were left to mature.

The history of Tullamore town itself starts 9,000 years ago with the formation of the bog. The centre explains raised bogs and the different uses of peat. The tour ends in the on-site bar with a complimentary glass of whiskey or Irish Mist Liqueur, both of which are on sale in the gift shop. Aside from the whiskey

bar, it's also worth staying for a meal in the excellent Bond Restaurant.

20

Emo Court

🅰 D4 🚗 13 km (8 miles) NE of Portlaoise, Co Laois 🚌 To Monasterevin or Portlaoise ⏰ Hours vary, check website 🌐 emocourt.ie

Emo Court, commissioned by the Earl of Portarlington in 1790, represents the only foray into domestic architecture by James Gandon, designer of

the Custom House in Dublin (p102). The grand Neo-Classical mansion, which can be explored by a guided tour only, has a splendid façade featuring a great green dome that tops the building and an imposing Ionic portico through which you enter. Inside are a magnificent gilded rotunda and fine stuccowork ceilings.

Emo Court became the property of the Office of Public Works in 1994. The grounds are adorned with fine statuary and include a path leading through the shrubberies to a tranquil lakeshore walk, which is ablaze with colour during early summer.

→

Aerial view of Emo Court and its beautifully manicured grounds

DRINK

The Thatch

One of south Offaly's oldest and best-loved pubs, the Thatch has open beams, antique fireplaces and - of course - a beautiful thatched roof.

C4 Military Rd, Crinkill, Birr thethatchcrinkill.com

→ The ruins of a 13th-century castle crowning the Rock of Dunamase

21

Birr

C4 Co Offaly Emmet Sq; 057 912 3936; Jun-Sep: Mon-Sat

Birr, a gentrified estate town, grew up in the shadow of the castle where the Earls of Rosse have resided for almost four centuries. It is famous for its authentic Georgian layout, with houses displaying original fanlights, door panelling and iron railings. Two particularly elegant streets are Oxmantown Mall, designed by the 2nd Earl of Rosse, and John's Mall.

Emmet Square may have sold its Georgian soul to commerce, but Dooly's Hotel is still a fine example of an old coaching inn. Foster's bar, in nearby Connaught Street, is one of many traditional shop-fronts to have been restored.

Birr Castle was founded in 1620 by the Parsons, later Earls of Rosse, and is still the family seat. They are most noted for a telescope named the Leviathan, built by the 3rd Earl in 1845. The 17-m (56-ft) wooden tube, supported by two walls, can be seen in the grounds. The Historic Science Centre traces the family's work.

The castle can be explored by pre-booked guided tours, although the real glory of Birr is its spectacular grounds. First landscaped in the 18th century, these are famous for their 9-m-(30-ft-) tall, 200-year-old box hedges and for the exotic trees and shrubs from foreign expeditions sponsored by the 6th Earl. The magnolias and maples are particularly striking.

Birr Castle

Rosse Row Garden: Mar-Oct: 9am-6pm daily; Nov-Feb: 9am-4:30pm daily 25-26 Dec, 1 Jan birrcastle.com

22

Slieve Bloom Mountains

C4 Co Offaly and Co Laois To Mountmellick slievebloom.ie

Journeying across the waist of Ireland, this low range of mountains rises unexpectedly from the bogs and plains of Offaly and Laois, providing a welcome change in the predominantly flat Midlands. The mountains are surprisingly wild, given their small compass. You can walk

Fast-flowing stream in the Slieve Bloom Mountains ↑

along the Slieve Bloom Way, a 77-km (48-mile) circular trail through an unspoiled area of open vistas, deep wooded glens and mountain streams. There are other marked paths too. Good starting points are Cadamstown, with an attractive old mill, and the pretty village of Kinnitty – both in the northern foothills.

Rock of Dunamase

🗺️D4 🚗5 km (3 miles) E of Portlaoise, Co Laois 🚌To Portlaoise

The Rock of Dunamase, which looms dramatically above the plains east of Portlaoise, has long been a military site. Originally crowned by an Iron Age ring fort, the 13th-century castle that succeeded it is now more prominent – though it was virtually destroyed by Cromwellian forces in 1651. You can reach the battered keep by climbing up banks and ditches, through two gateways and a fortified courtyard. The steep climb is rewarded with fine views from the Slieve Bloom Mountains to the Wicklow Hills.

Clonmacnoise

🗺️C4 🚗7 km (4 miles) N of Shannonbridge, Co Offaly 🚌🚆To Athlone, then minibus (090 647 4839/ 087 240 7706) 🚐From Athlone ⏱️Nov–mid-Mar: 10am–5:30pm daily (to 6pm mid-Mar–May, Sep & Oct; to 6:30pm Jun–Aug) 🚫25 & 26 Dec 🌐heritageireland.ie

This medieval monastery, standing in a remote spot by the River Shannon, was established by St Ciarán in AD 545–548. Clonmacnoise lay at a crossroads of medieval routes, linking all parts of Ireland. Known for its scholarship and piety, it thrived from the 7th to the 12th centuries, when many kings of Tara and of Connaught were buried here. Plundered by the Vikings and Anglo-Normans, it fell to the English in 1552. Today, a group of stone churches (temples), a cathedral, two round towers and three High Crosses remain.

Above the cathedral's 15th-century north doorway are carvings of saints Francis, Patrick and Dominic. Known as the Whispering Arch, the acoustics of this doorway are

↑ Replica of a High Cross at Clonmacnoise; originals are stored safely indoors

such that even a whisper is carried inside to a listener's ear pressed against the wall.

The visitor centre has a museum section which conains early grave slabs and the three remaining High Crosses, replicas of which now stand in their original locations (the originals are kept safely indoors, too precious to be exposed to the elements). The best-preserved, the Cross of the Scriptures, is decorated with biblical scenes, but the identity of most of the figures is uncertain.

NORTHERN IRELAND

The small country of Northern Ireland was written into being by the partition of Ireland in 1921, and is part of the United Kingdom. Its six counties (along with Donegal, Monaghan and Cavan) also make up Ulster, one of Ireland's four traditional provinces. Ulster has strong links to Irish Christianity; in AD 432 St Patrick landed at Saul in County Down and later founded a church in Armagh, which is still the country's spiritual capital.

The dominant political force in early Christian times was the Uí Néill clan. Their descendants, the O'Neills, put up fierce resistance to English conquest in the late 16th century, but were ultimately defeated and fled to Europe in 1607 in what became known as the "Flight of the Earls". Vacant estates were granted to individuals and companies, who planted them with English and Scottish Protestants. The arrival of new settlers meant that Irish Catholics were increasingly marginalized, thereby sowing the seeds of 400 years of conflict.

In the relative tranquillity of the 18th century, the Anglo-Irish nobility built stately homes, such as Mount Stewart House (p295) and Castle Coole (p290). Ulster also enjoyed prosperity in the 19th century through its linen, rope-making and ship-building industries, though outside the densely populated and industrialized city of Belfast, the region remained primarily agricultural.

In the late 20th century, Northern Ireland was a battleground for the sectarian violence of the Troubles. The signing of the Good Friday Agreement in 1998 paved the way for a new Northern Ireland Assembly, and hopes of peace.

NORTHERN IRELAND

1 Political murals, West Belfast.

2 Botanic Gardens.

3 Cathedral Quarter, full of pubs and restaurants.

4 Queen's University.

2 DAYS

A Weekend in Belfast

Day 1

Morning Allow a generous couple of hours to wander the Titanic Quarter and to explore the fascinating exhibits at the Titanic Belfast museum *(p274)*. The doomed ship was built in these docklands, and an award-winning museum now sits above its slipway. There are boat, bus and walking tours – led by a descendant of one of the crew members – to help you explore the area.

Afternoon At lunchtime, central Saint Anne's Square offers an abundance of tempting restaurants; try Coppi, a contemporary Italian in an industrial-chic setting that serves both small plates and heartier options. Spend the rest of the afternoon on a Black Cab Political Tour *(p273)*, visiting the murals of West Belfast and learning more about the city's rich but often troubled history.

Evening Head back to the city centre to sample as many of Cathedral Quarter's pubs *(p271)* as you have time for. Indulge in a spectacular dinner at the Muddlers Club, before rounding off the evening with a classy cocktail and live music in Bert's Jazz Bar.

Day 2

Morning Fuel up with breakfast at East Belfast's General Merchants café and continue along the Upper Newtownards Road to Stormont *(p273)*, seat of the Northern Ireland Assembly. Free tours of the parliament buildings are available, and the estate is a joy to walk. Head back to Ballyhackamore for lunch – the neighbourhood has been nicknamed "Ballysnackamore" thanks to the huge range of restaurants on offer.

Afternoon Head back across the city to explore University Quarter *(p272)*: start in the lush Botanic Gardens, and then wander the grounds of redbrick Queen's University, Northern Ireland's most prestigious (and photogenic) centre of learning. The Ulster Museum is next door, where a rich collection of art, local history, natural science and archaeology awaits.

Evening After a long day of walking, treat yourself to a leisurely dinner somewhere in the neighbourhood – The Barking Dog and Deanes at Queens are both local favourites. Then put your feet up fully with a movie screening in the QFT, the university's intimate independent cinema that does a strong line in art-house and classic films.

←

1 The Carrick-a-Rede Rope Bridge, Ballintoy

2 St George's Market, Belfast

3 Exhibits at the Tower Musuem, Derry

4 Dunluce Castle, Antrim

3 DAYS

Along the Northern Ireland Coast and Derry~Londonderry

Day 1

Morning Departing from Belfast city centre, pop into St George's Market to grab breakfast from one of the many local vendors, then head towards Ballycastle (*p285*). The drive takes a little over an hour, but *Game of Thrones* fans may want to stop for a photo op at the Dark Hedges (*p279*), an atmospheric tree-lined avenue that featured in the smash-hit TV series.

Afternoon Catch a ferry to Rathlin Island (*p285*) and spend a couple of hours roaming this craggy, beautiful spot. One of the best points to visit is the island's lighthouse, which offers stunning views of a thriving seabird colony.

Evening Ride the ferry back to the mainland and squeeze in a trip to walk across the vertiginous Carrick-a-Rede Rope Bridge (*p279*). Depending on how extreme the weather has been, you may be feeling in need of a little rest by now; check into the Bushmills Inn (*p284*), an excellent boutique hotel with a small cinema on site.

Day 2

Morning Make an early start to visit Northern Ireland's only UNESCO World Heritage Site, the Giant's Causeway (*p276*). The site's visitors' centre is interesting but limited, so avoid the official car park if you'd prefer to skip this and spend more time scrambling across the shining-black basalt stones. When you've worked up an appetite, seek out the nearby food truck Mini Maegden (29 Causeway Road), which serves gourmet grilled cheese during the summer season.

Afternoon Back in your car, drive west along the winding Causeway Coastal Route. The ruins of Dunluce Castle (*p278*), another *Game of Thrones* setting, make for an interesting stop-off. Arrive onto Portstewart Strand (*p284*) and spend the afternoon exploring the miles of golden sand. It's also a great surf and swimming spot, if you can brave the Atlantic temperatures.

Evening As the sun begins to set, stroll off the beach to dine at Harry's Shack (*p279*). It's a tiny, popular spot, so book ahead to end your day with ocean-fresh seafood.

Day 3

Morning Set off for Derry~Londonderry (*p280*), just under an hour's drive from Portstewart. It's Northern Ireland's second-largest city and the only complete walled city on the island, so walking the full loop is an excellent introduction for first-time visitors. Break for lunch at Pykes N Pommes (*p283*), which serves up tasty street food by the river.

Afternoon The Tower Museum (*p281*) is well worth a visit, with exhibits on the Spanish Armada as well as the area's more recent past. Afterwards, choose one of the many walking tours; take in some of the murals commemorating events in Derry during the Troubles (*p282*), or wander out to the city's iconic Peace Bridge.

Evening Enjoy a meal at Browns (*p283*), one of Derry's many excellent eateries, before setting course for Belfast again. If you have a hired car that can be returned in Derry, take the train back to the capital for a relaxing and scenic journey.

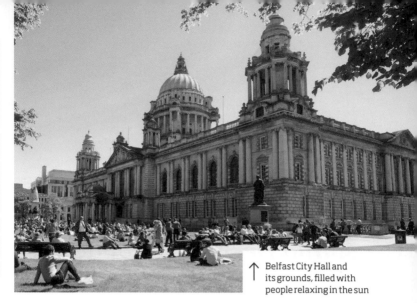

↑ Belfast City Hall and its grounds, filled with people relaxing in the sun

BELFAST

🅰 D2 🚗 Co Antrim ✈ Belfast City Airport, 6.5 km (4 miles) E; Belfast International, 29 km (18 miles) NW 🚉 Central Station; Great Victoria St Station 🚌 Europa Bus Centre; Laganside Bus Centre 🛈 9 Donegall Square North 🌐 visitbelfast.com

Northern Ireland's capital city experienced the full force of the Industrial Revolution; Belfast's ship-building, linen, rope-making and tobacco industries caused the population to rise to almost 400,000 by the end of World War I. The Troubles and decline of heavy industry somewhat hampered economic life, but the peace process and a burst of regeneration projects have revitalized this handsome, friendly city.

Did You Know?

The Grand Opera House became Northern Ireland's first listed building in 1974.

①

Belfast City Hall

🏛 Donegall Square 🕐 Grounds: 7am-7pm daily (May-Sep: to 9pm) 🌐 belfastcity.gov.uk

At the centre of Donegall Square stands the rectangular stone bulk of the 1906 City Hall. Here, along with an exhibition that recalls the city's history in six themed zones, there are free daily tours (check website).

Statues around the building include Queen Victoria outside the entrance and Sir Edward Harland – founder of the shipyard that built the *Titanic*. A memorial to those who died on the ship's 1912 maiden voyage stands close by.

②

Grand Opera House

🏛 Great Victoria St 🕐 Box office: 10am-5pm Mon-Sat; tours: check website 🌐 goh.co.uk

Designed by Frank Matcham, renowned theatre architect, this exuberant late-Victorian building opened its doors in 1895 and has been enter-taining Belfast's show-goers ever since. Bombings of the adjacent Europa Hotel ("Europe's most bombed hotel") at times disrupted business during the height of the Troubles, but the opera house, which under-went significant renovations in 2020, survives as a major venue for plays and theatre.

③

St Anne's Cathedral

🏛 Donegall St 🕐 9am-5pm Mon-Sat, 1-3pm Sun 🌐 belfastcathedral.org

Consecrated in 1904, this Anglican cathedral took over 100 years to be completed. The impressive interior includes elaborate mosaics – the one covering the baptistry ceiling contains over 150,000 pieces. Lord Carson (1854–1935), leader of the campaign against Home Rule, is buried in the south aisle. His is the only tomb in the cathedral.

---

④

Linen Hall Library

🏠 **17 Donegall Square North**
🕐 **9:30am–5:30pm Mon–Fri**
🌐 **linenhall.com**

Founded in 1788 as the Belfast Society for Promoting Knowledge, Belfast's oldest library has thousands of rare old books and is Ireland's last subscribing library. It is renowned for its Irish and Local Studies Collection, ranging from comprehensive holdings of printed books to the 250,000 items in the Northern Ireland Political Collection, the definitive archive of the recent Troubles. There is also a vast genealogical database, as well as regular exhibitions. Above the library door you will see the Red Hand of Ulster, emblem of the province. It is the subject of a gory legend about two Celtic heroes racing to see who would touch the land of Ulster first. In his determination to win, one cut off his own hand and threw it to shore.

⑤ (NT)

Crown Liquor Saloon

🏠 **Great Victoria St**
🕐 **Hours vary, check website** 🌐 **nationaltrust. gov.uk**

Even teetotallers should make a detour to this 1880s drinking palace. The Crown is Belfast's most famous pub; today it is a Grade A building and treasured landmark. The lovingly restored interior features stained glass, mosaics and cosy wooden snugs – the perfect place for a pint of the black stuff and some Strangford Lough mussels.

DRINK

Sample some of the city's best pubs along the picturesque cobbled streets of the Cathedral Quarter.

The Dirty Onion
🏠 **3 Hill Street**
🌐 **thedirtyonion.com**

Duke of York
🏠 **7-11 Commercial Ct**
🌐 **dukeofyork belfast.com**

The Thirsty Goat
🏠 **1 Hill Street**
🌐 **thethirstygoat.co.uk**

The Cloth Ear
🏠 **The Merchant Hotel, 16 Skipper Street**
🌐 **themerchant hotel.com**

The National
🏠 **62 High Street**
🌐 **thenational belfast.com**

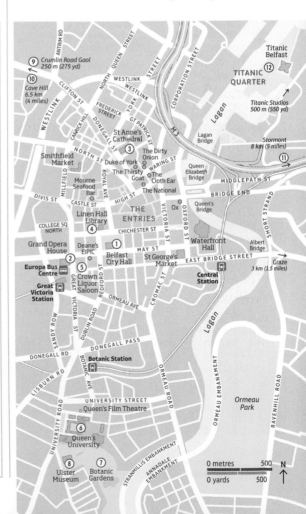

EAT

Belfast is packed with great restaurants; here are four favourites.

Deane's EIPIC
⌂ 28–40 Howard St
🌐 deaneseipic.com

£££

Graze
⌂ 402 Upper Newtownards Rd
🌐 grazerestaurantbelfast.com

£££

Mourne Seafood Bar
⌂ 34–36 Bank St
🌐 mourneseafood.com

£££

OX
⌂ 1 Oxford St
🌐 oxbelfast.com

£££

---

⑥ Ⓜ 🏛

Queen's University

⌂ University Rd 🌐 qub.ac.uk

Fifteen minutes from the city centre is Northern Ireland's most prestigious university. Queen's is part of the eminent Russell group, with famous alumni including David Trimble and Seamus Heaney. The main redbrick building, designed by Charles Lanyon in 1849, bears similarities to Magdalen College, Oxford. A towered gateway leads to a peaceful, colonnaded quadrangle.

---

⑦

Botanic Gardens

⌂ Botanic Ave 🕐 Hours vary, check website 🌐 belfastcity.gov.uk

Backing on to the university, these gardens provide a refuge from the bustle of campus. The 1839 Palm House is a superb example of curvilinear glass and cast-iron work, while visitors can look down from the Tropical Ravine, or Fernery, to a sunken glen of exotic plants.

---

⑧ 🖼 🏛

Ulster Museum

⌂ Botanic Gardens 🕐 10am–5pm Tue–Sun & Mon bank hols 🌐 nmni.com

Founded in 1929 as the Belfast Municipal Museum and Art Gallery, this excellent museum houses rich collections of art, local history, natural sciences and archaeology. The 6-m- (20-ft-) long Edmontosaurus dinosaur skeleton, the Egyptian mummy, Takabuti, and the stunning coiled Corrard torc are three of the most popular exhibits. The museum also has a number of engaging learning zones and a programme of temporary exhibitions and events.

↑ The ornate Lanyon Building, centrepiece of Queen's University

THE POLITICAL MURALS OF WEST BELFAST

During the Troubles (1968–98), popular art played a conspicuous role in proclaiming the loyalties of Belfast's two most intransigent communities, on the Protestant Shankill Road and the Catholic Falls Road. The gable walls of dozens of houses have been decorated with vivid murals expressing political and paramilitary affiliations. Similarly, kerbstones have been painted in the red, white and blue of the Union Jack or in Ireland's green, white and orange. Despite the successes of the current peace process, many are likely to remain. To view the murals, book a "Black Cab Tour" (028 9024 6609).

Crumlin Road Gaol

🏠 53–55 Crumlin Rd
🕐 11am–3:30pm (last adm) daily 🌐 www.crumlin roadgaol.com

Northern Ireland's only remaining Victorian-era prison, Crumlin Road Gaol

was in operation from 1845 to 1996. Today, the site is open for self-guided tours, with informative exhibits that relate to the gaol's colourful past touching upon escapes and executions, imprisoned suffragettes and De Valera's brief sojourn as an inmate in 1924. Most of the experience is indoors, but visitors are advised to wear warm, waterproof clothing as some outside locations – such as the underground tunnel that once connected the gaol to the Crumlin Road court-house – are included.

Cave Hill

🏠 Antrim Rd, 6.5 km (4 miles) N of city
🌐 belfastcastle.co.uk; belfastzoo.co.uk

One of the city's most visible landmarks, the whole of Belfast can be viewed from Cave Hill's 368-m- (1,207-ft-) high summit. The hill's craggy profile is said to have inspired the giant in Jonathan Swift's *Gulliver's Travels*, and it was next to MacArt's Fort (named after an Iron Age chieftain) that Wolfe Tone and the northern leaders of the United Irishmen met in 1795 to pledge themselves

to rebellion. The five artificial caves near the fort were carved out during the Neolithic period.

On the wooded eastern slopes of the hill stands Belfast Castle, built in 1870, while on the northeastern slopes is Belfast Zoo.

Stormont

🏠 Newtownards Rd, 8 km (5 miles) SE of city centre 🕐 9am–4pm Mon–Fri 🌐 parliament buildings.org

Built between 1928 and 1932, at a cost of £1,250,000, Stormont was designed to house the Northern Ireland Parliament. The huge Anglo-Palladian mass of Portland stone and Mourne granite stands at the end of a majestic avenue, 1.6 km (1 mile) long, bordered by parkland. A statue of Lord Carson stands near the front entrance.

Since the parliament was disbanded in 1972, the building has been used as government offices. The devolved Northern Ireland Assembly has sat here since the 1998 Agreement, although it has been suspended on several occasions, most recently for three years from January 2017 to January 2020.

The impressively designed Titanic Belfast museum ↑

⑫ 🍴 🖥 🏛

TITANIC QUARTER

🏠 Titanic House, Queen's Road, Belfast   🌐 Titanic Quarter: titanic-quarter.com;
Titanic Belfast: www.titanicbelfast.com; SS Nomadic: www.nomadicbelfast.com

Just a short walk from Belfast city centre, the Titanic Quarter is one of the largest waterfront regeneration projects in Europe. Centred around the former shipyard where the RMS *Titanic* was built and launched, it is home to Belfast's iconic yellow cranes, a sprawling film studio and Titanic Belfast, a world-class museum opened in 2012 to mark the fateful voyage's centenary.

TITANIC BELFAST

An eight-storey aluminium-clad building in the shape of a ship's prow, the Titanic Belfast is a impressive sight. Sitting above the original ship's slip-way, it is an expansive and eye-opening experience, with varied exhibits that guide visitors through both the construction of the *Titanic* and its recovery.

Attractions include a ride that shows how ships were built at the beginning of the 20th century, while exact replicas of the *Titanic*'s cabins and other parts of the ship allow visitors to imagine life as a passenger. Also, a moving account of the tragedy is presented, detailing the stories of those on board as well as the aftermath.

Beside the museum, the SS *Nomadic*, the world's last remaining White Star Ship, can also be visited .

STAY

Bullitt Hotel
This central hotel offers
"no frills" comfort -
including a rooftop bar.

🏠 40a Church Lane
🌐 bullitthotel.com

ⓔ ⓔ ⓔ

Titanic Hotel Belfast
A design hotel housed
in the former Harland &
Wolff headquarters.

🏠 8 Queens Rd 🌐 titanic
hotelbelfast.com

ⓔ ⓔ ⓔ

The Merchant Hotel
Luxurious interiors
beneath a period façade.

🏠 16 Skipper St
🌐 the merchant
hotel.com

ⓔ ⓔ ⓔ

TITANIC STUDIOS

The cornerstone of Belfast's growing Media Campus, Titanic Studios has a combined set area of over 9,800 sq m (106,000 sq ft) – making it one of the largest film studios in Europe. Attracting producers such as HBO and Universal, the set is best known for playing host to *Game of Thrones*. It has been the main studio and post-production facility for all eight seasons of the award-winning fantasy series, and the associated tours are extremely popular.

SAMSON AND GOLIATH

These twin yellow cranes dominate Belfast's skyline, and have come to be seen as symbols of the city. Named after two biblical figures renowned for their immense strength, the cranes tower over 90 m (300 ft) above the Harland & Wolff shipyard and can lift loads of up to 840 tonnes.

↑ Part of a *Game of Thrones* King's Landing set, constructed within Titanic Studios

2 (icons) NT

GIANT'S CAUSEWAY

🅐D1 🅐Co Antrim 🅘Visitor Centre: 44 Causeway Road, open daily 🆆nationaltrust.org.uk

Northern Ireland's north coast is home to some unique and unmissable landmarks, the most remarkable of which is the Giant's Causeway – the country's only UNESCO World Heritage Site.

The sheer strangeness of this place and the bizarre regularity of its basalt columns have made the Giant's Causeway the subject of numerous legends. Millions of years of geological activity can be seen in the eroded cliffs flanking the Causeway, including a band of reddish rock that is the inter-basaltic layer, formed during a long period of temperate climatic conditions. The site attracts many tourists, who are taken from the Visitor Centre down to the shore. Though usually busy, nothing can destroy the magic of this place, with its looming cliffs and shrieking gulls, and paths along the coast allow you to escape the crowds. Tickets need to be booked before 3pm the day before your visit.

THE LEGEND OF FINN MCCOOL

The most popular formation myth involves Finn McCool, a famous Irish giant. He laid the pathway to do battle with his great rival Benandonner, a Scottish giant. But Benandonner was bigger than Finn had expected, so he quickly tore up the Causeway - leaving just the ragged ends at either shore.

1. The unusual tapering rocks of the Giant's Causeway, shrouded in atmospheric sea mist at sunset.

2. The innovative glass-and-basalt design of the Visitor Centre is intended to mimic the Causeway itself.

3. Aird's Snout, a nose-shaped promontory, juts out from the 120 m (395 ft) basalt cliffs that soar above the Giant's Causeway.

↑ Walking along the hexagonal columns of the Giant's Causeway

Timeline

61 million years ago

In a series of massive volcanic eruptions, molten lava poured from narrow fissures in the ground, filling in the valleys and burning the vegetation that grew there.

60 million years ago

This layer of tholeiitic basalt lava cooled rapidly. In the process it shrank and cracked evenly into polygonal-shaped blocks, forming columnar jointing beneath the surface.

58 million years ago

New volcanic eruptions produced further lava flows. These had a slightly different chemical composition from earlier flows and, once cool, did not form such well-defined columns.

15,000 years ago

At the end of the Ice Age, when the land was still frozen, sea ice ground its way slowly past the high basalt cliffs, eroding the foreshore and helping to form the Giant's Causeway.

3 (NT)

CAUSEWAY COAST

 D1 Co Antrim nationaltrust.org

While the renown of the Giant's Causeway somewhat overshadows the rest of the North Antrim coast, there are plenty of other attractions to be found along this stretch. Head to the very tip of Northern Ireland to take in sandy bays, craggy headlands and dramatic ruins.

Dunluce Castle

87 Dunluce Road
9:30am–5pm daily
24–26 Dec, 1 Jan
discovernorthern
ireland.com

Approaching the Causeway from the west, visitors will pass the eerie ruins of Dunluce Castle, perched on a steep crag. The building dates from the 16th century and was the main fortress of the MacDonnell clan, chiefs of Antrim. Although the roof has gone, the rest of the castle is well preserved, with its twin towers, gateway and some cobbling intact. The iconic ruin can still be visited (with guided tours booked in advance), and the castle's

myths and quirky history – the castle kitchens fell into the sea during a storm in 1639 – make for a worthwhile trip.

Other fortresses along the Causeway Coast include Dunseverick Castle – a much earlier fortification than Dunluce, with only one massive wall remaining – and Kinbane Castle, a 16th-century ruin with spectacular views.

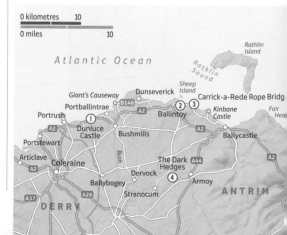

←

The ruins of Dunluce Castle, perched on Antrim's north coast

Ireland. First erected by salmon fishermen in 1755, the Carrick-a-Rede Rope Bridge hangs 30 m (100 ft) above the Atlantic Ocean and wobbles and twists as soon as you stand on it. Made of planks strung between wires, it provides access to tiny Carrick-a-Rede island across the 20-m (65-ft) chasm. There are strong handrails and safety nets, but it's definitely not for those with vertigo. A timed ticketing system ensures a regular flow of visitors to the island; once you make it across, take time to enjoy the isolation or a spot of bird-watching. The fisherman's cottage is open to the public on selected weekends throughout the year.

②

Ballintoy

📍 Ballintoy

Just past the attractive, sandy White Park Bay, a tight switchback road leads down to the picturesque harbour of Ballintoy, reminiscent – on a good day – of an Aegean fishing village. During some of Northern Ireland's less balmy weather, Ballintoy has been used as a *Game of Thrones* filming location, doubling as the inhospitable Iron Islands. Sheep Island, a rocky outcrop just offshore, is a cormorant colony, and boat trips run past it in the summer.

③

Carrick-a-Rede Rope Bridge

📍 119a Whitepark Road
🕐 Check website for times
🌐 nationaltrust.org

Just east of Ballintoy is one of the most unusual and hair-raising tourist attractions in

→

The Carrick-a-Rede Rope Bridge, stretching between two cliff faces

④

The Dark Hedges

📍 Bregagh Rd, Ballymoney
🌐 discovernorthern ireland.com

This extraordinary tree-lined avenue is also worth visiting on your way to or from the north coast. Planted in the 18th century to line the route to a Georgian mansion, the gnarled beeches have become an attraction in their own right. One of Northern Ireland's most-photographed natural phenomena, the spectacular stretch has also appeared as the King's Road on *Game of Thrones*. Its resultant popularity has led to non-essential traffic being banned from the road, but you can park nearby.

EAT

Harry's Shack
A tiny beach hut right on the strand offers diners idyllic views and fresh dishes served to perfection.

📍 116 Strand Rd, Portstewart
📞 028 7083 1783

£ £ £

Ramore Restaurants
A complex of six family-owned restaurants on Portrush's seafront. Arrive early to have a drink at the Gin Bar.

📍 1 Harbour Rd, Portrush
🌐 ramorerestaurant.com

£ £ £

4

DERRY~LONDONDERRY

🅰C1 🏠Co Londonderry ✈11 km (7 miles) E 🚉Waterside, Duke St (028 7134 2228) 🚌Foyle St (028 7126 2261)
ℹ44 Foyle St; www.visitderry.com

St Columba founded a monastery here in AD 546 and named the place Doire, later anglicized as Derry. The city acquired the prefix London in 1613 after it was selected as a major Plantation project, and its name has been a subject of fraught debate ever since, with the nationalist community using Derry, and the unionist community favouring Londonderry. Although the city suffered during the Troubles, heritage projects have been undertaken, resulting in it being named the 2013 UK City of Culture.

① Ⓜ 🏛
St Columb's Cathedral

🏠17 London St 🕐Mar-Sep: 9am-5pm Mon-Sat; Oct-Feb: 10am-2pm Mon-Sat
🅦stcolumbscathedral.org

Tucked away in the southwestern corner of the city, St Columb's was built between 1628 and 1633 in "Planters' Gothic" style, the first cathedral to be founded in the British Isles after the Reformation. The nave's wooden ceiling dates from 1862, and the corbels are carved with the heads of former bishops and deans. The interior was restored in the 19th century. A small museum in the Chapter House has relics from the siege of 1689, including the 17th-century locks and keys of the city. In the vestibule is a hollow mortar cannonball that was fired into the city by James II's army. It carried terms for capitulation, but the reply of the Protestants within the walls was a defiant "No surrender".

→
The Gothic façade of St Columb's Cathedral in the sunshine

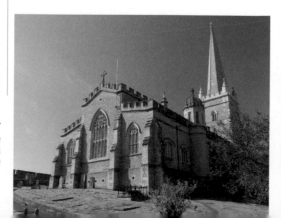

The Peace Bridge across the River Foyle in Derry, opened in 2011

② ⛴ Ⓜ

Tower Museum

🏛 Union Hall Place
🕐 10am–5:30pm daily
🌐 derrystrabane.com/towermuseum

Housed in O'Doherty Tower (a replica of the original 16th-century building on this site), this award-winning museum makes a great starting place for a visit to the city, tracing its history from Derry's foundation through to the Troubles using multimedia displays. The exhibits on local history include one on the mapping of the area during the reign of Elizabeth I, while upstairs there is an exhibition about

↑ A cannon on display in the Tower Museum

the 1588 Spanish Armada that includes artifacts from the *Trinidad Valencera*, wrecked in nearby Kinnagoe Bay. On the top level is the city centre's only open-air viewing facility, with stunning views across the river.

Did You Know?

Amelia Earhart landed the world's first transatlantic solo flight by a female pilot in Derry.

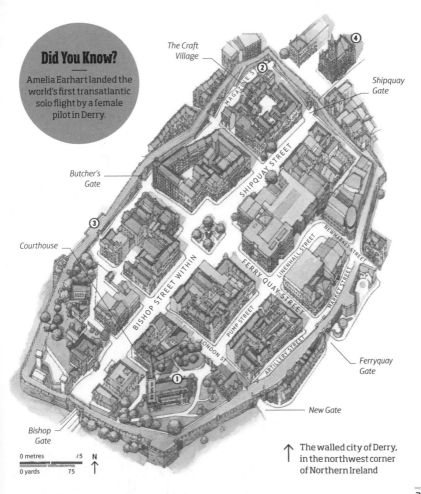

The Craft Village

Shipquay Gate

Butcher's Gate

③ Courthouse

Bishop Gate

0 metres 15
0 yards 75

N ↑

SHIPQUAY STREET
MAGAZINE ST
BISHOP STREET WITHIN
FERRY QUAY STREET
LINENHALL STREET
NEWMARKET STREET
MARKET STREET
PUMP STREET
LONDON ST
ARTILLERY STREET

Ferryquay Gate

New Gate

↑ The walled city of Derry, in the northwest corner of Northern Ireland

1972

The Troubles' Bloody Sunday sees 14 Catholics lose their lives during a peaceful protest.

→

The Guildhall and its striking clock tower, which was modelled on London's Big Ben

ART IN DERRY

Derry takes its art seriously. Contemporary spaces like Void and the Warehouse Gallery sit alongside the Bogside Murals, a series of large-scale murals depicting key events of the Troubles. It's a city that uses art to remember and reflect on the past, but, more importantly, it also looks to the future. A key symbol of this is the Derry Peace Bridge, which opened in 2011 and provides foot and cycle access across the River Foyle. It links the city walls and the Ebrington Centre, an arts and culture centre with a 14,000-capacity outdoor performance plaza and cinema.

The City Walls of Derry

🄰 Access from Magazine St

Derry is the only remaining completely walled city in Ireland and its fortifications are among the best preserved in Europe. The walls rise to a height of 8 m (26 ft) and in places are 9 m (30 ft) wide. Completed in 1618 to defend the new merchant city from Gaelic chieftains in Donegal, Derry's walls have famously never been breached. The biggest test came with the 1689 Siege of Derry. Part of the Williamite War between the Protestant William of Orange and the Catholic King James II, it lasted for 105 days and resulted in the deaths of over 7,000 people (out of a population of 20,000) from either starvation or disease.

→ A segment of Derry's historic city walls

The city gates were initially closed by a group of 13 apprentices, and the siege is commemorated every August with parades by the Apprentice Boys of Derry, a Protestant fraternal society founded in 1814.

Restoration work means that it is possible to walk right around the walls, which are approximately 1.5 km (0.9 miles) in circumference. Restored cannons are displayed along the walls, of which Roaring Meg is the most well known. Just outside the old fortifications, beyond Butcher's Gate, is the Bogside, a Catholic area with famous murals that depict more recent events in Northern Ireland's history.

④ Ⓜ️ 🗔

The Guildhall

🏠 Guildhall St 🕘 9am-7:30pm Mon-Fri, 10am-5:30pm Sat & Sun 🌐 derrystrabane.com/Guildhall

Between the walled city and the River Foyle, this Neo-Gothic building is one of Derry's most recognizable landmarks. It was built in 1890, but a fire in 1908 and then a bomb in 1972 led to major repairs. Stained-glass windows recount the history of Derry, including the Apprentice Boys shutting the city gates in December 1688. To the rear is Derry Quay, from where Irish emigrants sailed to America in the 18th and 19th centuries.

Must See

EAT

Brickwork
Laid-back, welcoming restaurant with a broadly Asian menu.

🏠 12-14 Castle St
🌐 brickworkderry.com

Cedar
Traditional Lebanese restaurant with a focus on sharing dishes.

🏠 32 Carlisle Rd
🌐 cedarlebanese.webs.com

Pyke 'N' Pommes
This local favourite serves great street food from a converted shipping container.

🏠 Strand Rd
🌐 pykenpommes.ie

The Sooty Olive
A modern Irish restaurant that became an instant hit when it opened in 2013. Their 3-course house menu for £24.95 is a steal.

🏠 162 Spencer Rd
☎ 021 7134 6040

Browns Bonds Hill
A Derry institution, the original Browns restaurant uses local ingredients in a creative menu.

🏠 1 Bonds Hill 🌐 brownsrestaurant.com

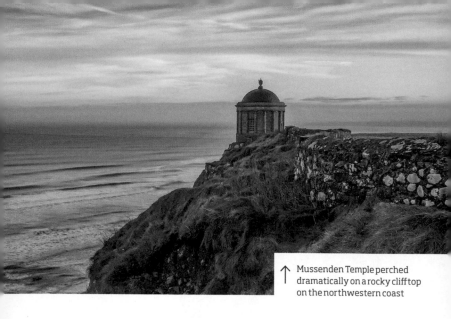

↑ Mussenden Temple perched dramatically on a rocky clifftop on the northwestern coast

EXPERIENCE MORE

5

Benone Strand

🅰 D1 🏠 Co Londonderry
ℹ Benone Tourist Complex, 53 Benone Ave, Limavady; 028 7775 0555

These wide, golden sands, also known as Magilligan Strand, sweep along the County Londonderry coastline. The magnificent beach has been granted EU Blue Flag status for its cleanliness. At the western extremity of the beach is Magilligan Point, where a Martello tower stands guard over the entrance to Lough Foyle.

6 (M) (NT)

Mussenden Temple

🅰 D1 🏠 Co Londonderry
🕐 Grounds: dawn-dusk daily (last adm: 30 mins before closing); Temple: Mar-Oct: 10am-5pm daily
🌐 nationaltrust.org.uk

An eye-catching sight along the County Londonderry coast is this small, domed rotunda

perched precariously on a headland outside the family resort of Castlerock. The temple was built in 1785 by Frederick Augustus Hervey, the eccentric Earl of Bristol and Protestant Bishop of Derry, as a memorial to his cousin Mrs Frideswide Mussenden. The design was based on the Temple of Vesta at Tivoli outside Rome.

The walls, made of basalt faced with sandstone, open

STAY

The Bushmills Inn

This charming coaching inn dates back to 1608, when the neighbouring distillery gained the world's first licence to distil whiskey. There's excellent dining here, too, and a lively bar.

🅰 D1 🏠 9 Dunluce Rd, Bushmills
🌐 bushmillsinn.com

💷💷💷

---

out at the four points of the compass to three windows and an entrance. Originally designed for use as a library, the structure is now maintained by the National Trust and is in excellent condition.

The bishop allowed the local priest to say Mass for his Roman Catholic tenants in the basement. The bishop's former residence, the nearby Downhill Demesne, was gutted by fire and is now little more than an impressive shell.

7

Portstewart

🅰 D1 🏠 Co Londonderry
🚉 To Coleraine or Portrush
🚌 ℹ Portrush; www. visitcausewaycoastand glens.com

A popular holiday destination for Victorian middle-class families, Portstewart is still a family favourite today. Its long, crescent-shaped seafront promenade is sheltered by rocky headlands. Just west of town, and accessible by road or by a cliffside walk, stretches

→
An idyllic stretch
of golden sands at
Portstewart Strand

Portstewart Strand, a long, sandy beach, protected by the National Trust.

On Ramore Head, just to the east, lies Portrush, a pleasant resort. The East Strand trails along sand dunes and runs parallel with the Royal Portrush Golf Club, which hosted the Open Championship in 2019.

Old Bushmills Distillery

D1 **Bushmills, Co Antrim** **From Giant's Causeway & Coleraine** **Hours vary, check website** **23 Dec–1 Jan** **bushmills.com**

The small town of Bushmills' main claim to fame is whiskey. The Old Bushmills plant prides itself on being the world's oldest distillery. Its Grant to Distil dates from 1608, but the spirit was probably made here at least 200 years before that.

Tours of the distillery end with a whiskey sampling in the 1608 Bar in the former malt kilns, which are home to a small museum with old distilling equipment on display.

Rathlin Island

D1 **Co Antrim** **Daily from Ballycastle (028 2076 9299)** **Boathouse Visitor Centre; www.rathlin community.org**

Narrow Rathlin Island is a short boat ride from Ballycastle – express services take only 25 minutes. The 150 or so residents make a living from fishing, farming and tourism. Facilities include a handful of guesthouses and hostels, a café and a pub. The fierce, salty Atlantic winds ensure that the landscape on Rathlin is virtually treeless. High white cliffs encircle much of the island, and at craggy Bull Point on the westerly tip, tens of thousands of seabirds make their home. At the opposite end of the island is Bruce's Cave, where, in 1306, Robert Bruce is said to have watched a spider climbing a thread. The spider's perseverance inspired the dejected Bruce to return and win back his kingdom.

Ballycastle

D1 **Co Antrim** **Portnagree House, 14 Bayview Rd; www. visitcausewaycoast andglens.com**

A resort town, Ballycastle is home to a pretty harbour and a sandy beach. Near the seafront is a memorial to Guglielmo Marconi, whose assistant sent the first wireless message across water from here to Rathlin Island in 1898. The town's Auld Lammas Fair in late August, held for nearly 400 years, is one of the oldest traditional fairs in Ireland.

On the outskirts of town, the ruined 15th-century Bonamargy Friary houses the remains of Sorley Boy MacDonnell, former chieftain of this part of Antrim. Sections of the church, gatehouse and cloisters are well preserved.

IRISH WHISKEY

Distillation was probably introduced to Ireland by monks from Asia over 1,000 years ago. Small-scale production became part of the Irish way of life, but in the 17th century the English introduced a licensing system and started to close stills. In the 19th century, post-Famine poverty and the Temperance movement lowered demand. The result was that Scotch whisky stole an export march on the Irish, but thanks to lower production costs, better marketing and a rise in popularity of Irish coffee, sales have increased.

11 Cushendall

D1 ▢ Co Antrim ▢
i 25 Mill St; Jun–Sep: 10am–5pm Tue–Sat; Oct–May: 10am–1pm Tue–Sat; www.visitcausewaycoast andglens.com

Three of the nine Glens of Antrim converge towards Cushendall, earning it the unofficial title of "Capital of the Glens". This attractive village has brightly painted houses and an edifice known as Curfew Tower, built in the early 19th century as a lock-up for thieves and idlers.

About 1.5 km (1 mile) north of the village stands Layde Old Church, which can be reached by a pretty walk along the cliffs. Founded by the Franciscans, it was a parish church from 1306 to 1790 and contains many monuments to the local chieftains, the MacDonnells.

Just over 3 km (2 miles) west of Cushendall, on the slopes of Tievebulliagh Mountain, lies Ossian's Grave, named after the legendary warrior-poet and son of the giant Finn McCool (p276). It is in fact a Neolithic court tomb: the area was a major centre of Stone Age tool-making and axeheads made of Tievebulliagh's hard porcellanite rock have been found at a wide range of sites all over the British Isles.

Other attractive villages further south along the coast road include Carnlough, with its sandy beach and a harbour, and Glenarm, which is set around a sunny bay overlooked by a castle.

12 Glenariff Forest Park

D1 ▢ Co Antrim ▢ Daily for car park ▢ discover northernireland.com

Nine rivers have carved deep valleys through the Antrim Mountains to the sea. Celebrated in song and verse, the Glens of Antrim used to be the wildest and most remote part of Ulster. This region was not "planted" with English and Scots settlers in the 17th century and was the last place in Northern Ireland where Gaelic was spoken.

Today the Antrim coast road brings all the glens within easy reach of any visitor. Glenariff Forest Park contains some of the most spectacular scenery. The main scenic path runs through thick woodland and wild-flower meadows and round the sheer sides of a gorge, past three waterfalls.

Did You Know?

The Mull of Kintyre, a Scottish headland, can be glimpsed from certain points in Glenariff Forest Park.

There are also optional trails to distant mountain viewpoints. William Makepeace Thackeray, the 19th-century English novelist, called the landscape "Switzerland in miniature".

ULSTER'S HISTORIC LINEN INDUSTRY

The rise in Ulster's importance as a linen producer was spurred on by the arrival from France of refugee Huguenot weavers at the end of the 17th century. Linen remained a flourishing industry for a further two centuries but, due mostly to expensive production processes, it is now made only in small quantities for the luxury goods market. Hundreds of abandoned mills dot Ulster's landscape.

13 Cookstown

D2 ▢ Co Tyrone ▢
i Burnavon Arts Centre, Burn Road; 028 8676 9949

Cookstown sticks in the memory for its grand central thoroughfare – 2 km (1 mile) long and perfectly straight. The road is about 40 m (130 ft) wide and, as you look to the north, it frames the bulky outline of Slieve Gallion, a prominent mountain in the Sperrin Mountains. A 17th-century Plantation town, Cookstown takes its name from its founder Alan Cook.

The countryside around the town is rich in Neolithic and

↑ Timber walkway running through a gorge, alongside a tumbling waterfall in Glenariff Forest Park

early Christian monuments. To the east, on a desolate stretch of Lough Neagh shoreline, the **Ardboe Old Cross** stands on the site of a 6th-century monastery. Although eroded, the 10th-century cross is one of the best examples of a High Cross *(p254)* in Ulster: its 22 sculpted panels depict Old Testament scenes on the east side and New Testament ones on the west. The **Wellbrook Beetling Mill**, west of Cookstown, is a relic of Ulster's old linen industry. "Beetling" was the process of hammering the cloth to give it a sheen. Set amid trees beside the Ballinderry River, the mill dates from 1768 and is a popular tourist attraction. The National Trust has restored the whitewashed two-storey building and its water wheel. Inside, working displays demonstrate just how loud "beetling" could be. From the mill, there are nice walks along the river banks.

Ardboe Old Cross
Off B73, 16 km (10 miles) E of Cookstown

Wellbrook Beetling Mill
Off A505, 6 km (4 miles) W of Cookstown, Co Tyrone Hours vary, check website nationaltrust.org.uk

← Snow-dusted stone circle monuments at the ancient Beaghmore site

14

Beaghmore Stone Circles

D2 Off A505, 14 km (9 miles) NW of Cookstown

On a stretch of open moorland in the foothills of the Sperrin Mountains lies a vast collection of stone monuments, dating from between 2000 and 1200 BC. Discovered during peat cutting in the 1940s, there are seven stone circles, several stone rows and a number of less prominent features (possibly collapsed field walls of an earlier period). Their exact purpose remains unknown, though in some cases their alignment correlates with movements of the sun, moon and stars. Three of the rows, for example, are clearly aligned with the point where the sun rises at the summer solstice.

The individual circle stones are small – none is more than 1.2 m (4 ft) in height – but their sheer numbers make them a truly impressive sight.

The Wilson Ancestral Home

A C2 **□** 28 Spout Road, Dergalt, Strabane, Co Tyrone **C** 028 7138 4444 **○** Jul–Aug: 2–5pm Tue–Sun (guided tour only). Visits at other times by arrangement

Located 3 km (2 miles) southeast of Strabane, off the road to Plumbridge, is the ancestral home of US President Thomas Woodrow Wilson (1856–1924). Woodrow's grandfather, Judge James Wilson, left this house for America in 1807 at the age of 20. Today, a visit to the thatched whitewashed house on the slopes of the Sperrin Mountains provides valuable insight into the history behind Ulster-American ties. The carefully conserved rooms contain original furniture, including kitchen utensils and farm implements. A portrait of James Wilson hangs over the traditional hearth fire.

Just outside the village of Newtownstewart, 12 km (7 miles) south of Strabane, is the medieval ruin of Harry Avery's Castle. This 14th-century Gaelic stone castle consisted of two storeys fronted by vast rectangular twin towers. These towers are still visible today.

Ulster-American Folk Park

A C2 **A** Co Tyrone **🚌** From Omagh **○** 10am–5pm Thu–Sun & bank hols **W** nmni.com

One of the best open-air museums of its kind, the Folk Park grew up around the restored boyhood home

← Forge demonstration at the Ulster-American Folk Park

of Judge Thomas Mellon (founder of the Pittsburgh banking dynasty). Its permanent exhibition, "Emigrants", examines why two million people left Ulster for America during the 18th and 19th centuries. It shows what became of them, with stories of both fortune and failure, including the grim lives of indentured servants and the

↑ A mock-up of a Pennsylvania log farmhouse at the Ulster-American Folk Park

15,000 Irish vagrants and convicts sent to North America in the mid-18th century.

The park has more than 30 historic buildings, some of them original, some replicas. There are settler homesteads (including that of John Joseph Hughes, the first Catholic Archbishop of New York), churches, a schoolhouse and a forge, some with craft displays, all with costumed interpretive guides. There's also an Ulster streetscape, a reconstructed emigrant ship and a Pennsylvania farmstead. The farmhouse is based on one built by Thomas Mellon and his father in the early years of their life in America.

The Centre for Migration Studies assists descendants of emigrants to trace their family roots. Popular American festivals such as Independence Day and Halloween are celebrated here and there is an Appalachian-Bluegrass music festival in early September.

Belleek Pottery

The border village of Belleek would attract few visitors other than anglers were it not for the world-famous Belleek Pottery, founded in 1857. The company's pearly coloured china is known as Parian ware. Developed in the 19th century, it was supposed to resemble the famous Parian marble of Ancient Greece.

Belleek is now best known for its ornamental pieces of fragile latticework decorated with pastel-coloured flowers. These are especially popular in the USA. Guided tours take in the stages of production, including mould-making and casting, while there are numerous elaborate showpieces on display in the small museum.

LOWER LOUGH ERNE

Fermanagh lakelands around Lower Lough Erne boast a rich combination of natural and historic sights. From pre-Christian times, settlers sought the security offered by the lough's forests and inlets. Monasteries were founded on many islands in the Middle Ages, and a ring of castles recall the Plantation era. The lake is a haven for waterbirds and the trout-rich waters attract anglers. In summer, ferries serve several islands.

↑ Potter making a Parian china ornament at the Belleek factory

The oval-shaped saloon at Castle Coole, with original Regency furnishings ↑

 18

Enniskillen

C2 **Co Fermanagh**
Enniskillen Castle, Wellington Road; www. fermanaghlakelands.com

Busy Enniskillen occupies an island between Upper and Lower Lough Erne. The town gained fame for the wrong reason in 1987, when 11 people died in an IRA bomb attack, but it deserves a visit for its setting and sights.

At the west end of town stands **Enniskillen Castle**, dating from the 15th century. It houses Fermanagh County Museum, which has exhibits on local history and crafts, and the Inniskilling Regimental Museum, which explores the military history of the region. Its most stunning feature, however, is the Watergate, a twin-turreted tower, best admired from the far bank of the river. Further west, Portora Royal School, founded in 1618, counts among its old boys the playwrights Oscar Wilde and Samuel Beckett. Tickets must be purchased in advance.

Just outside town, set in a park overlooking a lake, is

Castle Coole, one of the finest Neo-Classical homes in Ireland surrounded by beautiful parkland. It has a long Portland stone façade, with a central portico and small pavilions at each end. The first Earl of Belmore commissioned the house in the 1790s. The original design was by Irish architect Richard Johnston, but the earl then commissioned a second set of drawings by the English architect James Wyatt. The prodigal earl died in 1802, deep in debt, and it was left to his son to complete in the 1820s.

Family portraits from the 18th century line the walls of the dining room. In the lavish State Bedroom there is a bed made for King George IV on the occasion of his visit to Ireland in 1821, though in the end he never came here to sleep in it.

> ## Did You Know?
>
> The Marble Arch Caves featured in *Game of Thrones* as Beric Dondarrion's hideout.

One of the finest rooms is the oval saloon (or ballroom) at the back of the house. The furnishings may not be to everyone's taste, but the spacious oak-floored room produces an effect of unostentatious luxury.

Enniskillen Castle

⊗⊗⊗⊗ 🕘 9:30am–5pm Mon–Fri & bank hols, 11am–5pm Sat (Jun–Sep: 11am–5pm Sun) 🕘 24 Dec–1 Jan ⊠ enniskillencastle.co.uk

Castle Coole

⊗⊗⊗⊗ⓃⓉ ⊠ Off A4, 2.5 km (1.5 miles) SE of Enniskillen 🕘 Hours vary, check website ⊠ nationaltrust.org.uk

---

19

Marble Arch Caves Global Geopark

C2 **Marlbank Scenic Loop, Florencecourt, Co Fermanagh** 🕘 Mid-Mar–Jun & Sep: 10am–4pm daily; Jul–Aug: 9am–6pm daily; Oct: 10:30am–3pm daily ⊠ marblearchcaves geopark.com

The Marble Arch Caves are cut by three streams that flow

down the slopes of Cuilcagh Mountain, unite underground and emerge as the Cladagh River. Tours lasting 60 minutes guide visitors past stalagmites, calcite cascades and other limestone formations. The 9-m (30-ft) "Marble Arch" itself stands outside the cave system in the glen where the river gushes out from below ground. The caves are very popular, so book ahead, wear sensible clothing and ring to check the weather conditions before setting out. Visitors should arrive 30 minutes in advance of their tour's start time.

 20

Devenish Island

🅰 C2 📍 Co Fermanagh 🚢 Devenish Ferry (028 6862 1892) from Trory Point, 5 km (3 miles) N of Enniskillen; Mid-Jun–Sep: daily 🔲 discovernorthern ireland.com

St Molaise III founded a monastery on this tiny wind-swept island in the 6th century. Though raided by Vikings in the 9th century and burned in 1157, it remained an important religious centre up to the early 17th century.

Several fine buildings have survived, including Teampall Mor near the jetty. Built in 1225, this church displays the transition between Romanesque and Gothic styles. On the highest ground stands St Mary's Priory, an Augustinian church that was erected in the 15th century. An intricately carved stone cross close by dates from the same period.

The most spectacular sight, however, is the 12th-century round tower, which stands some 25 m (82 ft) tall. From the high windows the monks could spot approaching strangers. It is perfectly preserved, and the five floors can be reached by internal ladders. Supporting the roof is an elaborate cornice with a human face carved above each of the four windows; this is a unique feature in an Irish round tower. A small museum covers both the history and architecture of the island, and contains a collection of antiquities discovered at the site.

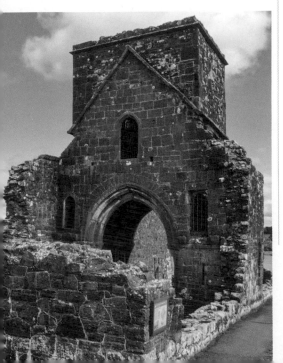

←
St Mary's Priory, located on Devenish Island in Lower Lough Erne

EAT

Café Merlot
Fine dining in a fabulously converted pub cellar, with vaulted ceilings and a well-priced wine list.

🅰 C2 📍 6 Church St, Enniskillen 🔲 cafemerlot.co.uk

€€€

 **21**

Florence Court

🅰 C2 📍 Co Fermanagh ⏰ Hours vary: check website 🔲 nationaltrust. org.uk

This three-storey Palladian mansion was built for the Cole family in the mid-18th century. The arcades and pavilions, which are of a later date than the main house, were added around 1770 by William Cole, first Earl of Enniskillen. The house features flamboyant Rococo plasterwork said to be by the Dublin stuccodore Robert West. Sadly, not much of what you see today is original as most of the central block was seriously damaged by fire in 1955. Much of the furniture was lost, but the plasterwork was painstakingly recreated from photographs.

The mansion's grounds are spectacular, and occupy a natural mountain-ringed amphitheatre. There are many enjoyable walks around the house. One woodland trail leads to the Florence Court yew tree, whose descendants are to be found all over Ireland. Closer to the house is a walled garden.

DRINK

The Craic'd Pot

This artisan espresso café is one of the best spots to get a caffeine fix in Armagh. Sample delicious pastries here too.

 D2 25 English Street, Armagh
 028 3778 9657

㉒
Lough Neagh

 D2 Co Armagh, Co Tyrone, Co Londonderry, Co Antrim

Legend has it that the giant Finn McCool *(p276)* created Lough Neagh by picking up a piece of turf and hurling it into the Irish Sea, forming the Isle of Man in the process. At 400 sq km (153 sq miles), the lake is the largest in the British Isles.

Bordered by sedgy marshland, it has few roads along its shore. The best recreational areas lie in the south: Oxford Island has walking trails, bird lookouts and the informative **Lough Neagh Discovery Centre**. In the southwest corner, a narrow-gauge railway runs through the bogs of **Peatlands Park**. The lake is famous for its eels.

Lough Neagh Discovery Centre

  Oxford Island Exit 10 off M1 Daily 24-26 Dec oxfordisland.com

Peatlands Park

 Exit 13 off M1 028 3885 1102 Apr–mid-Sep: 1–7pm daily; mid-Sep–Mar: noon–4pm Sat & Sun

㉓
Armagh

 D2 Co Armagh
 40 Upper English St; www.visitarmagh.com

One of Ireland's oldest cities, Armagh dates back to the age of St Patrick *(p296)* and the advent of Christianity. The streets in the city centre follow the ditches that once ringed the church, founded by the saint in AD 455. Two cathedrals, both called St Patrick's, sit on opposing hills. The huge Roman Catholic one is a twin-spired Neo-Gothic building covered in mosaic. The older Anglican Cathedral dates back to medieval times.

Armagh's gorgeous mall is surrounded by Georgian buildings. One of these houses the small **Armagh County Museum**, which has a good exhibition on local history. Off the mall, St Patrick's Trian is a heritage centre telling the story of the city. It also has a "Land of Lilliput" fantasy centre for children, based on *Gulliver's Travels* by Jonathan Swift. The **Armagh Planetarium**, up on College Hill, has interactive displays and shows on the solar system, although it is currently closed for renovations.

4,000 miles

Distance travelled by Lough Neagh's eels to breed in the Sargasso Sea.

To the west of Armagh stands Navan Fort, a large earthwork on the summit of a hill. In legend, Navan was Emain Macha, ceremonial and spiritual capital of ancient Ulster, associated with tales of the warrior Cúchulainn. The site may have been in use as much as 4,000 years ago, but seems to have been most active around 100 BC when a huge timber building, 40 m (130 ft) across, was erected over a giant cairn. The whole thing was then burned and the remains covered with soil. Archaeological evidence indicates that this was not an act of war, but a solemn ritual performed by the inhabitants of Emain Macha themselves. Below, the grass-roofed **Navan Centre** interprets the site.

Armagh County Museum

⊗ ☐ The Mall East 📞 028 3752 3070 ☐ Mon-Fri ☒ Some public hols

Armagh Planetarium

⊗ ☺ ☐ College Hill ☐ Grounds: Mon-Fri; Planetarium: closed for renovations ⓦ armagh.space

←

Hide for bird-watchers at Oxford Island on the shore of Lough Neagh

Navan Centre

 ☐ On A28 4 km (2.5 miles) W of Armagh 📞 028 3752 9644 ☐ Apr-Sep: 10am-5:30pm daily; Oct-Mar: 10am-4pm daily

---

24
Dungannon

☐ D2 ☐ Co Tyrone ⛟ ⓘ Ranfurly House, 26 Market Sq; www.flavour oftyrone.com

Dungannon's hilly location made an ideal site for the seat of government of the O'Neill dynasty from the 14th century until Plantation, when their castle was razed. The town's Royal School is one of the oldest in Northern Ireland, chartered in 1608 by James I. Opened in 1614, it moved to its present site in 1789.

Once a major linen centre, this market town was also known for its glass-making, as it was the base of the famous Tyrone crystal factory. The factory closed in 2010.

The Linen Green shopping centre in nearby Moygashel offers factory outlet shopping.

25
Seamus Heaney HomePlace

☐ D2 ☐ 45 Main St, Bellaghy, Co Londonderry ☐ 10am-5pm Mon-Sat, 1-5pm Sun ☒ 24-26 Dec & 1 Jan ⓦ seamusheaney home.com

The passing of Seamus Heaney in 2013 left a void in the Irish cultural landscape. The country's most beloved poet, he was also the most important, with a sensitive and lyrical voice that transcended the political divide. In the tiny

↑ Sculpture of the lauded poet Seamus Heaney, exhibited at HomePlace

village of Bellaghy, HomePlace is an interactive arts centre that celebrates Heaney's life and work, and contributes to his legacy. The modern building is filled with personal artifacts, photos, and recordings from friends, cultural figures and the poet himself. There is also a performance space (the Helicon), a library, a café, a shop and a community centre.

26
Larne

☐ E1 ☐ Co Antrim ☐ ⛟ ⓘ The Book Nook, 96b Main St; 028 2826 2450

Industrial Larne is the arrival point for ferries from Scotland. The town is not the finest introduction to Ulster scenery, but it lies on the threshold of the stunning Antrim coastline.

The sheltered waters of Larne Lough have been a landing point since Mesolithic times – flint flakes found here provide some of the earliest evidence of human presence on the island – nearly 9,000 years ago. Since then, Norsemen used the lough as a base in the 10th century, Edward Bruce landed his Scottish troops in the area in 1315, and in 1914 the Ulster Volunteer Force (UVF) landed a huge cache of German arms here during its campaign against Home Rule.

Ulster Folk and Transport Museum

🅰E2 🏠Cultra, near Holywood, Co Down 🚉 🚌 🕒Mar-Sep: 10am-5pm Tue-Sun & bank hols; Oct-Feb: 10am-4pm Tue-Fri, 11am-4pm Sat & Sun 🚫Mon 🌐nmni.com

This museum shows the life and traditions of people in Northern Ireland by demonstrating traditional industries, crafts and farming methods.

The A2 road splits the folk museum from the transport section. This is dominated by a hangar that houses the Irish Railway Collection. The smaller Transport Gallery exhibits machinery made in Ulster, including a saloon carriage from the tram service that ran from Portrush to Giant's Causeway (p276). Of particular note is a test model of the unsuccessful DeLorean car, made in Northern Ireland in the early 1980s with a huge government subsidy. There's also an exhibit on another ill-fated construction – the *Titanic*.

28

Carrickfergus

🅰E2 🏠Co Antrim 🚉 🚌 ℹCarrickfergus Castle; 028 9335 8222; Apr-Sep: 9am-4:30pm daily, Oct-Mar: 10am-4pm daily

This seaside town grew up around the massive castle begun in 1180 by John de Courcy to guard the entrance to Belfast Lough. De Courcy was the leader of the Anglo-Norman force that invaded Ulster following Strongbow's conquest of Leinster.

Carrickfergus Castle was shaped to fit the crag on which it stands overlooking the harbour. The finest and best-preserved Norman castle in Ireland, it even has its original portcullis. Many changes have been made since the 12th century, including wide

1760

Carrickfergus was captured by the French in this year, during the Seven Years' War.

EAT

The Bay Tree
Bistro famed for its cinnamon scones and Friday dinner menu.

🅰E2 🏠118 High St, Holywood 🌐bay treeholywood.co.uk.

ⓍⓍⓍ

Noble
Snug restaurant with a local, seasonal menu, prepared to perfection.

🅰E2 🏠27 Church Rd, Holywood 🚫Mon & Tue 🌐nobleholywood.com

ⓍⓍⓍ

Hara
A stylish restaurant, run by a husband-and-wife duo, serving creative dishes.

🅰D2 🏠16 Lisburn St, Hillsborough 🌐hara hillsborough.co.uk

ⓍⓍⓍ

↑ Old steam locomotive at the Ulster Folk and Transport Museum

ramparts to accommodate the castle's cannons. Life-size model soldiers are posed along the ramparts. The castle has changed hands several times over the years. Under Edward Bruce, the Scots took it in 1315, holding it for three years. James II's army was in control of the castle from 1688 until General Schomberg took it for William III in 1690. William himself stayed here before the Battle of the Boyne (p251) in 1690.

De Courcy also founded the pretty St Nicholas's Church. Inside are rare stained-glass work and a "leper window", through which the afflicted received the sacraments. Other attractions include the **Andrew Jackson Centre**, the ancestral home of the seventh president of the USA, and Flame Gasworks, a unique museum based on a Victorian coal gasworks.

Carrickfergus Castle
〄 〄 〄 **C** 028 9335 1273
O 9:30am–5pm daily **Q** 24–26 Dec, 1 Jan

Andrew Jackson Centre
〄 〄 **A** 2 Boneybefore
C 028 9335 8522 **O** 11am–3pm Wed–Sun (other times by appt)

29 〄 〄 〄 〄 〄 **NT**
Mount Stewart
A E2 **A** Portaferry Rd, Newtonards, Co Down
〄 From Belfast **O** House: Mar–Oct: 11am–5pm daily; Nov–Feb: 11am–3pm Sat & Sun; gardens: all year
W nationaltrust.org

This grand 19th-century house has a splendid interior, but the magnificent gardens are the main attraction. These were planted only in the 1920s, but the exotic plants and trees have thrived in the area's sub-tropical microclimate. Owned by the National Trust, Mount Stewart used to belong to the Londonderry family, the most famous of whom was Lord Castlereagh, British Foreign Secretary from 1812 until his death in 1822. The house has benefited from a restoration project by the National Trust.

30
Ards Peninsula
A E2 **A** Co Down 〄
〄 To Bangor **i** Regent St, Newtownards; www.visit ardsandnorthdown.com

The peninsula begins east of Belfast at Bangor. This resort town has a modern marina and well-known yacht clubs. A little way south is Donaghadee, from where boats sail to the Copeland Islands, inhabited only by seabirds since the last human residents left in the 1940s. The **Ballycopeland Windmill** (1784) is Northern Ireland's only working wind-mill and stands on the top of a hill a little further south.

Just across the peninsula is Newtownards, with shady Scrabo Country Park on a hill above the town. In the park stands the **Scrabo Tower**, built

→

Scrabo Tower, a prominent landmark of the Ards Peninsula

in 1857 as a memorial to the third Marquess of Londonderry.

Past the grounds of Mount Stewart House is the hamlet of Greyabbey, with its antique shops and Cistercian abbey ruins, founded in 1193.

On the tip of the peninsula, Portaferry overlooks the Strangford Narrows. Here the aquarium, **Exploris**, displays the diversity of life in the Irish Sea and Strangford Lough.

Ballycopeland Windmill
〄 **A** On B172, 2 km (1 mile) W of Millisle **C** 028 9082 3207
O Jul–mid-Sep: 10am–5pm Fri–Sun

Scrabo Tower
A Near Newtownards **C** 028 9082 3027 **O** Tower: Apr–Jun & Sep: daily (pm); Jul & Aug: daily; Oct: Sun (pm)

Exploris
〄 〄 〄 **A** Castle Street, Portaferry **O** 10am–5pm daily
Q 24–26 Dec **W** explorisni.com

Hillsborough

D2 **Co Down**
**The Square; www.
discovernorthern
ireland.com**

Dotted with craft shops and
restaurants, this Georgian town,
less than 16 km (10 miles)
from Belfast, is dominated by
Hillsborough Castle. It is the
official Northern Ireland residence of Queen Elizabeth II as
well as a popular venue for
visiting dignitaries. Guided
tours cover state rooms.

Located across the square
is **Hillsborough Fort,** which
was originally an artillery fort
before it was remodelled in the
18th century for feasts held by
the descendants of Arthur Hill,
founder of the town.

Hillsborough Castle

Apr-Sep: 10am-5pm
Thu-Sun; Oct-Mar: 10am-
4pm Thu-Sun 24-26 Dec
hrp.org.uk

Hillsborough Fort

Access from town square
or car park at Forest Park
028 9054 3030 Mon

Downpatrick

E2 **Co Down**
**St Patrick Centre, Market
St; www.visitstrangford
lough.co.uk**

Were it not for its strong links
with St Patrick, Downpatrick
would attract few visitors.
The Anglican Down Cathedral,
high on the Hill of Down, dates
from the early 19th century –
previous incarnations have
been razed. In the churchyard
is a well-worn 10th-century
cross and the reputed burial
place of St Patrick, marked by
a 20th-century granite slab
with the inscription "Patric".

Housed in the 18th-century
Old County Gaol, **Down County
Museum** has both refurbished
cells and exhibits relating to

St Patrick. One of the most
exciting exhibits is the remarkably intact, 10th-century
Downpatrick High Cross.

There are several sights
linked to St Patrick on the outskirts of Downpatrick. Struell
Wells, believed to be a former
pagan place of worship that
the saint blessed, has a ruined
church and 17th-century bath-
houses. Further out and to the
north at Saul, near where St
Patrick landed and began his
Irish mission in AD 432, is a
small memorial church. The
nearby hill of Slieve Patrick is
an important place of pilgrimage and has a granite figure
of the saint at its summit.

Not far from the banks of the
River Quoile is the Cistercian
Inch Abbey, founded by John
de Courcy in about 1180. Its
attractive marshland setting
is more memorable than its
remains, but it's worth a visit.

Down County Museum

English St, The
Mall 10am-4:30pm Mon-
Sat, 1:30-5pm Sun down
countymuseum.com

Inch Abbey

5 km (3 miles) NW of
Downpatrick 028 9181
1491 Daily

→

A beautiful sunrise over
the lakes and peaks of the
Mourne Mountains

Mourne Mountains

D2 **Co Down** **To
Newry** **To Newcastle**
**10-14 Central Promenade,
Newcastle; www.visit
mournemountains.co.uk**

These mountains occupy
just a small corner of County
Down, with no more than a
dozen peaks surpassing 600 m
(2,000 ft), and yet they attract
thousands of visitors each year.
Only one road of any size

LIFE OF ST PATRICK

Little hard information is
known about St Patrick,
the patron saint of Ireland,
but he was probably not
the first missionary to
visit the country. Most
stories tell that Patrick
was kidnapped from
Britain by pirates and
brought to Ireland to tend
sheep. From here he esca-
ped to France to study
Christianity. In AD 432, he
sailed back to Ireland and
converted the local chieftain in Saul, County Down.
He then travelled the
island convincing many
other Celtic tribes of the
truth of the new religion.

crosses the Mournes, making this ideal territory for walkers. A popular but tough trail runs from Newcastle up to the peak of Slieve Donard: at 850 m (2,790 ft), this is the highest mountain in the range. Part of the route follows the Mourne Wall, which was erected in 1904–22 to enclose the catchment area of the two reservoirs in the Silent Valley.

Over 20 short hikes are to be enjoyed in the area, ranging from easy strolls around Rostrevor Forest to rather more arduous treks up Slieve Muck and other Mourne peaks. Tourist information centres will have details.

Some 35 km (22 miles) north of Newcastle, the Legananny Dolmen is one of the finest and most photographed ancient sites in the country.

 34

Lecale Peninsula

🅰 E2 🏠 Co Down 🚌 To Ardglass 🚹 Downpatrick; www.discovernorthern ireland.com

A good way to get to this part of County Down is to take a car ferry from Portaferry on the Ards Peninsula to Strangford. Just outside this tiny port is **Castle Ward**, the estate of

Lord and Lady Bangor, who famously disagreed about everything – including the design of their 18th-century mansion. His choice, Palladian, can be seen at the front, while her favourite Gothic style influences the garden façade. Likewise, interiors are a mix of Classical and Gothic fantasy. Around the grounds are trails, gardens, and a farmyard with a working corn mill. Today the house is also famed for its role in *Game of Thrones*, where it doubles as the Stark stronghold, Winterfell.

About 4 km (2 miles) south of Strangford, the A2 passes 15th-century Kilclief Castle, one of the oldest tower houses in Ireland. The road continues to Ardglass, now a small fishing village but once Ulster's busiest harbour. A cluster of castles was erected between the 14th and 16th centuries to protect the port, of which six remain. St John's Point, 6 km (3.5 miles) southwest of Ardglass, offers a sweeping panorama over Dundrum Bay.

Castle Ward

🅰 On A25, 2.5 km (1.5 miles) W of Strangford 🕐 House: mid-Mar–Oct: noon–5pm daily; grounds: Apr–Sep: 10am–8pm daily; Oct–Mar: 10am–4pm daily 🌐 national trust.org.uk

 35

Castlewellan Forest Park

🅰 D2 🏠 Main St, Castlewellan, Co Down 📞 028 4377 8664 🕐 10am–sunset daily

The outstanding feature of Castlewellan Forest Park, in the foothills of the Mourne Mountains, is its magnificent arboretum. This has grown far beyond the original walled garden, begun in 1740, and now comprises hothouses, dwarf conifer beds and a rhododendron wood. Also of note is the Peace Maze, one of the world's largest permanent hedge mazes, which represents the path to a peaceful future for Northern Ireland. Elsewhere in the park are a 19th-century castle (now a conference centre), a lake and pleasant woodlands, at their most colourful in autumn.

> **Did You Know?**
>
> Scenery in the Mourne Mountains inspired Belfast-born C S Lewis's magical land of Narnia.

A DRIVING TOUR
THE MOURNE COAST

Length 85 km (53 miles) **Stopping-off points** Newcastle; Dundrum; Annalong; Kilkeel; Rostrevor **Terrain** Winding coastal roads

Driving up and down the dipping roads of the Mournes is one of the highlights of a trip to Northern Ireland. Along the coast, the Mourne Coastal Route drive skirts between the foothills and the Irish Sea, providing lovely views and linking a variety of fishing villages and historic castles. Heading inland, you pass through an emptier landscape of moorland, purple with heather. The Silent Valley, with a visitors' centre and well-marked paths, is one of the areas that have been developed especially for visitors.

NORTHERN IRELAND

The Mourne Coast

Locator Map
For more detail see p264

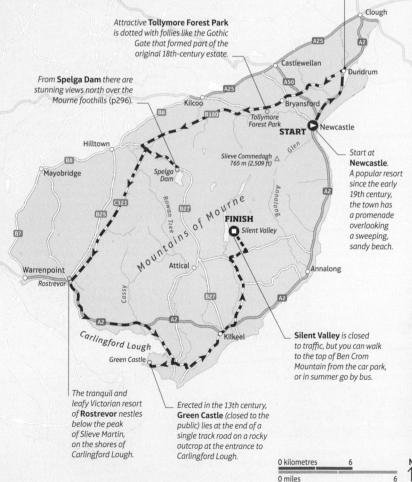

*The little town of **Dundrum** is overlooked by the ruins of a Norman castle (p297).*

Attractive **Tollymore Forest Park** is dotted with follies like the Gothic Gate that formed part of the original 18th-century estate.

*From **Spelga Dam** there are stunning views north over the Mourne foothills (p296).*

Clough

Castlewellan

Dundrum

Kilcoo

Bryansford

Tollymore Forest Park

START · Newcastle

Hilltown

Slieve Commedagh 765 m (2,509 ft)

*Start at **Newcastle**. A popular resort since the early 19th century, the town has a promenade overlooking a sweeping, sandy beach.*

Mayobridge

Spelga Dam

FINISH
Silent Valley

Mountains of Mourne

Attical

Annalong

Warrenpoint

Rostrevor

Kilkeel

Carlingford Lough

Green Castle

*The tranquil and leafy Victorian resort of **Rostrevor** nestles below the peak of Slieve Martin, on the shores of Carlingford Lough.*

*Erected in the 13th century, **Green Castle** (closed to the public) lies at the end of a single track road on a rocky outcrop at the entrance to Carlingford Lough.*

Silent Valley *is closed to traffic, but you can walk to the top of Ben Crom Mountain from the car park, or in summer go by bus.*

0 kilometres   6
0 miles   6

N

Mossy banks of
the Shimna River in
Tollymore Forest Park ↑

NEED TO KNOW

Healy Pass on the Beara Peninsula

BEFORE
YOU GO

Things change, so plan ahead to make the most of your trip. Be prepared for all eventualities by considering the following points before you travel.

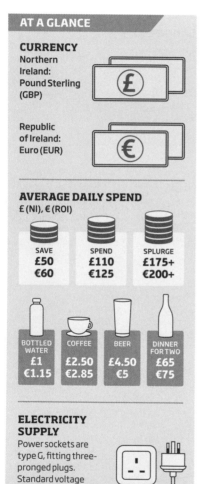

AT A GLANCE

CURRENCY
Northern Ireland:
Pound Sterling (GBP)

Republic of Ireland:
Euro (EUR)

AVERAGE DAILY SPEND
£ (NI), € (ROI)

SAVE	SPEND	SPLURGE
£50	£110	£175+
€60	€125	€200+

BOTTLED WATER	COFFEE	BEER	DINNER FOR TWO
£1	£2.50	£4.50	£65
€1.15	€2.85	€5	€75

ELECTRICITY SUPPLY
Power sockets are type G, fitting three-pronged plugs. Standard voltage is 230 volts.

Passports and Visas

For entry requirements, including visas, consult your nearest Irish or British embassy or the **INIS** or **UK Government** websites.
INIS
🅦 inis.gov.ie
UK Government
🅦 gov.uk

Government Advice

Now more than ever, it is important to consult both your and the Irish or UK government's advice before travelling. The **UK Foreign and Commonwealth Office**, the **US Department of State**, the **Australian Department of Foreign Affairs and Trade** and the **Ireland Department of Foreign Affairs** offer the latest information on security, health and local regulations.
Australian Department of Foreign Affairs and Trade
🅦 smartraveller.gov.au
Ireland Department of Foreign Affairs
🅦 dfa.ie
UK Foreign and Commonwealth Office
🅦 gov.uk/foreign-travel-advice
US Department of State
🅦 travel.state.gov

Customs Information

You can find information on the laws relating to goods and currency taken in or out of the Republic of Ireland on the **Tourism Ireland** website and those relating to Northern Ireland on the UK Government website *(above)*.
Tourism Ireland
🅦 ireland.com

Insurance

We recommend that you take out a comprehensive insurance policy covering theft, loss of belongings, medical care, cancellations and delays, and read the small print carefully.

EU citizens are eligible for free emergency medical care in the Republic of Ireland provided they have a valid **EHIC** (European Health Insurance Card). Check the **NHS** website for the latest details regarding emergency national health services in Northern Ireland.

EHIC
W ec.europa.eu
NHS
W nhs.uk

Vaccinations

No inoculations are needed for Ireland.

Booking Accommodation

Ireland offers a variety of accommodation, including luxury five-star hotels, family-run B&Bs and budget hostels. Lodgings fill up and prices are often inflated in the summer months (from June to September), so it's worth booking in advance to secure the best deal.

A comprehensive list of accommodation to suit any budget can be found on Tourism Ireland, Ireland's official tourist website (p302).

Money

Most shops and restaurants accept major credit and debit cards, while prepaid currency cards and American Express are accepted in some. Contactless payments are accepted by all major retailers, although not on public transport.

Tipping is optional. If you are pleased with the service in a restaurant it is customary to leave a tip of 10 per cent of the total bill. Porters and housekeeping appreciate €1 or £1 per bag. It is sufficient to round up taxi fares to the nearest euro or pound.

Travellers with Specific Requirements

Most of Ireland's main sights, public buildings and public transport have wheelchair access. Amenities in more rural parts of the country may be more limited, so it is worth calling ahead to check that your needs will be met. **Accessible Ireland** in the Republic of Ireland gives information on accommodation, transport and attractions for those with mobility, visual or hearing impairment, while **Disability Action** in Northern Ireland offers an advice service.

Accessible Ireland
W accessibleireland.com
Disability Action
W disabilityaction.org

Language

The Republic of Ireland is officially bilingual. Almost all road signs have place names in both English and Irish. English is the spoken language everywhere apart from a few parts of the far west, called Gaeltachts, but from time to time you may find signs written only in Irish.

Opening Hours

> **COVID-19** The pandemic continues to affect Ireland. Some sights and hospitality venues are operating on reduced or temporary opening hours, and require visitors to make advance bookings for a specific date and time. Always check ahead before visiting.

Mondays Some museums and tourist attractions are closed for the day.
Sundays Most shops and businesses are open for limited hours or closed for the day.
Public holidays Schools, post offices and banks close; shops and attractions close early or all day.

PUBLIC HOLIDAYS	
1 Jan	New Year's Day
17 Mar	St Patrick's Day
Mar/Apr	Good Friday (NI)
Mar/Apr	Easter Monday
First Mon May	Early May Bank Holiday
Last Mon May	Bank Holiday (NI)
First Mon Jun	Bank Holiday (ROI)
12 Jul	Battle of the Boyne (NI)
First Mon Aug	Bank Holiday (ROI)
Last Mon Aug	Bank Holiday (NI)
Last Mon Oct	Bank Holiday (ROI)
25 Dec	Christmas Day
26 Dec	Boxing Day (St Stephen's Day in ROI)

GETTING
AROUND

Whether you are visiting for a short city break or rural country retreat, discover how best to reach your destination and travel like a pro.

AT A GLANCE

PUBLIC TRANSPORT COSTS

DUBLIN

€3.30

Single bus journey

BELFAST

£4.20

All-day unlimited bus travel

BUS ÉIREANN OPEN ROAD PASS

€60

3 days unlimited country-wide travel

SPEED LIMIT (ROI)

MOTORWAY

120 kmph (75 mph)

NATIONAL ROADS

100 kmph (62 mph)

REGIONAL ROADS

80 kmph (50 mph)

URBAN AREAS

50 kmph (30 mph)

Arriving by Air

Ireland's four main airports – Dublin, Shannon, Cork and Belfast International – are well served by regular bus and rail services. The Republic's smaller airports depend mainly on local taxi services for transport to surrounding areas.

Dublin Airport is served by over 700 buses and coaches daily, including direct services between the airport, the city's main rail and bus stations and the city centre every 15 to 20 minutes. At Cork Airport, the Bus Éireann airport shuttle service runs every 30 minutes on weekdays and hourly at weekends. At Shannon Airport, Bus Éireann runs a regular service into Limerick. In addition, several buses a day go to the town of Ennis, about 20 km (12 miles) away.

All airports in the Republic have both long- and short-stay parking facilities.

In Northern Ireland, the Airport Express 300 shuttles passengers from Belfast International to the Europa Bus Centre every 20 minutes.

The table opposite lists popular transport options to and from Ireland's airports.

Public Transport

Ireland's main transport authorities, **Transport for Ireland** in the Republic of Ireland and **Translink** in Northern Ireland, provide information on safety and hygiene measures, timetables, ticket information, transport maps and more on their websites.

Translink
w translink.co.uk
Transport for Ireland
w transportforireland.ie

Train Travel

Regional Train Travel

The Republic of Ireland's rail network is run by **Irish Rail** (Iarnród Éireann). Note that no trains service Donegal. The service provided by **Northern Ireland Railways** is more limited, but fares are cheaper. The journey from Dublin to Belfast takes around two hours, with prices from £30 return.

GETTING TO AND FROM THE AIRPORT

Airport	Transport to City	Journey Time	Price
Dublin Airport	Bus (Airlink)	30–60 mins	€7
	Taxi	30 mins	€20-25
Cork	Bus (Éireann)	30 mins	€8
	Taxi	30 mins	€20-25
Shannon	Bus (Éireann) to Limerick	30–45 mins	€8
	Taxi to Limerick	25 mins	€35-40
Belfast International	Bus (Airport Express 300)	40 mins	£8
	Taxi	30 mins	£35-40
Belfast City Airport	Bus (Airport Express 600)	20 mins	£2.50
	Taxi	15 mins	£10

Irish Rail
W irishrail.ie
Northern Ireland Railways
W translink.co.uk/Services

Local Train Services

DART (Dublin Area Rapid Transit) electric rail serves 30 stations between Malahide and Greystones, with several stops in Dublin city centre. An all-day ticket allows unlimited travel on all DART trains for €12.15. Multi-day rail and bus tickets are also available. For ticket combinations and pricing, consult the DART website.

Dublin's light rail service, **Luas**, provides an easy way to reach suburban areas. The Luas lines connect with DART rail at Connolly Station.

In Belfast, train services are operated by Northern Ireland Railways. All trains leave from Central Station, which is not in fact in the centre, but has regular links to Great Victoria Street Station in the heart of the city. Tickets can be purchased online or at stations.
DART
W irishrail.ie
Luas
W luas.ie

Bus Travel

Long-Distance Bus Travel

The Republic of Ireland's national bus company, **Bus Éireann**, operates a country-wide network of buses. Journeys cost about half the price of the equivalent train trip, cheaper still if you book in advance or opt for a same-day return. Timetables and fares are listed online. Private bus companies serve many rural areas, covering routes not serviced by Bus Éireann. In Dublin, the main bus station is Busáras.

Ulsterbus/Translink operates throughout Northern Ireland and provides express links between major towns. Timetables and tickets are available online and at major bus stations. Belfast has two main bus stations – the Europa Bus Centre and Laganside Bus Station.
Bus Éireann
W buseireann.ie
Ulsterbus/Translink
W translink.co.uk

Local Bus Services

A number of local bus services operate in the Republic and Northern Ireland.

Dublin Bus runs the bus services in Dublin and the Greater Dublin area. In the rest of the Republic the bus services are mainly operated by Bus Éireann.

Ulsterbus/Translink operates Belfast's local service, called **Metro**.

Visitors to Dublin, Limerick , Galway, Cork and Waterford can purchase a **Leap Card** which offers discounts on public transport services.
Dublin Bus
W dublinbus.ie
Leap Card
W leapcard.ie
Metro
W translink.co.uk

Taxis

Apart from in Dublin, where they are plentiful, cruising taxis are a rarity. The best places to find taxis are at train or bus stations, hotels and taxi ranks – your hotel or B&B will also be able to provide details. Taxis are identified by an illuminated sign on the roof displaying the driver's licence number. Four- or eight-seater taxis are available and prices are usually based on metered mileage; if not, it is always best to confirm the fare to your destination before travelling. A taxi fare estimator and a tool to check whether your driver is properly licensed are available on the Transport for Ireland website (p304).

Taxis in Northern Ireland are reasonably priced; journeys within the centre of Belfast will usually cost no more than £10 by mini-cab or black cab. In most large towns in Northern Ireland you will find a taxi rank where you can wait for a cab. A taxi plating scheme is in place, with large plates at the front and rear of the vehicle to identify official taxis.

Lynk and **Fonacab** are taxi services in Dublin and Belfast, respectively, that can be booked online or by phone.

Lynk
W lynk.ie
Fonacab
W fonacab.com

Driving in Ireland

Driving is perhaps the best way to take in all that Ireland has to offer. Drivers must carry their passport and insurance documentation if driving their own vehicle. Driving licences issued by any of the EU member states are valid throughout the European Union.

If visiting from outside the EU, you may need to apply for an International Driving Permit. Check with your local automobile association.

Roads are well surfaced and are generally in good condition. Many sections have been upgraded to motorways, and there has been extensive construction of two-lane carriageways across the country, including in remote areas such as County Donegal. For roadside assistance, contact the **AA** or **AA Ireland**.

AA
W theaa.com
AA Ireland
W theaa.ie

Car Rental

All the international car rental firms operate in the Republic and are also well represented in Northern Ireland. Rental – particularly in the Republic – is quite expensive and the best rates are often obtained by booking in advance.

Car rental usually includes unlimited mileage plus passenger indemnity insurance and coverage for third party, fire and theft, but not damage to the vehicle. If you plan to cross the border in either direction, however briefly, you must tell the rental company, as there may be a small insurance premium.

To rent a car, you must be over 21 years of age and have a full driver's licence held for two years without violation.

Parking

Due to increased congestion, the majority of towns have paid on- and off-street parking. Dublin, Belfast and a few other cities have either parking meters or designated car parks.

Parking on the street is allowed, though a single yellow line along the edge of the road means there are some restrictions (there should be a sign nearby showing the permitted parking times). Double yellow lines indicate that no parking is allowed at any time.

Disc parking operates in most large towns and cities in the Republic and in the north. Discs can be purchased from fuel stations, roadside machines, tourist offices and many shops.

In Northern Ireland, almost all towns and villages have Control Zones, which are indicated by large yellow or pink signs. For security reasons, unattended parking in a Control Zone is not permitted at any time of the day.

Rules of the Road

Northern Ireland uses the same Highway Code as Great Britain. The Republic of Ireland's Highway Code is very similar.

Road signs in the Republic are in English and Irish, and distances are shown in kilometres, as opposed to miles in the north. Speed limits in the Republic differ slightly from those in Northern Ireland; be sure to follow signage when crossing the border.

On both sides of the border, drive on the left. When approaching a roundabout, give way to traffic from the right, unless otherwise indicated. All vehicles must give way to emergency service vehicles. Motorists must always overtake on the outside or right-hand lane.

It is compulsory for the driver and all passengers to wear seat belts at all times. Third-party insurance is obligatory. Motorcyclists and their passengers must wear helmets. Children up to 135 cm (53 in) in height or aged 12 or under must travel with the correct child restraint for their weight and size.

Mobile phones may not be used while driving, with the exception of a "handsfree" system. Random breath-testing is common in both the Republic and Northern Ireland, especially during public holidays. The drink-drive limit (p309) is strictly enforced.

Plotting the main driving routes according to journey time, this map is a handy reference for travelling between Ireland's main towns and cities by car. The times given reflect the fastest and most direct routes available. Tolls may apply.

Belfast to Donegal	2.5 hrs
Belfast to Derry	1.75 hrs
Cork to Killarney	1.5 hrs
Dublin to Belfast	2 hrs
Dublin to Galway	2.5 hrs
Dublin to Kilkenny	2 hrs
Dublin to Limerick	2.75 hrs
Dublin to Waterford	2.5 hrs
Galway to Sligo	2 hrs
Limerick to Cork	1.5 hrs

Derry~
Londonderry
Donegal
Belfast
Sligo
Galway
Dublin
Limerick
Kilkenny
Waterford
Killarney
Cork

••• Major road connections

Cycle Hire

Ireland's quiet country roads make touring by bicycle a real joy. The unreliable weather, however, can be something of a hindrance.

Bike rental companies rent bikes to tourists and are usually open at least six or seven days a week. It is often possible to rent a bike in one town and drop it off at another for a small charge. You can also take bikes on buses and trains, usually for a small surcharge. Bike share schemes operate in main cities, including Dublin, Cork, Galway, Limerick and Belfast.

Be aware that the legal drink-drive limit (p309) also applies to cyclists.

Boats and Ferries

Travelling by ferry is a popular way of getting to Ireland, especially for groups or families intending to tour the country by car. Nine ports in Great Britain and two in France provide ferry crossings to Ireland's six main ports, all of which have adequate bus and train connections, as well as taxi ranks. Most ferries offer drive-on/drive-off facilities for vehicles. **Brittany Ferries**, **Irish Ferries**, **P&O Ferries** and **Stena Line** run regular domestic ferries and international

services to Ireland from the UK and France. Many ferry companies offer a rail-and-sail service, through which it is possible to travel from any train station within the UK to any specified destination in Ireland on a combined ticket. These tickets are bookable online, by telephone or in person at port offices.

There are also a great number of shorter crossings within Ireland itself. Prices and availability can vary widely depending on the time of year. It is always best to book well in advance.
Brittany Ferries
W brittany-ferries.co.uk
Irish Ferries
W irishferries.com
P&O Ferries
W poferries.com
Stena Line
W stenaline.co.uk

Walking

An extensive network of footpaths covers the entire country. Most of Ireland's main cities, including Dublin and Belfast, are compact enough to explore on foot, and walking is the most agreeable way to admire the architecture and soak up the local atmosphere.

PRACTICAL
INFORMATION

A little local know-how goes a long way in Ireland. Here you can find all the essential advice and information you will need during your stay.

AT A GLANCE

EMERGENCY NUMBERS

NORTHERN IRELAND	REPUBLIC OF IRELAND
999	**112**

TIME ZONE
GMT
British and Irish Summer Time (BST and IST) runs from the last Sunday in March to the last Sunday in October.

TAP WATER
Unless stated otherwise, tap water in Ireland is safe to drink.

WEBSITES AND APPS

Wild Atlantic Way App
An app for anyone planning to travel Ireland's rugged west coast.
www.discoverireland.ie
Fáilte Ireland's website covering things to see and do throughout Ireland.
www.discovernorthernireland.com
The official tourism website for Northern Ireland.

Personal Security

Ireland is generally a very safe travel destination. In Northern Ireland during July, visitors may find themselves caught up in slow-moving traffic behind an Orange march. Tensions between local communities can be higher at this time, but the affected areas are easily avoided. If you see a sign while driving that indicates you are approaching a checkpoint, slow down and use dipped headlights.

ITAS, the Irish Tourist Assistance Service, provides confidential support to visitors who have been victims of crime or have experienced other traumatic events while visiting Ireland.

Pickpocketing can be a problem in the larger towns. If you have anything stolen, report the crime as soon as possible to the nearest police station. Get a copy of the crime report in order to claim on your insurance. Contact your embassy if you have your passport stolen, or in the event of a serious crime or accident.

As a rule, the Irish are accepting of all people regardless of their race, gender or sexuality. Northern Ireland recognized the right to legally change your gender in 2005, followed by the Republic in 2015, while same-sex marriage was legalized in 2015 in the Republic and in 2020 in Northern Ireland. The main cities have vibrant LGBT+ scenes. However, smaller towns and rural areas can be more conservative in their views, as are some individuals, particularly if they are of a strong faith. **Outhouse** in Dublin, the **Rainbow Project** in Belfast and the **LGBT Ireland Helpline** offer support services for the LGBT+ community.

ITAS
🅦 itas.ie
LGBT Ireland Helpline
🅦 lgbt.ie
Outhouse
🅦 outhouse.ie
Rainbow Project
🅦 rainbow-project.org

Health

Ireland has a very good healthcare system. Emergency medical care for EU citizens is free

of charge for all those that have an EHIC card *(p303)*. Be sure to present the card as soon as possible. You may have to pay for treatment and reclaim the money later. For non-emergencies and non-EU visitors, payment of medical expenses is the patient's responsibility. It is therefore important to arrange comprehensive medical insurance before travelling. Check the NHS website *(p303)* for emergency healthcare services in Northern Ireland.

Advice and medical supplies for minor ailments are available at pharmacies.

In a medical emergency that does not require an ambulance, visit a general practitioner (GP) or the out-patients, accident and emergency or casualty department of the nearest public hospital. In the Republic, you may need to pay a fee if you are not referred to the hospital by a GP.

Smoking, Alcohol and Drugs

A smoking ban is enforced inside all public places, including bars, cafés, restaurants and hotels. The possession of illegal drugs is prohibited and could result in a prison sentence.

The legal limit for drivers in the Republic is 50 mg of alcohol per 100 ml of blood and in Northern Ireland it is 80 mg of alcohol per 100 ml of blood. This is roughly equivalent to a small glass of wine or a pint of regular-strength lager.

ID

There is no requirement for visitors to carry ID, but due to occasional checks you may be asked to show your passport. If you don't have it with you, you may be asked to present the original document within 12 hours.

Local Customs

Although Northern Ireland is on the whole a safe travel destination, visitors should be aware of the tensions between North and South and their tumultuous history. Be respectful of the religious beliefs and political opinions of the local people.

The Republic of Ireland is 87 per cent Roman Catholic, which means that it may be difficult to find a non-Catholic church. When visiting a Catholic church, dress respectfully: cover your torso and upper arms, and ensure shorts and skirts cover your knees.

Mobile Phones and Wi-Fi

Free Wi-Fi hotspots are available in main towns and cities. Cafés and restaurants usually permit the use of their Wi-Fi if you make a purchase.

Visitors travelling to Ireland with EU tariffs are able to use their devices without being affected by data roaming charges. Users will be charged the same rates for data, SMS services and voice calls as they would pay at home. This situation may change in Northern Ireland as a result of the UK's departure from the EU.

Post

Stamps can be bought from post offices, supermarkets and newsagents. Allow three to four days when sending post to Great Britain and at least six days for the United States.

Taxes and Refunds

The rate of VAT is 23 per cent in the Republic of Ireland, while in Northern Ireland it is in line with the UK's standard rate of 20 per cent. Non-EU residents are entitled to a tax refund subject to certain conditions. In order to claim this, request a tax receipt and relevant documentation when you purchase your goods. When leaving the country, present these papers, your receipt and ID at Customs to receive your refund.

Discount Cards

Many destinations offer a visitor's pass or discount card for exhibitions, events, museum entry, guided tours and more. Valid for one, two, three or five consecutive days, the **Dublin Pass** includes free access to top attractions, restaurant discounts and a tour on the hop-on hop-off bus. The **Belfast Vistor Pass** includes travel on public transport and discounts to sights and restaurants for one, two or three days. The **Heritage Card** gives free admission to heritage sites in Ireland for a year. All passes are available online and from participating tourist offices.
Belfast Visitor Pass
ⓦ visitbelfast.com
Dublin Pass
ⓦ dublinpass.com
Heritage Card
ⓦ heritageireland.ie

INDEX

ACKNOWLEDGMENTS

DK would like to thank the following for their contribution to the previous edition: Darragh Geraghty, Lisa Gerard-Sharp, Darren Longley, Tim Perry, Helen Peters

The publisher would like to thank the following for their kind permission to reproduce their photographs:

Key: a-above; b-below/bottom; c-centre; f-far; l-left; r-right; t-top

123RF.com: bloodua 277cla; Alberto Loyo 291bl.

4Corners: Francesco Carovillano 18, 184-5.

Alamy Stock Photo: 19th era 50-1tc; 500px / stephenemerson 10-1b; Phil Crean A 99c; AA World Travel Library 237br; age fotostock 195tr, 216tl, 260b; Aitormmfoto 116-7t; Ambling Images 183br; Per Andersen 255br; Art Directors & TRIP / Helene Rogers 49tr; Artokoloro Quint Lox Limited 85br; Stephen Barnes 266crb, 294-5t, / Arts and Crafts 286bl, / Entertainment 275br, / Food and Drink 45br, / Northern Ireland 266cr; Eduardo Blanco 266t; Hans Blossey 199b; Paul Briden 195bl; David Broadbent 24-5c; Chris Bull 52tl; James Byard 88tl; Alexandre Cappellari 102tc, 109tl; Peter Cavanagh 46bl; ClickAlps Srls 163cr; David Clynch 133tl; Thornton Cohen 105cl, 281tr, 268cr; Gary Cook 215tr; Chris Cooper-Smith 101tr; Roger Covey 211tr; culliganphoto 98; Cultura RM 239br; Richard Cummins 48br, 296bc; Ian G Dagnall 22bl, 44-5b, 50cb, 151t, 174-5b, 243tl, 274-5t; dbimages 58cr, 190cla; Design Pics Inc 20cb, 89b, 99cr, 104t, 113tl, 119b, 128cr, 135br, 140t, 143bl, 189tr, 197bl, 244-5, 289tr; dominic dibbs 145tl; Werner Dieterich 103br; Ros Drinkwater 58crb; Joe Dunckley 176-7b; Andrew Egan 253t; Stephen Emerson 19, 20tl, 206-7, 224-5, 292-3b; Eye Ubiquitous 84bl, 86b, 133tr, 135tr, 135ca, 256tr, 288b, / Hugh Rooney 40tr; David Flanagan 39cr; Kevin Foy 71cr; Ian Pollock James Joyce / geogphotos 41cla, 212bl; H.S. Photos 83br; Rik Hamilton 69tr; Justin Hannaford 43cl; Kim Haughton 106tr; Hemis.fr 234t, 238b, / Gregory Gerault 47bl, / Jacques Sierpinski 33br; Hi-Story 116clb; Chris Hill 213clb; Hufton+Crow-VIEW 277ca; imageBROKER 153bc; incamerastock 40-1b; Brian Irwin 249cl; JLBvdWOLF 115tr; Inge Johnsson 94-5; Victor Lacken 279br; Lebrecht Music & Arts 49br, 85bc; Vincent Lowe 38bl, 229crb; David Lyons 24cla, 24-5t, 258bl; Gavin Lyons 145cra; Jack Maguire 239t; Martin Thomas Photography 13t, 115cl; Barry Mason 74br;

mauritius images GmbH 114cla, / Walter Bibikow 182cl; Angus McComiskey 46br; Gareth McCormack 39bl, 152clb, 152b, 169tl, 191cr, 229bl, 232tr, 254t; Paul McErlane 41tr, / Carolyn Mulholland *Seamus Heaney Bust* 2016 293tr; John A Megaw 58bl; Andrew Melbourne 179tl; Mike Kipling Photography 172t; Mikel Bilbao Gorostiaga Travels 35crb, 196tr; Ashley Morrison 47c; John Morrison 52cr; George Munday 31br, 148bl; Juan Carlos Muñoz 162-3b; Michael David Murphy 189cra; National Geographic Creative 287bl, 288cl, / Catherine Karnow 45tr, 58t; Niday Picture Library 251cr; linda nolan 142t; North Wind Picture Archives 65clb; J Orr 266bl, 268bl; Peter Oshkai 85crb; Pictorial Press Ltd 49bl, 50cla, 52bc; Radharc Images 252bl; reallifephotos 35cla; Republic of Ireland 38-9t; David Ribeiro 114-5b; Richard Wareham Fotografie 69tl; RM Ireland 236t; robertharding 105b, 235b, / Francesco Vaninetti 268t, / Nigel Hicks 22cr; Olle Robin 189br; De Rocker 112cl; Invictus SARL 203br; scenicireland.com / Christopher Hill Photographic 13cr, 21, 25tr, 149b, 233b, 262-3, 276-7b, / Paul Lindsay 47br; Nazrie Abu Seman 112-3b; Kathleen Smith 17t, 124-5; Stephen Saks Photography 192cb; travelib 73t; Ferenc Ungor 110l; Universal Images Group North America LLC / DeAgostini 213bl; Ivan Vdovin 181tr; Vito Arcomano Photography 10clb; Richard Wayman 29cb, 228clb; Ken Welsh 147br; Tim E White 86tc.

AWL Images: Walter Bibikow 140br; Marco Bottigelli 8-9b; Danita Delimont Stock 4; Cahir Davitt 28bl; Shaun Egan 26-7c, 60-1; Hemis 10ca; Nick Ledger 12clb; Maurizio Rellini 6-7, 17bl, 74t, 87tl, 107tl, 154-5, 210t.

Bantry House and Garden: 166clb.

Bridgeman Images: The Board of Trinity College/MS 58 fol.202v *The Devil Tempting Christ to cast Himself down from the Temple*, illumination to the Gospel of St. Luke, from the Book of Kells, c.800 (vellum), Irish School, (9th century) 66tl.

Christ Church Cathedral: 85tr, 85cr.

Coppi: Geoff Telford 11br, 44tl.

Dalkey Book Festival: Conor McCabe 41br.

Depositphotos Inc: Patryk_Kosmider 49tl, 198bl.

Front flap images:
4Corners: Francesco Carovillano c, br; **Alamy Stock Photo:** Ian Dagnall t; Stephen Emerson cla, cra; Inge Johnsson bl.

Cover images:
Front and Spine: **Getty Images:** Marius Roman. *Back:* **123RF.com:** James Byard c; **AWL Images:** Maurizio Rellini tr; **Getty Images:** Marius Roman b; **iStockphoto.com:** JoeDunckley cl.

For further information see:
www.dkimages.com

Illustrations:
Draughtsman Maps, Maltings Partnership, Robbie Polley, Richard Bonson, Brian Craker, John Fox, Paul Guest, Stephan Gyapay, Ian Henderson, Claire Littlejohn, Gillie Newman, Chris Orr, Kevin Robinson, John Woodcock, Martin Woodward

This edition updated by
Contributors Darren Longley, Sean Sheehan, Rachel Thompson
Senior Editor Alison McGill
Senior Designers Tania Da Silva Gomes, Stuti Tiwari
Project Editors Parnika Bagla, Rada Radojicic
Project Art Editor Ankita Sharma
Editors Avanika, Chhavi Nagpal, Kanika Praharaj
Picture Research Coordinator Sumita Khatwani
Assistant Picture Research Administrator Vagisha Pushp
Jacket Coordinator Bella Talbot
Jacket Designer Laura O'Brien
Cartography Manager Suresh Kumar
DTP Designer Rohit Rojal
Senior Production Editor Jason Little
Production Controller Kariss Ainsworth
Managing Editors Shikha Kulkarni, Hollie Teague
Deputy Managing Editor Beverly Smart
Managing Art Editors Bess Daly, Priyanka Thakur
Art Director Maxine Pedliham
Publishing Director Georgina Dee

First edition 1995

Published in Great Britain by Dorling Kindersley Limited, One Embassy Gardens, 8 Viaduct Gardens, London SW11 7BW

Published in the United States by DK Publishing, 1450 Broadway, Suite 801, New York, NY 10018

Copyright © 1995, 2021 Dorling Kindersley Limited
A Penguin Random House Company
21 22 23 24 10 9 8 7 6 5 4 3 2 1

The publishers cannot accept responsibility for any consequences arising from the use of this book, nor for any material on third party websites, and cannot guarantee that any website address in this book will be a suitable source of travel information.

A CIP catalogue record for this book is available from the British Library.

A catalogue record for this book is available from the Library of Congress.

ISSN: 1542 1554
ISBN: 978-0-2415-1059-9

Printed and bound in China.

www.dk.com

MIX
Paper from responsible sources
FSC™ C018179

This book was made with Forest Stewardship Council ™ certified paper – one small step in DK's commitment to a sustainable future. For more information go to www.dk.com/our-green-pledge

A NOTE FROM DK EYEWITNESS

The rapid rate at which the world is changing is constantly keeping the DK Eyewitness team on our toes. While we've worked hard to ensure that this edition of Ireland is accurate and up-to-date, we know that opening hours alter, standards shift, prices fluctuate, places close and new ones pop up in their stead. So, if you notice we've got something wrong or left something out, we want to hear about it. Please get in touch at travelguides@dk.com